PLANTING A GARDEN

PLANTING A GARDEN

*Choosing • designing
planting • growing*

COLLINS & BROWN

First published in Great Britain in 2001
by Collins & Brown Limited
London House
Great Eastern Wharf
Parkgate Road
London SW11 4NQ

3 5 7 9 8 6 4 2

British Library Cataloguing-in-Publication Data:
A catalogue record for this book
is available from the British Library.

ISBN 1-85585-874-6

A Berry Book, conceived, edited and designed by
Susan Berry for Collins & Brown Limited

Gardening Consultant: Joanna Chisholm
Editors: Alison Freegard, Jacqueline Jackson,
Amanda Lebentz, Hilary Mandleburg and Ginny Surtees
Editorial Assistant: Lisa Pendreigh

Senior Designer: Kevin Williams
Designers: Dave Crook, Claudine Meissner and Allan Mole
Design Consultant: Tim Foster
Art Director: Roger Bristow

Special photography: Howard Rice and George Taylor
Illustrations: Ian Sidaway
Garden designs: Tim Newbury
Planting plans: Yvonne Innes

Reproduction by Hong Kong Graphic and Printing Ltd, Hong Kong
Printed and bound in Hong Kong by Paramount Printing Company

CONTENTS

PLANTS FOR THE GARDEN

To enable the different elements of a garden to blend comfortably and attractively, there has to be balance, which can to a large degree be dictated by the trees, shrubs and flowers that you choose. By opting for plants that complement and harmonize with other aspects of the garden, such as the paving or lawn, and its overall size and shape, you can create a framework in which art and nature reach a happy equilibrium. To help you choose plants to suit your garden's needs, concise descriptions of a wide range of trees, shrubs, roses, climbers, perennials, ground cover, bamboos, grasses, bulbs and annuals and biennials have been included. Each entry provides vital details as to what the plant looks like, how high it will grow, what kind of growing conditions it prefers, how hardy it is and when it flowers, if appropriate. This section also provides a host of helpful ideas on where to position plants, how to use and combine flower colours, design borders and incorporate different styles.

Principles of planting

'Harmony' is perhaps the most important word in making a garden. You want somewhere that is relaxing but also stimulating to the senses, where art and nature have reached a happy equilibrium. Creating a balance between the different elements of a garden, such as the paving, lawn, trees, shrubs and flowers, is crucial to the end result.

Colour is an essential design element, but because flowers are relatively fleeting, it can be difficult to maintain interest all year long. The stronger the framework of the garden, with plenty of 'architectural' plants (those with strong and distinct shapes), the less vital it will be to have flowers all year round.

Small gardens are especially difficult to plan. All plants are highly visible, so there is no room for the spectacular flowering plant that looks messy for the rest of the year. Good foliage and flowers with a long season are vital.

Creating a design core
This cottage garden has a formal plan. The gravel paths provide the 'bones' of the design while the planting is sympathetically unstructured.

Creating a structure

It is the larger or more upright plants that do most to develop the garden frame-work, dividing it into sections and serving as a guide as you walk or look round. Trees or shrubs with a narrow, vertical, columnar habit have lots of impact, but are useful in that they take up little space. Trees, under whose branches you can walk, hedges that act as green walls, or plants with strong shapes, all provide the visual 'bones' for the garden. The softer, more formless shrubs and flowering perennials are the 'flesh'. Some of the most successful gardens are those that balance the formality of clearly designed shapes, such as clipped hedges and topiary, with the informality of burgeoning borders of flowers and shrubs.

Informal design
This simple garden has all the ingredients for success: an enclosing structure of trees and hedges, space for relaxation and an impeded view so that the garden appears larger, and more inviting.

Year-round interest

Some gardeners are happy to have most of their garden flowering at once. They like to see a spring garden with lots of bulbs, or an early summer garden with roses and perennials, and they are happy to let it rest for the remainder of the year. Most gardeners, though, prefer to attempt a long season of interest, which involves trying to interweave plants so that there is always something, or some part, that looks good.

A garden takes time to develop, and never stands still. Planning planting for the short, medium and long term helps avoid the great gaps that can try the patience of even the most dedicated. Trees, needless to say, are the most long term, often maturing long after we have gone.

Shrubs, too, can take many years to look their best, which can mean that a garden that is heavily reliant on them may take rather a while

Spring colour
An unusual contrasting bedding scheme with magenta tulips and yellow wallflowers brings strong colour to the garden in spring.

to develop. Herbaceous perennials look established with remarkable speed, whereas annuals fulfil their promise and disappear within a year. It makes good sense, then, to include all these different plant forms in a garden.

Autumn foliage
A dramatic canopy of foliage can provide both colour and interest in the garden, as the contrasting golds of this Liquidambar orientalis *and (behind) the reds of Japanese maple (*Acer palmatum *'Osakazuki') demonstrate.*

Harmony and contrast in the garden

Making a garden is an intensely personal business. What one person loves, another may hate. Such varying reactions are often to do with the level of harmony and contrast in the planting. Very harmonious gardens, where all the colours match, and clashes or surprises are avoided, are soothing, restful places. Those who like more stimulation may prefer gardens with lots of vivid, contrasting colours, or a wide and dramatic range of leaf shapes and plant forms.

Harmony in gardens is relatively easy to achieve with single colour schemes. 'White gardens' are particularly rewarding and straightforward. Plantings based on colour contrast are more difficult to get right, and are much more personal. Mixing strong colours can create results that are vibrant to some, but too obtrusive and clashing to others.

Mixing colours and shapes
Big, bold shapes, like this spiky variegated agave (left), make a striking feature against softer planting. Vibrant colour contrast is also provided by the yellow/green agave and the pink sedum.

Soft harmonies
The delicate blues, mauves and pinks and the softly billowing shapes of a herbaceous perennial border in summer (right) are a study in gentle harmony.

Plants for particular situations

To make a successful garden it is crucial to choose plants that are suitable for the prevailing conditions. All plants have preferences: moist or dry soils, acid or limey, warm climates or cold. Traditionally, gardeners have expended energy on making conditions suit particular plants, in places where they would not naturally grow, by changing the nature of the soil or using copious quantities of water. However, water shortages, and the pollutant effects of chemicals have compelled people to think in terms of a more natural approach. Instead of changing conditions to suit plants, today the trend is towards choosing plants to suit the place.

Sympathetic planting
Damp areas of the garden, in particular water features, need to be planted sympathetically. Moisture-loving plants have large lush foliage at the expense of brilliant flower colour. Use features, like this little bridge, to create colour accents instead.

What grows best?

Before you select plants for your garden, it is advisable to learn as much as you can about the area in which you live, as this will determine what you can grow. A good way of finding out which plants will grow well is to visit local parks and gardens that are open to the public. An area where everyone seems to have rhododendrons means that you can grow these acid-lovers, too, as well as azaleas, camellias and many more.

Keep a notebook handy to record plants that you like and that thrive in gardens with similar conditions to yours. It is a good way of building up your own body of knowledge. Once you have a clear idea of what the area can or cannot offer, you will be in a position to select plants that will succeed with little effort on your part.

Climate is the place to start. Is your area one that regularly experiences cold winters or hot, dry summers? If it is, then the hardiness of plants or their drought tolerance are two important limiting factors. Then there is the 'microclimate', which refers to factors that affect the overall climate on a small scale and of your garden in particular.

A wall or hedge that protects the garden from the prevailing wind may mean you are able to grow a range of more tender plants than anyone else in your neighbourhood. On the other hand, being in an exposed position, or in a frost hollow, where cold, heavy air gathers, can mean the opposite.

Sheltered spots
If you are lucky enough to have a walled garden, you can grow more tender plants that require protection from cold winds. Your perennial borders will flower earlier than your neighbour's in these conditions.

Light is yet another very important factor. Is your garden shaded by trees, or is it on the sunless side of a hill or your house? If it is, then you will need to concentrate your efforts on growing shade-tolerant plants.

The soil is the other major consideration. Is it generally damp or even wet, or is it very free-draining and so liable to dry out in summer? Is it fertile, or acid, or rich in lime? You may not require a soil-testing kit to find out – gardening neighbours can often supply the answers.

Hardiness ratings
In the following plant directory pages, plants that will not survive temperatures less than 5°C (40°F) are described as 'tender' in individual entries. Other plants are hardier, and are given ratings as follows:

★ will survive 4 to -1°C (30–40°F)
★★ will survive -1 to -7°C (20–30°F)
★★★ will survive -7 to -17°C (0–20°F)
★★★★ will survive -17 to -30°C (0 to -20°F)

Choosing your plants

Any garden benefits from having a good mixture of plants, both in terms of height and shape, and in the variety of foliage and flower form and colour. However, it is surprising how much diversity and interest you can create without flower colour.

Plants for shady parts of the garden will inevitably major on leaf form and shape; plants for full sun will have more flower power. Make sure that you choose those that do well for these differing situations, and look, too, at the soil conditions. Some plants prefer acid soil, others alkaline. Rhododendrons and azaleas, for example, refuse to grow on alkaline soil but will quickly provide useful ground cover for large gardens on peaty soil.

Hopefully, the differing habitats in your garden will allow you to choose a variety of plants from dry-loving to damp-loving, sun-loving to shade-loving.

Plants for dry sun
Many grasses like dry, sunny conditions. Big, clump-forming Miscanthus sinensis 'Variegatus' (right) is a handsome architectural plant for a dry border.

Plants for shade
Some euphorbias (left), and most dicentras, cope well with partial shade. Among the many plants that enjoy shady conditions are those that grow naturally in woodland. Some prefer damp, while others prefer dry shade (see list below).

Natural planting

The next time you take a country walk, or go on holiday, look at the plants around you. Notice how those that grow in exposed places usually have tiny, closely packed leaves, how those in hot, dry areas have a tendency to grey foliage or succulent leaves, and how woodland plants are often evergreen or dormant in the summer. All these are adaptations plants have evolved over millions of years to enable them to grow successfully in different environments.

It makes sense to take advantage of this, and select plants for our gardens that are naturally adapted to our particular type of soil and climate, whatever it is.

Gardeners often complain of bad drainage, or of dry, or clay, or limestone soil. They never seem satisfied, and are prone to label anything that is not a perfect loam as a 'problem garden'. However,

the fact is that nature has developed a wonderful and beautiful flora for every 'problem', at least those that are of natural origin.

A good start is to consider growing more wild plants native to your region. They are often very beautiful, but underrated for being wild, and at least they are perfectly adapted and will not have

difficulty growing. If there are no local nurseries selling local wild plants, you can collect seed (but *never* dig up the plants) and propagate them yourself.

Natural planting
A woodland edge provides the ideal habitat for shade-loving perennials, including geraniums, ferns and these foxgloves.

Trees for the framework

Trees and large shrubs are an essential part of most landscapes, and by planting trees you are not only planting for the future, but also contributing to the appearance of the whole neighbourhood for generations to come – which means that it is very important to get it right!

There are plenty of trees that are suitable even for small gardens, although their mature shape can vary considerably. Some are very narrow, columnar varieties, which will cast little shade but form a striking part of the garden framework. Others may not reach a great height, but develop a broad canopy which requires a fair bit of space. Trees with fine, elegant forms make a great contribution to the overall structure of the garden.

Achieving a balance
Trees surround this country garden, giving it shelter and privacy. Choose carefully to create different forms and colours, and mix evergreens and deciduous trees to give the garden balance.

Choosing trees

It is of fundamental importance to know the eventual size of any tree that you plant, not only for the effect it will have on your own garden, but on the neighbours' too. Also bear in mind the kind of shade it will cast: light like a birch, or so heavy that little will grow beneath it,

Siting trees
This old apple tree, carefully sited at the corner of a perennial border, is just the right size and scale for this garden and also offers the bonus of delicious fruit in late summer.

such as with a beech. There are safety considerations, too. Any tree right next to a house may undermine foundations. Some, such as willows and poplars, may cause damage from a distance. If strong winds are frequent, you need to ensure that whatever you plant is wind resistant, or cannot blow over onto someone's home. You should also consider whether it will block anyone's view or light when it matures.

Since a tree will have an effect on the wider landscape, consider what this might be. Country districts can be depressingly suburbanized by

trees that are not characteristic of the local area, but which are mass planted in towns and industrial sites. Conversely, you can contribute positively to your local landscape by planting native trees.

A tree may be chosen simply for its shape or the play of its branches. However, good foliage is particularly important if we have to look at the tree a lot. This may mean coloured foliage, such as purple or yellow-tinged, or simply quietly attractive green leaves. Evergreens are popular, many considering them essential for providing interest

and structure in the winter. However they have drawbacks. One is that very little will grow beneath them, and the other is that their never-changing quality can become boring after a while.

Perhaps even more than with deciduous trees, it is extremely important not to choose evergreens that will become too large in time.

Shady places
Small and large trees have their place in the garden. Shade provided by larger trees is ideal for creating a secluded sitting area. Smaller trees can act as punctuation points at the end of a border.

Planting a tree

Young trees need support in windy areas. Hammer a stake into the base of the planting hole before inserting the tree, to avoid damaging roots, and tie the tree to the stake about 50cm (20in) above ground level. Use an angled stake (right) for container or root-balled trees, place at a 45° angle and secure with a tie. When filling the hole, look for the soil mark on the base of the trunk and plant at the same depth as it was before transplanting. Remove or loosen the tie around the trunk as the tree grows.

1 *In autumn or spring, dig a large hole, roughly two and half times the width of the root-ball, and deep enough so that the base of the trunk is just below the surface of the soil. Add a general purpose fertilizer to the base of the hole.*

2 *For container-grown or root-balled trees, insert a stake at a 45° angle and secure loosely with a tie. Spread the roots out well to enable the tree to get off to a good start. Make sure that the earth around the hole has been well dug and is friable.*

3 *Backfill the hole, and firm the tree in by treading down around the base carefully. Pull the stem gently to ensure it is firmly fixed. (Windrock will damage the tree and stunt its eventual growth). Water well and regularly.*

Hedging

Sometimes we need to plant trees for purely functional reasons, such as for screening or for hedging. Fast-growing, upright trees are useful for the former, and those with a dense, twiggy habit are ideal for the latter.

However, there is a temptation to plant fast-growing trees for these purposes, such as poplars for screening and Leyland cypress (x *Cupressocyparis leylandii*) for hedging. Both of these can rapidly become too large, shading you and your neighbours and robbing gardens of light, moisture and nutrients. It is therefore often better to be patient and stick to less aggressive, slower-growing alternatives. Hedges are often a useful backdrop against which borders and groups of containers can be displayed. Not only do they provide a visual context, they also give much-needed shelter from cold or damaging winds.

Yew (*Taxus baccata*), although slow growing, is ideal for this purpose as it forms a thick, impenetrable hedge that needs only infrequent clipping.

Private view
A hedge can form a useful backdrop for groups of containers as well as providing a secluded, sheltered area for seating.

Trees and shrubs for colour

Flowering trees are understandably popular, with flowering cherries and plums (*Prunus* spp.) among the most widely planted. Ornamental apples (*Malus* spp.) and rowans and whitebeams (*Sorbus* spp.) are well-loved, too, because they have a dual season; flowers in spring and coloured fruit in the autumn.

However, if you want to plant a flowering tree, why not plant a culinary one? An apple or cherry tree will produce fruit you can eat and flowers that are every bit as good as the purely ornamental varieties.

Autumn colour is a good basis on which to select trees; after all, at its best it can rival flowers for sheer impact. It is as well to remember, though, that good autumn colour largely depends on there being sharp frosts at the right time in autumn, so areas with mild climates rarely see a good show of colour.

Many of the best trees are large, but there are smaller ones, such as amelanchiers, and several shrubs, like *Euonymus alatus* and species of rhus. Remember, too, that it is worth having at least one tree for winter colour. A little witch-hazel (*Hamamelis mollis*), with its bright yellow flowers on bare, midwinter branches, or the winter-flowering cherry, *Prunus* x *subhirtella* 'Autumnalis', are a source of great joy in what would otherwise be a flowerless period.

Foliage colour
For dramatic colour in autumn, Japanese maples (Acer palmatum) are hard to beat, with their beautiful filigree leaves which turn a range of russet tones from scarlet to burnt orange.

Trees

A mixture of evergreen and deciduous trees provides the best framework for a garden. Even a small garden needs at least one small tree for vertical interest. The trees here include evergreens, deciduous trees and conifers. A few are magnificent large trees, appropriate only for large gardens. Most are medium or small trees that can be grown in an average sized-garden. Trees are a permanent feature of the landscape, so plant them sensibly. Do not site them near buildings, and consider their height when full grown, even though some may take years to mature. Take care when pruning, as poor cuts lead to disease. The pruning of large trees is best left to experts.

Acer pseudoplatanus **'Brilliantissimum'**

Aesculus x *neglecta* **'Erythroblastos'**

Amelanchier lamarckii

Betula utilis **var.** *jacquemontii*

ACER DAVIDII
H 10–15m (30–48ft) ★★★★
Useful, small deciduous tree, known as Snake-bark Maple, with whitish-striped, green to dull-red bark. Leaves oval, mid-green, yellow to orange-flushed in autumn. Grow in any reasonably moist soil, sheltered from strongest winds in sun or partial shade. *A. palmatum,* Japanese Maple, has rounded leaves with 5 to 9 pointed lobes turning bright red to orange or yellow in autumn. H 6–8m (18–24ft). Best in neutral to acid soil. The variety 'Dissectum' has finely cut leaf-lobes and a mound-forming habit, H 2m (6½ft). *A. pseudoplatanus* 'Brilliantissimum', has 5-lobed leaves, bright pink when young, turning yellow then green, H 6m (18ft).

AESCULUS x CARNEA 'BRIOTII'
H 10–20m (30–64ft) ★★★★
Known as Red Horse Chestnut, this handsome, round-headed, deciduous flowering tree has deep green leaves. Flowers dark red in panicles in early summer. Fruits globular, smooth to sparsely spiny. Grow in fairly fertile, moist soil in sun or partial shade. *A.* x *neglecta* 'Erythroblastos', Sunrise Horse Chestnut is a conical tree, the leaves unfolding cream and bright pink on red leaf-stalks, becoming yellow then green with age. Flowers are yellow, flushed with red.

AMELANCHIER LAMARCKII
H 6–10m (18–32ft) ★★★★
Attractive, small deciduous flowering tree, also called Shadbush or Snowy Mespilus, is suitable for the small garden. Leaves oval, often bronze-tinted when young, becoming green then turning red to orange in autumn. Flowers 5-petalled, white, freely produced in loose spikes in late spring followed by edible, sweet, juicy fruits ripening purple-black. Grow in moderately fertile, moist soil in sun or partial shade. 'Ballerina' H 6m (18ft) is a more spreading tree, the leaves broadly elliptic, emerging bronze-tinted but becoming green by mid-summer, turning red and purple in mid-autumn. Flowers in arching spikes in mid- to late spring.

BETULA PENDULA
H 18m (60ft) ★★★★
An elegant, deciduous, medium-sized tree, the Silver Birch is erect with pendulous branchlets and a trunk covered with peeling white bark. Its triangular, mid-green leaves turn yellow in autumn. Catkins before the leaves, yellowish to brownish yellow. Grow in fertile soil in sun or partial shade. 'Laciniata' (often labelled 'Dalecarlica' by nurseries), H 15-18m (48-60ft), differs in having deeply lobed and toothed leaves. *B. nigra,* Black or River Birch, has more spreading branches and red-brown, peeling bark.

Leaves are diamond-shaped, glossy above, deep green, yellow in autumn. *B. utilis* var. *jacquemontii,* Himalayan Birch, H 15–18m (48–60ft), has white, peeling bark and oval leaves. Catkins are yellow, and red-tinted.

CARAGANA ARBORESCENS
H 6m (20ft) ★★★★
Known as the Pea Tree, this deciduous, hardy, small tree makes a good windbreak. It has spiny branches, attractive light green leaves of up to l2 leaflets, and pale yellow, pea-like flowers in late spring. Prefers well-drained soil and full sun. 'Nana' is a dwarf form, H l.5m (5ft).

CARPINUS BETULUS
H 20–25m (64–80ft) ★★★★
A handsome, deciduous specimen tree, the Hornbeam is grown for its habit and foliage, but is only suitable for larger gardens. Broadly pyramidal when young, later rounded with a smooth, fluted bark. Leaves are mid-green turning yellow or orange-yellow in autumn. Yellowish male catkins in spring, female ones followed by pendent spikes of winged nutlets. Grow in moist garden soil in sun or partial shade. 'Fastigiata' ('Pyramidalis'), H 12-15m (38–48ft), erect and narrowly pyramidal when young, broadens with age.

CERCIDIPHYLLUM
JAPONICUM
H 18–20m (60–64ft) ★★★★
Also known as Kadsura, this is an attractive, deciduous specimen tree for the larger garden, pyramidal when young, later broadening and becoming rounded. It is grown for its foliage. Oval to rounded leaves emerge bronze and mature to mid- to bluish green, turning yellow, orange and red in autumn, particularly on acid soil. Grow in reasonably moist, neutral to acid soil in sun or partial shade.

CERCIS SILIQUASTRUM
H 8–10m (24–30ft) ★★★★
The flowering Judas Tree is a beautiful, rounded to spreading, deciduous tree suitable for smaller gardens. Flowers pea-shaped, magenta to pink or white, in profuse clusters on bare stems before the leaves which are kidney-shaped to inversely heart-shaped, bronze when young, usually changing to yellow in autumn. Grow in any reasonably moist soil, sheltered from cold winds, in full sun. *C. canadensis,* Eastern Redbud, has heart-shaped, pointed leaves. Flowers purple or pink, occasionally white. 'Forest Pansy' has red-purple leaves.

CORNUS KOUSA
H 5–7m (15–21ft) ★★★★
Showy, deciduous, flowering tree suitable for smaller gardens. Broadly conical to rounded, erect when young, with flaking bark. Leaves oval, wavy-margined, usually turning crimson-purple in autumn. Flowers in greenish, button-like clusters surrounded by four, large, conspicuous white, petal-like bracts, followed by strawberry-like fleshy, red fruits. Grow in fertile, moist soil, ideally sheltered from cold winds, in sun or partial shade. The variety *chinensis* has leaves with flat margins and floral bracts which age pink. 'China Girl' is free-flowering when young.

CRATAEGUS LAEVIGATA
(C. OXYACANTHA)
H 6–8m (18–24ft) ★★★★
Attractive, small- to medium-sized flowering and fruiting deciduous tree, also known as Midland Hawthorn, of erect to spreading habit. Leaves oval, mid-glossy green, bearing 3-5 broad lobes. Flowers 5-petalled, white to red in clusters in spring, followed by globular, red fruits. Grow in ordinary garden soil in sun or partial shade. 'Paul's Scarlet' or

Caragana arborescens

Cercis siliquastrum

Craetaegus laevigata 'Paul's Scarlet'

Flowers of *Davidia involucrata*

'Coccinea Plena', bears fully double, reddish-pink flowers. *C. persimilis* 'Prunifolia' (*C.* x *prunifolia*), H6–8m (18–24ft) is a thorny-stemmed, bushy-headed tree. Leaves glossy deep-green, often turning orange to red in the autumn. White flowers followed by rounded, bright red fruits.

DAVIDIA INVOLUCRATA
H 10–15m (30–48ft) ★★★★
An outstanding deciduous specimen tree for larger gardens, also known as the Dove, or Handkerchief Tree. Broadly pyramidal, spreading with age. Leaves heart-shaped, mid- to deep green above, downy beneath. Flowers tiny, petal-less in clusters enclosed by two large, unequal-sized creamy white pendent bracts, followed by green, plum-like fruits. Grow in fertile, moist soil, sheltered from cold winds in sun or partial shade. The variety *vilmoriniana* has smooth, paler green leaves.

Eucalyptus gunnii

EUCALYPTUS GUNNII
H 15–25m (48–64ft) ★★
An evergreen specimen tree, also called Cider Gum, with attractive, flaking, whitish-green bark. Leaves are blue-white and rounded on young plants, lance-shaped and green with maturity. (If plants are cut back annually they become bushy and retain their juvenile leaves). Grow in any well-drained garden soil in full sun, sheltered from cold winds. *E. pauciflora* ssp. *niphophila* (*E.*

Gleditsia triacanthos 'Sunburst'

Laurus nobilis

Magnolia x soulangeana

Prunus 'Taihaku'

niphophila), the Snow Gum, H 6m (18ft), is a rather bushy, spreading tree with waxy-white twigs and peeling white to pale brown bark. The hardiest eucalpyt.

GLEDITSIA TRIACANTHOS 'SUNBURST'
H 10–12m (30–38ft) ★★★★

Also called Golden Honeylocust, this is a fast-growing, deciduous tree, conical when young, spreading with age. It is grown for its striking, ferny and colourful foliage, the long yellow leaves divided into 15 to 25 narrow, oval leaflets. The greenish-white flowers are insignificant. Grow in reasonably moist garden soil in full sun.

LABURNUM ALPINUM
H 6m (18ft) ★★★★

A colourful, deciduous tree for the smaller garden, also called Scotch Laburnum. It has smooth bark and trifoliate leaves, which are rich green and glossy. The bright yellow, pea-shaped flowers hang in pendent chains in late spring, followed by bean-like seed pods which are poisonous if eaten. Grow in moist, well-drained soil, sheltered from strong winds in sun or partial shade. Remove suckers from the stem and base. *L. anagyroides* (*L. vulgare*), Common Laburnum, has a spreading habit and hairy shoots. The leaves, with dark green elliptic leaflets, are silky haired beneath. *L.*

x *watereri* 'Vossii', Golden Rain, is similiar but has chains of bright yellow flowers to 60cm (2ft) long.

LAURUS NOBILIS
H 12m (40ft) ★★

Commonly known as Sweet Bay, this evergreen is grown for its aromatic glossy, dark green leaves (which are used as a flavouring in cooking). It bears clusters of insignificant flowers in spring and female plants bear small black berries after flowering. It prefers full sun and partial shade, and some shelter from cold winds. 'Aurea' has golden foliage.

LIQUIDAMBAR STYRACIFLUA
H 20–25m (64–80ft) ★★★★

Known as Sweet Gum, this deciduous tree often has richly coloured autumn foliage. Broadly conical in habit, spreading with age, the young stems often have corky wings. Leaves rounded, cut into 5 to 7 glossy, mid-green, pointed lobes turning orange red and purple in autumn. Flowers inconspicuous, yellow-green in small globular clusters which ripen into spiky seed pods. Grow in moist, neutral to acid soils for best autumn colour, in full sun, sheltered from strongest winds.

MAGNOLIA x SOULANGEANA
H 6m (18ft) ★★★★

This Magnolia is a small specimen tree is grown for its large, showy, goblet-shaped, many-petalled flowers which vary from deep purplish-pink to white and which are borne with or before the leaves. Leaves oval, often somewhat broader near the tip, medium-green above, paler beneath. Grow in fertile, reasonably moist soil with shelter from strong, cold winds. 'Brozzoni' has pure white flowers. 'Lennei' bears dark purple-pink flowers. 'San José' has white flowers flushed deep pink. *M. kobus*, H 10–12m (30–38ft), is a

broadly conical, deciduous tree. Leaves oval, usually broader at the tip, often turning yellow in autumn. Flowers saucer-shaped, white, profusely borne on bare twigs in spring.

MALUS FLORIBUNDA
H 8–10m (24–30ft) ★★★★

This beautiful, small, flowering deciduous tree, also called Japanese Crab-apple, is for medium-sized gardens. Leaves oval, toothed. Flowers 5-petalled, pale pink from red buds in profuse clusters, in late spring followed by globular yellow fruits. Grow in ordinary garden soil in full sun. 'Golden Hornet' H 8–10m (24–30ft) is a rounded- to oval-headed tree with white flowers from pink buds in late spring followed by a profusion of ovoid, golden yellow fruits which often last through winter. 'Profusion' is a spreading tree with bronze-green leaves. Flowers are purplish-pink in late spring, followed by glossy reddish-purple fruits.

PRUNUS (SYN. AMYGDALUS)
H 5–10m (15–40ft) ★★★★

Also known as Ornamental Cherry, there are more than 200 species in this genus of deciduous or evergreen, small garden trees. They are highly decorative with clusters of white or pink flowers in spring; there are single, semi-double and double forms. Certain species are grown for their edible fruits (plums, almonds and peaches among them). Among the popular ornamental hybrids, grown for their spring blossom, are 'Kanzan', H 10m (30ft), with double, deep-pink, large flowers, and 'Taihaku', H 8m (25ft), with large, bowl shaped, single white flowers.

ROBINIA PSEUDOACACIA 'FRISIA'
H 15m (48ft) ★★★★

Also known as False Acacia, this is a popular, goldenfoliaged, deciduous tree of elegant habit. The leaves age to yellow-green, turning orange-yellow in autumn. Insignificant flowers in summer. Grow in moist, well-drained soil in full sun.

SORBUS AUCUPARIA
H 10–15m (32–48ft) ★★★★
Deciduous small tree, also called Mountain Ash, of broadly conical to rounded habit. Leaves dark green, composed of several oblong to lance-shaped, toothed leaflets turning yellow or red in autumn. Flattened heads of small white flowers in late spring, followed by orange-red berries. Grow in well-drained soil in sun or partial shade. 'Aspleniifolia' has deep, dissected leaflets. 'Fastigiata' has a conical to columnar habit. *S. aria*, Whitebeam, is broadly columnar to rounded in habit with oval, leaves dark green above and downy white below. 'Lutescens' has narrower, grey-green leaves.

TAMARIX RAMOSISSIMA
H 5m (15ft) ★★★★
Also known as Tamarisk, this deciduous small tree does well in coastal areas. It is grown for its graceful feathery foliage and plumes of 5-petalled pink flowers in late summer and early autumn. Grow in well-drained soil in full sun. Prune hard after planting for a more shrub-like form. *T. tetrandra* has 4-petalled pale pink flowers.

Conifers

ABIES KOREANA
H 8–10m (24–30ft) ★★★★
Also known as Korean Fir, this striking conical conifer has glossy, deep green needle-like leaves which are silver beneath. The erect, cylindrical violet-blue cones are produced on the upper branches, often on young trees. Grow in moist, well-drained, ideally neutral to acid soil, in full sun.

CHAMAECYPARIS LAWSONIANA
H 15–25m (48–80ft) ★★★★
One of the best-known conifers, also called Lawson Cypress, of columnar habit composed of minute, bright green, scale leaves in flattened sprays. The tiny male cones are crimson in spring. Grow in moist, well-drained soil in sun or light shade. 'Chilworth Silver' is slow-growing, with awl-shaped, blue-green leaves. 'Pembury Blue' is conical with sprays of blue-grey leaves. 'Ellwoodii' is dense and conical with blue-grey young leaves. 'Winston Churchill' is narrowly conical with golden foliage. *C. obtusa* Hinoki Cypress, shorter and slower-growing, has deep green leaves, white banded beneath.

CRYPTOMERIA JAPONICA
H 15–25m (48–80ft) ★★★
Also called Japanese Cedar, this handsome, large specimen tree of conical to columnar habit has mid- to deep green, awl-shaped leaves and small, prickly cones. Grow in fertile, moist but well-drained, humus-rich soil in sun or partial shade. 'Bandai-sugi' H 2m (6½ft), forms an irregularly rounded shrub with dense foliage turning bronze in winter. 'Elegans', H 6–10m (18–30ft), has a dense, conical habit, with bluish-green foliage turning bronze to reddish-brown in winter.

PICEA PUNGENS
H 15m (48ft) ★★★★
Also known as Colorado Spruce, this small, broadly columnar tree has upward-pointing orange-brown shoots covered in glaucous bluish-grey, sharply pointed leaves, arranged radially, and cylindrical long cones. It prefers a slightly acid soil and full sun. Other varieties include those with bluish-white and silvery blue foliage, and there are also dwarf forms, like 'Mrs Cesarini' which is only 2m (6½ft) tall.

Robinia pseudoacacia 'Frisia'

Tamarix tetranda

Chamaecyparis lawsoniana

Picea pungens 'Koster'

Using shrubs

For many gardeners, shrubs are the most important part of the garden. Quite apart from whatever intrinsic beauty of flower or foliage they may have, they create a sense of fullness, smoothing the rough edges of corners and walls and making the garden feel occupied. They enable the gardener to 'sculpt space', so that particular views through the garden can be shut off.

It is important to choose shrubs with different forms of growth, to give a variety of shapes. Some form neat, low mounds (such as *Skimmia japonica*), while others have a tall arching habit (like many of the buddlejas). Many of the evergreen shrubs can be clipped (below) into predetermined shapes, or trained to form standards, bushing out at the top of a slender stem.

Using shrub forms
Different forms of shrub have been used to create a change of pace where two compartments of the garden join.

Size and scale

The majority of shrubs can become quite substantial in time. Many small gardens become thickets as shrubs grow and get tangled up in each other. Since they take many years to reach their full size, there is also a tendency to plant too many together. It is vital to find out the eventual sizes of any shrubs you are considering planting, and plan accordingly. Large gaps between young shrubs can be filled with perennials, to be gradually displaced as the shrubs grow. One reason for the popularity of shrubs is their supposed low maintenance. This is true, if you have space to let them grow and grow. But if you have a small garden and several vigorous shrub species you may end up spending a lot of time pruning. Those with small gardens should look at using dwarf shrubs and perennials more extensively.

Shrubs in variety
This garden shows how varied shrubs can be in form, size and colour. Dogwoods (cornus), elaeagnus and viburnum grow to different sizes, in different forms, to add interest, even without flower colour.

Improving shape

Although shrubs are principally bought for their foliage form or flower colour or shape, their habit or form is important, too. Certain shrubs, many of them evergreen, have a naturally interesting form. *Viburnum davidii*, for example, makes a neat mound shape, as does *Skimmia japonica*. Others are notable for their arching shape, like *Buddleja alternifolia* or *Forsythia suspensa*.

However, most popular shrubs have an informal, rather amorphous, shape, yet this is easily overcome by clipping. Many gardeners train shrubs as standards, or clip them into shapes, so that they can be made part of a classically formal garden. Their primary appeal is sculptural and architectural rather than floral.

Historically, certain species have been used extensively for this, such as box (*Buxus sempervirens*). Yet most species can be clipped or trained, the only drawback being that such shaping reduces flowering.

Formal shapes
Many evergreen shrubs can be clipped to create formal shapes, as this little parterre with its clipped box demonstrates.

Using shrubs for colour

It is for their flowers that most shrubs are grown, which allows you to have something blooming at most times of the year.

Start in late winter with the brilliant yellow of forsythia, progress through spring with viburnums and camellias, through early summer with rhododendrons and ceanothus and end with roses, many of which flower until autumn. Apart from roses, though, there are few shrubs that flower in summer, which is something to bear in mind when planning. Indeed, many shrubs with beautiful flowers look dull after flowering, thus limiting their use in smaller gardens.

Autumn, again, sees certain shrubs come into their own. Many species bear brightly coloured berries; pyracanthas are notably dramatic with clusters of golden-yellow berries throughout winter. Some have good texture, too, such as amelanchiers and deciduous *Euonymus* varieties. Evergreen shrubs are very valuable for their attractive foliage and golden variegated plants, such as varieties of *elaeagnus* or the evergreen *euonymus*, remind us in winter of summer sunshine.

Those with coloured foliage can be a great asset in colour-schemed borders, their long season enhancing the look of any flowers. For example, yellow leaves go well with blue and purple flowers, and silver foliage sets

Colourful foliage
Shrubs like euonymus, holly (ilex) and elaeagnus are evergreens with the bonus of interesting coloured foliage. Species with variegated leaves, such as Euonymus 'Emerald 'n' Gold' are worth looking out for.

off pink flowers. Varieties with silver, grey or white variegated foliage provide flashes of light in the garden, especially against a dark evergreen backdrop. You will add to the variety and interest of the garden if you consider these various different attributes when choosing which shrubs. Ideally, a good mixture of leaf forms and colours should be chosen, as well as varying habits and sizes.

Dwarfs and heathers

Dwarf, often ground-hugging, shrubs are characteristic of harsh environments. Think of aromatic-leaved lavenders and herbs of Mediterranean climates, or the heathers (*Calluna* and *Erica* spp.) of windswept moorlands. These plants are obviously useful in gardens in such areas, but as they are so versatile, they can be used in any unshaded garden where low-maintenance ground cover is needed.

The vast majority of these low-growing shrubs are evergreen, often with attractive foliage, making them very useful garden plants indeed. Those from drought-prone habitats tend to be grey or

Heather beds
For gardens with acid soil, heather beds are a good source of colour and, since they cover the ground well with very little maintenance, are an excellent solution for large gardens.

silver, those from cooler areas green, although many of the latter have golden-leaved varieties. Among good small shrubs for dry gardens are hebes, lavenders and santolinas, all with a mound-forming habit and tough, small leaves. For example, they can be used to create a low edging to a path, softening its harder outlines.

Acid soils
Another difficult environment for many plants is any area that has infertile, acid soil, where very few herbaceous perennials grow well, leaving certain distinctive, shrubby plants as the dominant vegetation. Chief amongst these are rhododendrons and azaleas. They make socalled 'problem soil' into something of an asset, as they are surely the most varied and striking group of garden shrubs.

Rhododendron yakushimanum

Large shrubs

Buddleja alternifolia

Buddleja globosa

Camellia japonica
'Debutante'

Cotinus coggygria

AUCUBA JAPONICA
H 3m (10ft) or more ★★★

Useful, very shade-tolerant, rounded, evergreen shrub with large, oval, glossy, mid- to deep green leaves. Insignificant male and female flowers are borne on separate plants and both are needed to produce the glossy red berries. Grow in moist, well-drained soil. Propagate by semi-hardwood cuttings in late summer or by seed sown in a cold frame when ripe. 'Crassifolia', male, has large, deep green leaves. 'Salicifolia', female, has narrow, rich green leaves. 'Gold Dust', female, has leaves dusted with golden yellow.

BUDDLEJA DAVIDII
H 3–5m (10–15ft) ★★★★

Also known as Butterfly Bush, this popular deciduous shrub has arching stems and

Choisya ternata

slender, lance-shaped, grey-green leaves. Long spikes of small, fragrant, lilac flowers are borne in succession from summer to autumn. Grow in ordinary soil in full sun. Cut back hard in late winter. Propagate by semi-hardwood cuttings in late summer or hardwood cuttings in autumn. 'Black Knight' is dark purple-blue; 'White Profusion' has white flowers with yellow eyes in panicles. *B. globosa*, Orange Ball Tree, has clusters of orange to yellow flowers. *B. alternifolia* bears dense, rounded clusters of intensely fragrant lilac flowers.

CAMELLIA JAPONICA
H 3m (15ft) or more ★★★

Beautiful, erect to spreading, usually rounded evergreen shrub, with very glossy, deep green, leathery leaves. Large, single to double rose-like flowers in shades of pink, red and white from early to late spring. Grow in partial shade in humus-rich, neutral to acid soil in a sheltered site. Propagate by semi-hardwood or leaf-bud cuttings in a frame from late summer to winter. Single, semi and fully-double cultivars are available in many shades including bicolours.

CHIMONANTHUS PRAECOX
H 2.5–4m (8–12ft) ★★★

Also called Wintersweet, this is a delightful, strong-growing, erect to spreading deciduous shrub with slender pointed, lance-shaped, mid-green leaves. Sweetly fragrant, sulphur-yellow, brownish-purple centred, bell-shaped flowers wreathe the bare branches in late winter. Grow in fertile, well-drained soil in sun or partial shade, in a sheltered site. Propagate by softwood cuttings in a frame in summer or seed sown in a cold frame when ripe. 'Grandiflorus' has larger, richer yellow flowers. var. *luteus* is clear yellow.

CHOISYA TERNATA
H 2–2.5m (6½–8ft) ★★★

Charming, bushy, rounded evergreen shrub, also known as Mexican Orange Blossom, thickly set with glossy, deep green, rounded leaves divided into three oval leaflets. From late spring to late summer it bears terminal clusters of pure white, 5-petalled, fragrant flowers. Grow in well-drained soil, in sun, in a site sheltered from freezing winds. Propagate by semi-hardwood cuttings in summer. 'Sundance' has bright yellow foliage, particularly when young.

COTINUS COGGYGRIA
H 3–5m (10–15ft) ★★★★

Also known as Smoke Bush, this bushy, erect, deciduous shrub has mid-green, oval leaves that turn orange or red in autumn. Insignificant flowers give way to smoke-like clusters of downy filaments and seeds. Grow in any fairly fertile, well-drained soil in a sunny site. Propagate by softwood cuttings in summer or by layering in late winter. 'Royal Purple' has dark purple foliage, turning red in autumn.

ELAEAGNUS COMMUTATA
H 4m (12ft) ★★★★

Also known as Silver Berry, this hardy, evergreen shrub is useful for hedging and bears very fragrant, tiny flowers in autumn, followed by silvery red fruit. It has small downy mid-green leaves. Does well in sun or partial shade, and will cope with salt spray and dry soil, but not lime. Propagate from semi-ripe cuttings in summer.

HIBISCUS SYRIACUS
H 2–3m (6½–10ft) ★★★★

Ornamental, erect, deciduous shrub with oval leaves, usually shallowly to deeply three-lobed, coarsely toothed and mid- to deep green. Large,

Elaeagnus commutata

funnel-shaped, pink flowers open in succession from late summer to autumn. Grow in fertile, moist, well-drained soil in full sun. Propagate by semi-hardwood cuttings in a frame in summer or by layering in late winter. Colour forms occur in shades of blue, purple, pink and white.

KOLKWITZIA AMABILIS
H 2.5–3m (8–10ft) ★★★★

Also known as Beauty Bush, this lovely, erect then spreading, deciduous shrub has arching stems and broadly oval, slender pointed mid- to deep green leaves. The shoots are wreathed with clusters of bell-shaped, pale to deep pink flowers with yellow-flushed throats from late spring to early summer. Grow in fertile, moist, but well-drained soil in full sun. Propagate by semi-hardwood cuttings in summer.

MAGNOLIA STELLATA
H 2–3m (6½–10ft) ★★★★

Delightful, compact, spreading, deciduous shrub with oblong to narrowly paddle-shaped mid-green leaves. The silky-white buds open to pure white, star-shaped flowers before the leaves in early- to mid-spring. Grow in sun or partial shade in fertile, moist, but well-drained soil, ideally neutral to acid. 'Royal Star' has pink buds. 'Rubra' has flowers opening red.

OSMANTHUS HETEROPHYLLUS
H 2.5–4m (8–15ft) ★★★

Intriguing, holly-like evergreen shrub of dense, rounded habit with oval to elliptic, spine-toothed, leathery, deep green leaves. Small, tubular, fragrant white flowers open in small clusters from late summer to autumn, followed by blue-black berries. Grow in fertile, moist but well-drained soil in sun or partial shade. Propagate by semi-hardwood cuttings in summer or layering in autumn or winter. 'Aureomarginatus' has yellow margined leaves.

PHILADELPHUS CORONARIUS
H 2–2.5m (6½–8ft) ★★★★

Also known as Mock Orange, this is an appealing, rounded, deciduous, hardy shrub with somewhat arching stems and narrow, pointed, mid-green leaves. Small clusters of fairly large, fragrant, white bowl-shaped flowers in early summer. Grow in well-drained soil in sun or partial shade. Propagate by softwood cuttings in summer or hardwood cuttings in autumn. P.c. 'Aureus' has golden leaves, 'Variegatus' has leaves with white markings.

PYRACANTHA
H 2.5–3m (8–10ft) ★★★

This showy, erect, evergreen, hardy shrub has red-flushed young stems and broadly elliptic, glossy deep green leaves. In summer, a profusion of small white flowers is followed by masses of golden-yellow berries which can last all winter. Grow in fertile garden soil in sun. Propagate by semi-hardwood cuttings in late summer. 'Orange Glow' has orange-red berries. 'Mohave' has red berries. 'Mohave Silver' has white-variegated leaves.

SYRINGA VULGARIS
H 3–3.5m (10–11ft) ★★★★

Deservedly popular, often tree-like, hardy, deciduous shrub also known as Lilac. It bears mid- to bright green, smooth, heart-shaped leaves. Tubular, 4-petalled, very fragrant lilac flowers are produced in dense, conical clusters in late spring and early summer. Grow in moist but well-drained soil in sun or partial shade. Propagate by softwood cuttings in summer or by layering in autumn or winter. Many cultivars are available, some with larger flowers, others double, in shades of lilac, purple, white to creamy yellow and near red.

VIBURNUM TINUS
H 2–3m (6½–10ft) ★★★

Also known as Laurustinus, this hardy, winter-flowering shrub of bushy, rounded habit is thickly set with oblong to narrowly oval, deep green leaves. The small, somewhat starry, 5-petalled flowers are gathered into rounded, dense, flattened clusters, which open between late winter and spring. These may be followed by deep blue berry-like fruits. Grow in well-drained garden soil in sun or partial shade. Propagate by semi-hardwood cuttings in summer or by layering in winter. V. x burkwoodii is semi-evergreen with larger, fragrant, white flowers, often from pink buds, and has a looser habit. V. x bodnantense is an erect, robust, deciduous shrub with pendent clusters of longer, tubular, pink to white fragrant flowers.

Hibiscus syriacus 'Oiseau Bleu'

Kolkwitzia amabilis

Philadelphus coronarius 'Aureus'

Syringa vulgaris 'Vestale'

Viburnum x burkwoodii

Medium shrubs

Buxus sempervirens

Ceanothus thyrsiflorus **var. repens**

Chaenomeles **x** *superba*

Cornus alba 'Elegantissima'

Exochorda racemosa

BUXUS SEMPERVIRENS
H 5m (15ft) ★★★★

Also known as Box, this hardy, evergreen shrub has a bushy habit. The small, glossy dark green leaves are densely packed, making it ideal for topiary. It is also slow-growing. It prefers partial shade and fertile soil. Propagate from semi-ripe cuttings in summer. Some varieties have larger leaves, such as 'Handsworthiensis' which is good for hedging. 'Marginata' (syn. 'Aurea Marginata') has golden-margined leaves.

CEANOTHUS 'GLOIRE DE VERSAILLES'
H 1.5–2m (5–6½ft) ★★

This charming, deciduous shrub has finely toothed, mid- to deep green leaves. Each stem tip bears a large truss of tiny, 5-petalled, pale blue flowers from mid-summer to autumn. Grow in fertile, well-drained garden soil in a sunny position. Propagate by semi-hardwood cuttings in late summer. Best hard pruned in spring.

CHAENOMELES X SUPERBA
H 1.5–2m (5–6½ft) ★★★★

Also called Flowering Quince, this is an attractive, bushy, rather rounded, deciduous shrub with spiny, wiry stems and oval, mid-green, glossy leaves. Cup-shaped, pink to red flowers appear on bare stems in spring, sometimes continuing into summer. Grow in fairly fertile, ideally neutral to acid, well-drained soil. It prefers a position in full sun. Propagate by semi-hardwood cuttings in a frame in late summer or layering in autumn. 'Crimson and Gold' has a compact habit and rich red flowers with golden stamens. 'Pink Lady' has early, deep pink flowers.

CORNUS ALBA
H 2m (6½ft) or more ★★★★

A very valuable, strong growing, erect, deciduous shrub, also known as Red-barked Dogwood, with red winter stems and smooth, elliptic to oval dark green leaves which may turn red or orange in autumn. The small white, starry flowers are carried in dense, flattish clusters from late spring to early summer. They are followed by white, sometimes blue-tinted berries. Grow in moist garden soil in sun or partial shade. Propagate by hardwood cuttings in autumn or semi-hardwood cuttings in summer. 'Elegantissima' has grey-green leaves which are variegated with white.

DEUTZIA 'MONT ROSE'
H 1.5m (5ft) or more ★★★★

This delightful, bushy, erect, deciduous shrub has narrowly oval, pointed, deep green leaves and attractive star-shaped, rose-pink flowers that appear in early summer. Grow in ordinary, well-drained soil in sun or partial shade. Propagate by hardwood cuttings in autumn. *D. scabra* has stems with peeling, brown bark and spikes of white or pink-tinted flowers in early to mid-summer. *D. s.* 'Candidissima' has double white flowers and 'Pride of Rochester' has double, pink-tinted flowers.

ESCALLONIA 'DONARD SEEDLING'
H 2m (6½ft) or more ★★★

This pretty, evergreen shrub has arching stems and narrow to spoon-shaped, glossy, toothed, rich green leaves. In summer, stems are wreathed with clusters of little, tubular, white, pink-tinted flowers opening from pink buds. Grow in fertile, well-drained soil in sun or partial shade. Propagate by semi-hardwood cuttings in a frame in late summer. 'Donard Radiance' is more compact with slightly larger, rich pink flowers.

EUONYMUS ALATUS
H 1.5–2m (5–6½ft) ★★★★

Interesting, bushy, spreading deciduous shrub, with mid- to deep green leaves that usually turn brilliant red in autumn. Insignificant greenish flowers give way to spherical, purplish-red fruits which split open to reveal bright orange seeds. Grow in moist, well-drained, preferably acid soil in either sun or partial shade. Propagate by semi-hardwood cuttings in summer.

EXOCHORDA X MACRANTHA
H 1.5–2m (5–6½ft) ★★★★

This beautiful, hummock-forming, dense, deciduous shrub has lots of spoon-shaped, light- to mid-green leaves. From late spring to early summer it is smothered with spikes of white flowers. Grow in fertile, moist but well-drained soil in full sun. Propagate by softwood cuttings in a frame in summer. *E. racemosa* bears slightly larger pure white flowers.

FORSYTHIA X INTERMEDIA
H 2m (6½ft) or more ★★★★

Showy, erect, bushy, deciduous shrub with oval to lance-shaped, sharp toothed mid-green leaves, occasionally with two basal lobes. From late winter to mid-spring bright yellow, bell-shaped flowers appear on leafless stems. Grow in ordinary soil in sun or partial shade. Propagate by semi-hardwood cuttings in a frame in late summer.

HYDRANGEA MACROPHYLLA
H 1.5–2m (5–6½ft) ★★★★
Popular, rounded, deciduous shrub with robust, erect stems and large, broadly oval, toothed, glossy, rich-green leaves. From mid- to late summer, clusters of tiny, star-shaped blue, pink or white flowers are surrounded by a ring of larger, sterile ones: these are the Lace-caps. Grow in fertile, well-drained but moist soil in sun or partial shade. Propagate by softwood cuttings in early summer or semi-hardwood cuttings in late summer. Best-known Lace-cap is 'Mariesii Perfecta' (syn. 'Blue Wave') with rich blue or mauve flowers. Among the Hortensias (mop-head) are 'Deutschland' with large mauve heads, 'Europa' purple-blue and 'Madame Emile Mouillière' with white flowerheads which become pink-tinted with age.

MAHONIA JAPONICA
H 2m (6½ft) ★★★
Erect, evergreen, fragrant shrub with dark green, leathery leaves. From autumn to spring, small, pale yellow, bell-shaped flowers are produced in arching chains, often followed by purple-blue, white-bloomed berries. Grow in moist but well-drained, fertile soil in partial shade. Propagate by semi-hardwood or leaf-bud cuttings from late summer to autumn in a frame. M. x media 'Charity' is taller and more robust with richer yellow, denser flower spikes.

PIERIS JAPONICA
H 2m (6½ft) ★★★★
Striking, rounded, dense ever-green shrub, also known as Firecrest, with elliptic to narrow, spoon-shaped, toothed,

leathery, mid-green leaves which are bright red when young. From late winter to spring, clusters of small, white, bell flowers appear. Grow in humus-rich, moist, acid soil in partial shade. Propagate by semi-hardwood cuttings in late summer.

RIBES SANGUINEUM
H 2–3m (6½–10ft) or more ★★★★
Popular, erect, deciduous shrub, also called Flowering Currant, with rounded, 3 to 5-lobed, toothed, curiously aromatic mid- to deep green leaves. In early spring tubular, 5-petalled, reddish-pink flowers are borne in dense, arching clusters. Grow in ordinary soil in sun or partial shade. Propagate by hard-wood cuttings in autumn. 'Pulborough Scarlet' has rich red, white-centred flowers. 'Tydeman's White' has pure white flowers. 'Brocklebankii' is smaller and slower-growing with golden-green leaves.

SKIMMIA JAPONICA
H 1–2m (3–6½ft) or more ★★★
Attractive, rounded to hum-mock-forming, evergreen shrub with oval, slightly aro-matic mid- to deep green leaves. The small, star-shaped, often fragrant, white flowers are carried in dense, terminal clusters from mid- to late spring. Male and female flow-ers are carried on separate plants. If both are grown together, the female plant will produce a crop of long-last-ing bright-red berries. Grow in fertile, ideally humus-rich soil in partial shade. Propagate by semi-hardwood cuttings in late summer or by seed sown when ripe in a cold frame.

SPIRAEA 'ARGUTA'
H 2m (6½ft) ★★★
Also known as Bridal Wreath, this pretty, rounded, freely-branching, deciduous shrub has slim stems which tend to arch at the tips and

are clad with lance-shaped to narrowly oblong, bright green leaves. The small, pure white, 5-petalled flowers are carried in flattened clusters in spring. Grow in well-drained soil in a sunny or partially shaded site. Propagate by semi-hardwood cuttings in summer or hard-wood cuttings in autumn.

WEIGELA FLORIDA
H 2m (6½ft) ★★★★
This attractive, spreading, deciduous shrub has arching shoots and oval, toothed, mid-green leaves. The fun-nel-shaped flowers are pink and freely borne in clusters from late spring through until early summer. Grow in fertile garden soil in sun or partial shade. Propagate by semi-hardwood cuttings in late summer or by hardwood cuttings in autumn. There are many hybrid cultivars avail-able which have larger flow-ers and leaves.

Hydrangea macrophylla

Mahonia x media 'Charity'

Ribes sanguineum

Skimmia japonica 'Tansley Gem'

Weigela 'Florida Variegata'

Small shrubs

Daphne mezereum

Euonymus fortunei 'Silver Queen'

Fuchsia magellanica

Genista hispanica 'Compacta'

BERBERIS CANDIDULA
H 60cm (2ft) ★★★★

Attractive, evergreen, densely hummock-forming shrub with oval, spine-tipped, glossy green leaves, waxy-white beneath. Bright yellow, bowl-shaped flowers open in late spring, followed by oval purple fruit. Grow in ordinary soil in sun or light shade. Propagate by suckers in winter. *B. wilsoniae* is mound-forming to 1m (3ft), semi-evergreen with small, spoon-shaped leaves and pale yellow flowers in summer followed by globular, pink fruits.

BUXUS SEMPERVIRENS 'SUFFRUTICOSA'
H 1.5m (5ft) ★★★★

This small, hardy evergreen variety of box is one of the best for low hedging, being dense, compact and slow-growing. The glossy green leaves are notched at the tips. Flowers are insignificant. Grow in fertile soil, ideally in partial shade as hot sun may scorch its leaves. Propagate from semi-ripe cuttings in summer. Many other varieties with yellow or variegated leaves are available.

CALLUNA VULGARIS
H 30–90cm (1–3ft) ★★★★

Popular, bushy, evergreen shrub, also known as Heather, with mid-to deep green, minute, sometimes hairy, scale-leaves and spikes of small bell-flowers in shades of pink, purple, red and white. Grow in moist but well-drained, acid soil in full sun. Propagate by semi-ripe cuttings in late summer in a cold frame or by layering in late winter. Hundreds of cultivars are available in many colours.

CISTUS SALVIIFOLIUS
H 60–75cm (24–28in) ★★★

Also known as Sun Rose, this attractive, dense, rounded evergreen shrub bears a profusion of white flowers with yellow centres that resemble species roses, in summer. The oval, deep green leaves are boldly veined. Hardy in all but the severerest of winters. Grow in well-drained soil in full sun. Propagate by semi-hardwood or softwood cuttings in summer.

COTONEASTER HORIZONTALIS
H 60–90cm (2–3ft) ★★★★

Intriguing, deciduous shrub with a neat herringbone branch formation and low arching habit. Stems are covered with small, rounded, glossy, deep green leaves usually turning red in autumn. Pinkish-white flowers in late spring are followed by bright red berries. Grow in ordinary soil in either sun or partial shade. Propagate by seed sown when ripe in a cold frame or by semi-ripe cuttings in late summer. *C. microphyllus* is more hummock-forming with narrower, glossy, evergreen leaves and larger, pinker fruits.

DAPHNE MEZEREUM
H 90–120cm (3–4ft) ★★★★

Showy, erect, deciduous shrub, also known as Mezereon, which in late winter and early spring becomes thickly wreathed with many, small, tubular, 4-petalled, pink to rose-purple fragrant flowers. They are followed by bright red, inedible berries. The lance-shaped to narrow spoon-shaped leaves are pale to greyish-green. Grow in fertile, well-drained, ideally limy soil in sun or partial shade. Propagate by seed sown as soon as ripe in a cold frame. 'Bowles' Variety' and f. *alba* varieties both have white flowers.

ERICA CARNEA
H 15–20cm (6–8in) ★★★★

Also known as Winter Heath, this is an invaluable, mat-forming, evergreen shrub smothered in winter and spring with short spikes of tiny, narrow bell-flowers in shades of pink to purple or white. The densely-borne leaves are deep green and needle-shaped. It prefers sun or light shade and a moist but well-drained, ideally neutral soil (though some lime is tolerated). Propagate by layering in winter or semi-hardwood cuttings in late summer. Many cultivars are available in many shades, some with the young foliage tinted yellow, bronze or red. *E. cinerea*, Bell Heather, is somewhat taller with broader bell-shaped flowers in summer, on some cultivars ranging to magenta and almost red. Some also have golden foliage. Requires neutral to acid soil to thrive.

EUONYMUS FORTUNEI
H 30–120cm (1–4ft) ★★★★

Hummock-forming evergreen shrub grown for its glossy, green leaves. The oval, toothed, glossy leaves are deep green and insignificant flowers give way to whitish globular fruits which burst to show orange seeds. Grow in ordinary soil in full sun. Propagate by semi-hardwood cuttings in late summer in a frame. 'Emerald 'n' Gold' has leaves with a broad, bright yellow margin. 'Silver Queen' is more erect in habit with white-margined leaves.

FUCHSIA MAGELLANICA
H 1–1.5m (3–5ft) ★★★

Attractive, erect, deciduous shrub producing many pendent flowers in shades of red and purple in summer. The oval, toothed leaves are mid- to deep green. Grow in ordinary garden soil in sun or partial shade. Prune hard annually in early spring. Propagate by softwood cuttings in summer in a frame. 'Tom Thumb' is a normally small hybrid which rarely exceeds 30cm (1ft). 'Riccartonii' is a hardier hybrid with somewhat more rounded flowers. There is a large number of cultivars in a variety of colours and forms, chiefly of hybrid origin.

GENISTA LYDIA
H 45–60cm (1½–2ft) ★★★

Also known as Lydian Broom, this bright, cheerful, domed deciduous shrub has numerous slender arching branches and very narrow blue-green leaves which are soon shed. In early summer it is smothered with clusters of small, bright yellow, pea-shaped flowers. Grow in a sunny position in well-drained, ideally limy soil. Propagate by semi-ripe cuttings in summer in a frame. G. hispanica, Spanish Gorse, is more rounded and denser in habit to 75cm (2½ft) tall with prickly foliage and equally profuse darker yellow flowers.

HEBE ALBICANS
H 45–60cm (1½–2ft) ★★★

Neat, rounded, dense evergreen shrub, thickly set with firm, oval, grey leaves. The small, tubular, 4-petalled white flowers are carried in dense, terminal spikes in summer. Grow in ordinary soil in sun or partial shade.

Propagate by cuttings in late summer in a cold frame. H. pinguifolia 'Pagei' is mat-forming, rarely above 15cm (6in) high with bright blue-grey leaves and white flowers in late spring.

HELIANTHEMUM NUMMULARIUM
H 10–15cm (4–6in) ★★★★

Also named Rock Rose, this showy, mat-forming, evergreen shrub is closely set with small, elliptic, deep-green leaves. The flat, 5-petalled, freely produced, summer borne flowers are bright yellow with an orange eye. Grow in well-drained, ideally limy soil in a sunny position. Propagate by softwood cuttings in summer in a frame. The best known cultivars are of hybrid origin with a larger growth habit. The bigger flowers come in a range of colours from white to red and leaves which can also be grey or grey-green. The 'Ben' series of cultivars is recommended.

LAVANDULA ANGUSTIFOLIA
H 60–90cm (2–3ft) ★★★★

Much loved, compact, bushy shrub, also known as lavender, thickly set with small, strap-shaped, aromatic grey-green leaves. The dense spikes of small, tubular, purple flowers are borne on slender stems above the leaves. Grow in ordinary, ideally limy garden soil in full sun. Propagate by semi-hardwood cuttings in late summer in a frame or hardwood cuttings in the open garden. 'Hidcote' is more compact with greyer leaves and deeper flowers.

POTENTILLA FRUTICOSA
H 75–90cm (2½–3ft) ★★★★

Ornamental, rounded, bushy, deciduous shrub, also known as Shrubby Cinquefoil, with small, fingered deep green leaves. The 5-petalled flowers look like tiny wild roses and appear from late spring to autumn. Grow ideally in limy garden soil in sun or partial

Helianthemum '**Ben Heckla**'

Potentilla fruticosa
'**Primrose Beauty**'

shade. Propagate by semi-hardwood cuttings in summer or by seed sown in a cold frame when ripe. Many cultivars are available (some taller than 1.5m/5ft) with green to grey foliage and flowers primarily in shades of yellow, plus white, pink, orange and red.

RHODODENDRON WILLIAMSIANUM
H 90–150cm (3–5ft) ★★★

Beautiful, domed evergreen shrub with broadly oval to rounded, glossy rich green leaves which are grey beneath when mature. Rather large, bell-shaped flowers in shades of pink appear in late spring. Grow in humus-rich, acid soil in sun or partial shade. Propagate by semi-hardwood cuttings in a cold frame in late

Lavandula angustifolia
'**Hidcote**'

Santolina chamaecyparissus

summer. R. impeditum rarely exceeds 60cm (2ft) with much smaller, aromatic grey-green leaves and smaller, funnel-shaped lavender-blue flowers in mid to late spring.

SANTOLINA CHAMAECYPARISSUS (S. INCANA)
H 45–60cm (1–2ft) ★★★

Useful, rounded, evergreen shrub primarily grown for its densely borne, finely dissected grey-white leaves. In summer, bright yellow, button-shaped flowerheads are borne singly on slender stems above the foliage. Grow in well-drained soil in full sun. Propagate by semi-ripe cuttings in a frame in summer. 'Lemon Queen' has lemon-yellow flowerheads. 'Weston', H 15–20cm (6-8in) is dwarf and rarely flowers.

Roses

Favourites for several hundred years, today roses have never been more popular. Originally, only wild species were available, with single, five-petalled, usually fragrant flowers. Once attention had switched to the double-bloomed forms that occurred occasionally as natural mutations, man then took the lead with purposeful cross-breeding and selection which continues unabated today. Over the years many thousands of different roses have arisen, at least 2,000 of which are at present available.

Roses vary greatly in habit, from tall, thorny clinbers to miniature thornless bushes. The leaves are formed of several, oval, mid-green leaflets and the flowers range in size from 2.5–13cm (1–5in) across, usually semi- or fully double, in shades of pink, red, purple, yellow and white. All are hardy and like fertile, moist, well-drained soil in a sunny site, although some are shade-tolerant. Most roses need hard pruning after flowering or in early spring, or, in the case of climbers and ramblers, thinning out in autumn.

Rosa 'Maigold'

Rosa 'Alberic Barbier'

Rosa 'Peace'

Rosa 'Fragrant Cloud'

Rosa 'Iceberg'

CLIMBING
H 3–10m (10–30ft)

Generally vigorous, erect roses which extend almost indefinitely, though more slowly when older. The taller ones are best cascading from a redundant tree, the smaller ones on walls, pergolas and pillars. They prefer sun or partial shade. Pruning is mostly cutting out dead or weak stems in autumn or early spring, but to maintain vigour and curb ultimate size, thin out the oldest stems every two to four years. *R.* 'Mermaid' ★★★ H 6m (20ft) has deeper, glossy leaves and large, light yellow single flowers with reddish-amber stamens. *R.* 'Madame Grégoire Staechelin' ('Spanish Beauty') ★★★★ H 5–6m (15–20ft) has clusters of large, loosely double, pink flowers in early summer, followed by orange to red hips.

RAMBLER
H 2–5m (6½–15ft)

A group of freely-flowering cultivars producing strong stems from near the ground each year which bloom the next. The smallish, often double flowers are carried in large clusters in summer. Grow in full sun. Pruning consists of removing some or all of the flowered stems after blooming, just above strong new shoots. 'American Pillar' ★★★★ H 3–4m (10–12ft) is a vigorous, 1902 vintage that is still popular, with glossy leaves and freely-borne trusses of carmine-pink, white-eyed, single, almost scentless flowers. 'Veilchenblau' ★★★★ is almost as tall, with paler green leaves and double flowers in a unique dusky blue-violet. 'Goldfinch' ★★★★ H 2.5m (8ft) has plentiful, light green leaves and abundant, neat, yellow, double blooms that age to cream. 'Albéric Barbier' ★★★★ H 5m (15ft) has clusters of creamy white double flowers, which fade to white, set off against glossy, dark green leaves. *R. filipes* 'Kiftsgate' ★★★★ H 10m (30ft) has paler leaves and small, creamy white single flowers in late summer.

MINIATURE
H 15–45cm (6–18ins)

A group of very small, twiggy stemmed roses, freely producing small, double flowers from summer to autumn. Ideal for rock gardens or small borders in sunny sites. 'Angela Rippon' ★★★★ bears fully double, rose to salmon-pink flowers. 'Darling Flame' ★★★★ has glossy leaves and cup-shaped, orange-red flowers. 'Little Artist' ('Top Gear') ★★★★ has semi-double red flowers with white markings.

LARGE-FLOWERED BUSH
(Hybrid Tea)
H 54–90cm (1½–3ft)

Erect, thorny bushes with robust shoots and usually small clusters of large, double, often scented flowers. Prune by removing one-third of the oldest stems to the base each year and reduce the remaining stems by two-thirds. 'Fragrant Cloud' **** is strongly scented, with rich scarlet flowers. 'Pascali' **** is cup-shaped, double, creamy white flowers. 'Grandpa Dickson' **** fully double, large, pointed, primrose-yellow flowers. 'Blue Moon' **** fully double, fragrant, mauve-lilac flowers. Large-flowering 'Peace' **** H 1.2m (4ft) is very popular, with fully double, scented yellow flowers and a beautiful, old-fashioned rose shape.

CLUSTER-FLOWERED BUSH
(Floribunda)
H 45–90cm (1½–3ft)
Similar to Large-flowered Bush roses, but with larger clusters of smaller flowers, sometimes only semi-double. Prune by removing one-third of the oldest stems to the base each year and reduce the remaining stems by one-third. Grow in full sun. 'Elizabeth of Glamis' ('Irish Beauty') **** has elegant sprays of cupped, double, scented, orange-pink flowers. 'Iceberg' **** is tall-growing and vigorous, with large clusters of loosely double white flowers. 'Lilli Marlene' **** has loosely double, crimson flowers. 'Glenfiddich' **** rounded, loosely double, amber to yellow flowers. The modern Patio roses are dwarf, compact forms. 'Cider Cup' **** has glossy foliage and double, apricot-pink flowers. 'Tip Top' **** has glossy leaves and rich pink flowers. 'Wee Jock' has fully double, deep crimson flowers.

POLYANTHA
H 45cm–2m (1½–6½ft)
Similar to Cluster-flowered Bush roses but often somewhat smaller with a more twiggy growth habit and smaller, single to double, rarely scented flowers from summer to autumn. Prune by removing about one-third of old stems annually and short-en the side stems by one-third to one-half. 'White Pet' **** H 45cm (1½ft) vigorous, spreading habit, with deep green leaves and fully double, rosetted, white flowers from red-flushed buds.

MODERN SHRUB (including Hybrid Musk)
H 1–2.5m (3–8ft) or more
A variable group of bushy roses, mostly of fairly recent origin with few- to many-flowered clusters of usually scented, single to double flowers, some followed by red hips. Little pruning is necessary, except to remove dead and weak stems and thin out congested ones. Grow in a sunny position. 'Ballerina' **** usually of dense and spreading habit, H 1-1.5m (3-5ft), with large clusters of bright, light pink, white-centred, single flowers. 'Cerise Bouquet', vigorous with arching habit, greyish leaves and semi-double, cherry-red flowers. 'Constance Spry' **** vigorous with arching habit, climbing if supported, greyish green leaves and large, fully double, glowing pink, richly fragrant flowers. 'Nevada', vigorous with spiny, arching red stems and flat, semi-double, glowing pink, richly fragrant flowers. 'Frühlingsgold' ****, strong growing, bristly stems, H 2.5m (8ft), with cupped, semi-double, fragrant, light yellow flowers. 'Graham Thomas' **** H 1.2m (4ft), quartered-rosette to cupped, fully double, fragrant, yellow flowers.

OLD-FASHIONED SHRUB
H 1–2.5m (3–8ft)
This name covers at least a dozen smaller groups of varied cultivars, most of which are 100 years old or more. All are erect to spreading shrubs with green to grey-green leaves and single to double, usually scented flowers, in shades of red, pink, purple and white. Grow in full sun. Pruning comprises cutting

Rosa 'Ballerina'

Rosa 'Graham Thomas'

Rosa 'Louise Odier'

Rosa xanthina 'Canary Bird'

out dead and weak stems and shortening back long ones by one-third to one-half. 'Alba Maxima' **** the White Rose of York, H 2.2m (7ft), vigorous, erect habit, greyish green leaves and loosely double, sweetly scented, white flowers. 'Charles de Mills' **** H 1.5m (5ft) or more, erect habit, densely petalled, bright magenta, fragrant flowers. 'Louise Odier' **** H 2m (6½ft), spreading habit with double, pink, scented flowers from summer to autumn. 'Mme Hardy' **** H 1.5m (5ft), erect habit, leathery, dark green leaves and very fully double, fragrant, white flowers with a green-button eye. 'William Lobb' **** vigorous, with arching stems to 2m (6½ft) and fully double, cupped, fragrant, purple-crimson flowers tinged lavender grey.

SPECIES
H 1–3m (3–10ft)
This includes all the cultivated wild roses ranging across the northern hemisphere. All have single flowers followed by hips in shades of purple-black to orange and red and some have autumn tinted foliage. Little pruning other than removing dead stems and thinning crowded ones. *R. rugosa* **** H 2m (6½ft), sparingly branched, suckering stems, leathery, deep green leaves and large, single, scented carmine pink flowers followed by large, orange-red hips. Var *rosea* **** has rose pink flowers, var *rubra* **** has purplish red ones and 'Alba' **** is white. *R. xanthina* 'Canary Bird' **** H 2m (6½ft) or more, erect habit with red-flushed stems and ferny leaves. Flowers are yellow with a musky scent.

Using climbers and wall shrubs

Climbers have an innate flexibility, which makes them extremely useful to the gardener, who can bend and train them in all sorts of ways on a variety of supports. They also have different mechanisms by which they pull themselves up, which can determine how they are used in the garden. When considering climbers it is useful to look at 'wall shrubs' as well. These are grown against walls, either because they have a lax, floppy habit and need something to lean against, or because they are slightly tender and benefit from a wall's protection.

Climbers have a distinctly romantic appeal and are perfect for clothing eyesores, like outbuildings. They are a boon in small urban gardens, where they can do much to introduce a note of greenery and nature into a brick or concrete-dominated environment.

Vertical bonus

A high wall provides an opportunity to increase the capacity for flowering plants in the garden. Roses and clematis are an obvious choice, but it is worth mixing evergreens with deciduous climbers, and using the shelter of walls to grow tender wall shrubs.

Planting a climber

Most climbing garden plants climb by means of twining stems or tendrils, which means that they must have something to cling onto, and preferably not so wide that their tendrils cannot grip on. It is often necessary to attach wire to walls, or other structures, to help them to climb.

As with shrubs in the garden, it is important that the eventual size of any climber is understood. Several years' growth of stem and leaf can not only smother original supports, but exert a considerable amount of weight.

There are those, however, that are conveniently self-clinging, ivies (*Hedera* spp.) for example, which use aerial roots or suckers that emerge from the stems. They are especially useful for sending up big expanses of wall, to which they will tightly cling.

1 *Create a generous-sized planting hole 30-45cm (12-18in) away from a wall. Add fertilizer, tease out the roots of the plant and insert in the hole.*

2 *Backfill the hole, firm down and water well. As the plant grows, tie in the shoots, if necessary to a supporting structure of wire or trellis.*

Combining climbers

Where space is at a premium, you can greatly enhance the garden's visual beauty by combining climbers that will grow into one another.

Clematis and roses are the most commonly combined climbers, since both have a relatively short flowering season. By planting them together so that the clematis uses the rose as support, you extend the flowering value without actually adding to the space requirements.

When combining climbers in this way you need to be careful that the vigour of one does not completely overwhelm the growth of the other.

Macropetala type clematis are ideal companions for some of the less vigorous climbing roses. However, the big scrambling forms of the latter, such as *Rosa* 'Kiftsgate' or 'Bobbie James' should be left to strut their stuff alone.

Useful combinations

When combining climbers, it is important that they complement one another in terms of colour as well as scale and vigour. Roses and clematis, used to adorn this arch, make successful partners.

Knowing how far they go

Wall shrubs may be grown simply against a convenient wall, preferably one facing the sun, as most are sun lovers. The heat radiated by the wall will give protection from severe frosts and enhance the effect of summer sun, enabling you to grow species that might not be hardy elsewhere in the garden. The wall will also protect against damaging winds.

More creative, and useful in confined spaces, is training appropriate shrubs against walls. You can tie them to wires or trellis and cut back branches that thrust out too far, so that they are held close to the wall. This can be an effective way to treat, not only slightly tender species, but also certain other, bone-hardy, shrubs. Pyracantha, smothered in fiery, bright berries in autumn, looks stunning grown like this.

More difficult to guide in the right direction are plants, notably climbing roses, with strong stems that, in nature, can haul themselves up by means of sharp thorns. In the garden, their stems must be tied to supports at intervals, otherwise they will flop down and become an unmanageable mess.

Vigorous climbers
Wisteria is one of the most popular climbers for covering walls, but it is exceptionally vigorous and will need regular tying in and pruning to keep it in check.

Wall shrubs
Some shrubs, like winter-flowering jasmine (Jasminum nudiflorum) are not self-clinging, but can be trained to climb if a suitable supporting structure is provided.

Structures and supports

Given that in many gardens there is a limit to the amount of wall or fence space for climbers, various structures have been developed for supporting and displaying them. Pergolas, where supports carry the weight of an overhead structure with a walkway underneath, are suitable for medium-sized or larger gardens. Archways are more suited to the smaller garden, and are particularly useful as 'doors' between one part of the garden and another. Free-standing supports have recently become popular, enabling climbers to be grown in borders without having to rely on a convenient stretch of wall space. These vary from obelisks which are ideal for formal situations to 'wigwams' made from willow which are more rustic in feel. Established trees or shrubs can also be home to climbers. Using a late-flowering climber on an early-flowering shrub is a good way of capitalizing on space, although it is vital that the host plant is not smothered by too vigorous a choice of climber.

Overhead canopy
A pergola provides an ideal structure over which climbers can be grown to give shade in summer. Here, rustic wooden poles support a climbing rose.

Trellis arbour
Adding trellis to a garden fence or wall can create additional height, and provide a home for climbers. Here ivy has been grown over a trellis arbour in a shady city garden to give shelter and privacy.

Climbers and wall shrubs

Actinidia kolomikta

Campsis x tagliabuana

Garrya elliptica

Humulus lupulus 'Aureus'

Jasminum humile

ACTINIDIA KOLOMIKTA
H 5–7m (15–22ft) ★★★★

Deciduous, twining climber grown for its unique foliage. The oval to heart-shaped, mid-green leaves are flushed with white and pink for up to two-thirds of their surface. The bowl-shaped, white flowers appear in summer but are rather hidden by the foliage. Grow in moist but well-drained fertile soil in sun or partial shade. Propagate by semi-ripe cuttings in late summer.

CAMPSIS RADICANS
H 10m (30ft) or more ★★★★

Also known as Trumpet Creeper, this showy, deciduous, self-clinging climber has prominent clusters of tubular, 5-petalled, scarlet flowers in late summer. The dark green leaves are composed of several toothed, oval leaflets. Grow in moist but well-drained soil in a sunny site. Propagate by semi-ripe cuttings in summer or seed in spring. *C.* x *tagliabuana* 'Mme Galen' is a hybrid with orange-red flowers, which clings as vigorously as *C. radicans*.

CHIMONANTHUS PRAECOX
H 3–4m (10–12ft) ★★★

A deciduous, erect shrub, also called Wintersweet, grown for its very sweetly scented, sulphur-yellow, pendant bell-shaped flowers in winter. The large, rough-textured mid-green leaves are lance-shaped. Grow in moist but well-drained soil in a sunny position. Propagate by softwood cuttings in summer or by seed when ripe in a cold frame. Best trained out flat on a wall when young, then allowed to grow more freely. *C.p.* var. *luteus* has clearer, yellow flowers which open more widely.

CYTISUS BATTANDIERI
H 3–5m (10–15ft) ★★★

Also known as Pineapple or Moroccan Broom, this is a handsome, deciduous to semi-evergreen shrub bearing dense, erect spikes of strongly pineapple-scented, yellow pea flowers in summer. Leaves are composed of three oval, silky, silver-haired leaflets. Grow in well-drained, ideally limy soil in full sun. Propagate by semi-ripe cuttings in late summer. Best trained out flat on a wall when young, then allowed to grow more freely.

GARRYA ELLIPTICA
H 3–4m (10–12ft) ★★

Also called Silk Tassel Bush, this popular bushy, evergreen shrub or small tree is grown for its long, silvery grey, male catkins in winter. Female plants have shorter, less showy catkins and are seldom seen. The deep green, oval, leathery leaves have strongly waved margins. Grow in ordinary soil in sun or partial shade. Propagate by semi-ripe cuttings in summer. 'James Roof' bears clusters of longer, more silvery catkins.

HUMULUS LUPULUS
H 5–6m (15–20ft) ★★★★

Twining, herbaceous climber, also known as Hop, with striking foliage of large, 3 to 5-lobed, boldly toothed, rough-textured leaves. Female plants may bear soft, pale green, cone-like fruits (hops) in late summer. Grow in moist but well-drained fertile soil in sun or partial shade. Propagate by seed or softwood cuttings in spring. *H.l.* 'Aureus', with suffused golden yellow leaves, is most commonly grown but does not come true from seed.

HYDRANGEA ANOMALA SSP. PETIOLARIS)
H 10–15m (30–50ft) ★★★★

Also known as Climbing Hydrangea, this attractive, self-clinging, deciduous climber has lacy, flat heads of small, white flowers in summer surrounded by larger, sterile florets. The rounded to broadly oval toothed leaves are mid- to deep green, turning yellow in autumn. Grow in moist but well-drained soil in sun or partial shade. Propagate by softwood cuttings in summer or hardwood cuttings in winter.

JASMINUM OFFICINALE
H 8–12m (25–40ft) ★★★

Twining climber, also known as Jasmine, with fragrant, white flowers in clusters from summer to early autumn. Grow in ordinary soil in sun or partial shade. Propagate by cuttings in summer or layering in autumn. The form *affine* has pink-tinted flowers. *J.* x *stephanense* is less vigorous with fragrant, pale pink flowers and matt green leaves, sometimes flushed with cream. *J. humile,* Yellow Jasmine, is semi-evergreen or evergreen with bright yellow, sometimes fragrant flowers. *J. nudiflorum,* Winter Jasmine, is a deciduous shrub with long, slender, arching green stems and bright yellow flowers in winter and early spring.

LONICERA PERICLYMENUM
H 5–8m (15–25ft) ★★★

Deciduous, vigorous, twining climber, also known as Common Honeysuckle, with clusters of tubular, fragrant flowers which open white and age to yellow. Broadly spoon-shaped leaves are mid-green. The flowers are followed by bright red berries. Grow in ordinary soil in sun or partial shade. Propagate by semi-ripe cuttings in summer. *L.p.* 'Belgica', Early Dutch Honeysuckle, has earlier flowers which are strongly suffused red. *L. caprifolium* is less vigorous with creamy white to yellow, pink-flushed, scented flowers in summer, borne at the stem tips in the centre of a cup-like leaf.

SOLANUM CRISPUM
H 4–6m (12–20ft) ★★★

Also known as Chilean Potato Tree, this showy, scrambling climber produces a profusion of starry, purple-blue flowers with cone-shaped, yellow centres in terminal clusters in summer. Grow in ordinary soil in full sun, sheltered from cold winds and secured to its support. Propagate by semi-ripe cuttings in summer. 'Glasnevin' ('Autumnale'), flowers freely from summer to autumn.

VITIS COIGNETIAE
H 10–15m (30–50ft) ★★★★

Vigorous, deciduous, woody, tendril climber with large, heart-shaped, deep-green leaves which turn bright red in autumn. Small flowers may be followed by blue-black, unpalatable grapes. Grow in moist, well-drained, fertile soil in full sun. Propagate by hardwood cuttings in winter, layering in autumn or by bud-cuttings in early spring.

WISTERIA FLORIBUNDA
H 8–10m (25–30ft) ★★★★

A vigorous, deciduous, twining climber bearing many loosely pendent spikes of fragrant, pea-shaped flowers in shades of lavender to purple and white. Long leaves consist of lance-shaped, mid-green leaflets. Grow in fertile, well-drained soil in sun. Propagate by softwood cuttings in summer or layering in autumn. 'Alba' has white flowers, 'Multijuga' ('Macrobotrys'), lilac-blue flowers in spikes 90-120cm (3–4ft) long. *W. sinensis* has lilac-blue to white flowers in denser spikes.

Jasminum nudiflorum

Lonicera periclymenum 'Belgica'

Solanum crispum 'Glasnevin'

Wisteria floribunda 'Multijuga'

Clematis

This large group of often fast-growing climbers comes in a wide variety of flower shapes and sizes. The leaves can be simple or dissected into three or more mid- to deep green leaflets, the stalks of which coil like tendrils around any available support. All clematis prefer a moist, but well-drained, rich soil where the roots are shaded and the top is in the sun. Propagate by layering in late winter, softwood cuttings in spring or semi-hardwood ones in summer. Prune the early, large-flowered cultivars by cutting the previous season's stems back to the highest and plumpest expanding bud. Cut late flowerers to 10–15cm (4–6in), above ground level, both in spring.

LARGE-FLOWERED – EARLY GROUP H 2.5–3.5m (8–11ft)

Moderately vigorous growers with 3 to 5 or more leaflets and 8-petalled, or more, flowers 15–25cm (6–10in) across in late spring and early summer and again in late summer. A wide range of excellent cultivars is available.

LARGE-FLOWERED – LATE GROUP H 2.6m (8½ft)

Vigorous growers with 1–3 or more leaflets and flowers 10–20cm (4–8in) across composed of six or more petals from midsummer to autumn. A wide range of excellent cultivars is available.

SPECIES H 2–15m (6½–48ft)

Some early flowering species are evergreen or semi-evergreen but the three listed here are deciduous.

C. macropetala ★★★★ H 2–3m (6–10ft), has a slender-stemmed, bushy habit with 6 to 9, coarsely toothed leaflets and nodding, bell-shaped, blue to violet, pink or white, 4-petalled flowers with a central boss of petaloid stamens from mid- to late spring, followed by decorative seed-heads. *C. montana* ★★★★ H 7–15m (21–48ft) is very vigorous with trifoliate, lobed and toothed leaflets and many 4-petalled, white flowers in late spring to early summer. 'Elizabeth' has pink flowers and purple-flushed leaves. *C. tangutica* ★★★★ H 4–6m (12–20ft) is vigorous, with irregularly shaped, toothed leaflets and nodding, lantern-shaped flowers of pointed, yellow petals from midsummer to autumn followed by striking silvery seedheads.

Clematis montana 'Odorata'

Clematis 'Jackmanii'

Using perennials

Herbaceous perennials are, for most people, what gardening is all about: flowers and colour. They are generally long-lived, resilient species that die back every autumn to re-emerge the following spring (which is what is meant by the word 'herbaceous'). Quicker to establish than shrubs, they are invaluable for the impatient gardener. Being smaller, too, they suit restricted spaces.

The seasonal habit of growth of perennials gives them a strongly dynamic character, many being practically invisible over the winter, yet growing to over 2m (6½ft) by the end of the year. This creates a strong sense of change in the garden, quite different to one dominated by shrubs or conifers. Winter, when the majority are dormant, need not be dull, as many perennials have dead stems and seedheads that are attractive in a ghostly way, especially in low winter light.

Cottage-garden border
A perennial planting of cottage garden favourites – foxgloves (Digitalis), poppies (Papaver orientale), flax (Linum) and burning bush (Dictamnus albus) – is an ideal choice for a country garden.

Perennials for colour

In many gardens it is shrubs and, perhaps, trees that make up the framework, with perennials being the 'infill'. Given that they take up relatively little space, and flower over a long period, it makes

Perennials for colour
Bright summer border Asters (Aster amellus 'King George') and Japanese anemones (Anemone x hybrida 'Prinz Heinrich') mingle in a vibrant late summer border (below).

sense to rely on perennials for the bulk of the garden's floral interest. The perennial year starts off in late winter with a limited number of extremely versatile plants, notably hellebores and pulmonarias, with their often strangely coloured flowers and attractive evergreen leaves. While there are certainly a number of attractive, spring-flowering perennials and plenty of spring-flowering bulbs, it is not until early summer that perennials really get into their stride, with the pinks and blues of the hardy geraniums ('cranesbills').

Because perennials have to renew all their above-ground growth every year, it is not, perhaps, surprising that the majority flower later in the

Naturalistic forms
Planting in large groups, or drifts, to echo the way that plants grow in the wild, gives the garden a natural appearance and reduces labour. Here grasses and perennials are grown in a relaxed border.

year. Numbers build up through midsummer to a peak in late summer and early autumn. Midsummer sees monardas in pinks, purples and mauves, later months

a huge variety of species from the daisy family, such as asters and rudbeckias. Yellow is the dominant late colour, although there are plenty of good blues and violets too.

Evergreens and architecturals

Although their growth is replaced every year, there are certain species that are effectively evergreen. These are usually rather statuesque plants, such as varieties of hellebore and euphorbia, whose attractive foliage alone is reason enough to grow them. They are vital in providing some interest for perennial plantings in winter, especially appreciated in smaller gardens.

While flowers are the main attraction for most gardeners, and good-looking leaves an additional boon, it is the habit of certain perennials that earns them a place in the garden, a quality best described as architectural. Examples include the eryngiums, upright growers with the atmosphere of refined thistles, and macleayas, large growers with a combination of bulk and elegance.

Grasses, too, play an extremely useful role in adding structure and form to a perennial border. Their slender leaves and arching habit make a welcome counterpoint to smaller flowering perennials.

Strong architecture
Giant thistles, such as Onopordum acanthium, *with their large, steely-blue leaves, make an eye-catching feature in any perennial border.*

Graceful elegance
The elegant shape and arching habit of the silver-leaved grass, Miscanthus sinensis *'Variegatus', gives a border striking architectural form.*

Naturalistic and border planting

The border may be the traditional place to grow perennials, but there is now interest in more innovative ways, such as alongside grasses in wildflower meadow or prairie plantings, or in naturalistic, wild garden drifts.

Such plantings are low maintenance once established, but need as much care and attention as any other planting for the first few years. The core idea of these naturalistic plantings is the selection of appropriate perennials (and grasses). They must be plants that are naturally adapted to the prevailing conditions, and which stand a reasonable chance of competing together.

Shady border
Restrained colour, in a variety of shades of blue, is the keynote of a shady perennial border where forget-me-nots (Myosotis), Lunaria rediviva *and grasses, such as this Bowles' golden grass* (Milium effusum) *predominate.*

Selecting for success

Selecting perennials suited to the environment of your garden is an important part of success. Herbaceous perennials have a reputation for needing a lot of maintenance. This is largely to do with the way they were grown in the past, when they were fed well and grown in distinct and separate clumps. They would become top heavy, as a result, and so needed staking. The choice of more robust, modern varieties or natural species helps to reduce the need for support, as does avoiding heavy feeding. The range of perennials available today is far more suited to mixed borders and informal styles of planting than those of the past. These are plants that are becoming increasingly important in modern gardening.

Damp lovers
Next to a gulley, various moisture-loving perennials do well, including irises, euphorbia, ferns, Heuchera *'Palace Purple' and* Alchemilla mollis.

Perennial borders

Given that most of us only have limited space in the garden, achieving a border with as long a period of interest as possible is crucial. Many gardeners decide to colour-scheme a border, by including only pink or only yellow flowers, for example, or a mix such as blue and white. Others simply want to include as many of the plants they like as possible. No matter how well colour-schemed, a border will never be an entire success unless there is also foliage interest. Leaves have a longer season, give the border structure and also make a contribution in terms of colour. Because most plants, perennials and shrubs tend to be fairly shapeless, a border will greatly benefit from the inclusion of clearly defined, contrasting shapes.

Vibrant summer border
Seen in early summer, this perennial border features a number of cottage garden perennials, including delphiniums, flax (Linum spp.), astrantia, inula and pyrethrums (Tanacetum coccineum).

Height in the border

A perennial border is normally organized with the tallest plants at the back, medium ones in the middle and smaller perennials at the front. Failure to plan your border in this way will mean that some plants are obscured by others as the seasons progress.

The perennials on the following pages therefore, are organized from the tallest to the smallest. It also helps to have a few punctuation points in the border created by larger plants, such as shrubs.

Punctuation points
Give the border shape and form by including a few shrubs to add height. A clipped yew (Taxus baccata) pyramid gives definition to a border of African lilies (agapanthus) and fuchsia.

Colour in the border

Planning a colour scheme for a border is a complex task, since you have to orchestrate the flowering times as well. Limiting the colour choices helps not only to produce greater impact but it means that you do not have to worry so much about what is flowering when.

You can therefore opt for a single colour theme border – all white flowers or all blue for example. This means that you do not have to worry about whether colours 'go' together. In general, when mixing colours in the border aim either for all pastel shades – pale pinks, blues, mauves, creamy yellows – or strong contrasting colours - red, yellows, strong blues or purples. Problems may arise when you mix strong colours with pastels as the bright colours will swamp or overwhelm the pale ones.

Single theme
Opting for a single colour theme, such as white, means that you do not have to worry about whether colours 'go' together.

Designing a border

It is all too easy to plant a border that becomes a jumbled collection of plants without a real theme. A few distinct 'theme plants' can make all the difference.

Dotting a few of the same variety through a border can do wonders in unifying it and developing a sense of rhythm. Such plants need to have a distinct colour and a reasonably long flowering season. If there is space, it is possible to use a particularly effective colour combination as a repeating element.

It pays when planning a border to go for simplicity. Repeat groups of plants at intervals, and keep the colour palette limited. The

Colour co-ordination

This backed border has been carefully designed with a yellow and blue colour theme. Delphiniums and catmint (Nepeta) *create the blue areas; mulleins, helenium and thalictrum the yellow. Limiting the colour palette in this way greatly increases the impact.*

border, below, is effective because it is created from blue and yellow plants only. The contrast gives interest without appearing either bitty or unstructured.

Plant small plants in odd-numbered groups – 3, 5 or 7. Use quick-growing annuals to fill those holes where

plants inevitably die or fail. Busy lizzies (*Impatiens* spp.) or large annuals, such as *Nicotiana sylvestris* are excellent plants for this purpose.

Remember to have some plants in the border for foliage interest – big thistles, grasses, euphorbias, irises, and the large hellebores are ideal for this purpose – so that once the main flower-

ing period is over, there will still be something interesting to look at. An occasional evergreen will help give the border form in winter.

Remember that not all plants like the same soil conditions, or the same climate, so for the best results, it is advisable to choose those that enjoy the conditions you have.

Planning the planting

To create a border, mark the planting down on paper and plant in groups of at least three to give the border bulk. The plan, right, is for a similar blue and yellow border to that shown above, for an area about 2.4m (8ft) x 1.2m (4ft). Repeat the planting for a longer border.

1 *Verbascum* 'Gainsborough'
2 *Delphinium* x *belladonna* 'Blue Bees'
3 *Thalictrum flavum*
4 *Aster frikartii* 'Monch'
5 *Solidago* 'Laurin'
6 *Hosta* 'Gold Standard'
7 *Nepeta mussinii*
8 *Hemerocallis* 'Canary Glow'
9 *Salvia* x *sylvestris* 'Indigo'
10 *Helenium* 'Butterpat'
11 *Geranium* 'Johnson's Blue'

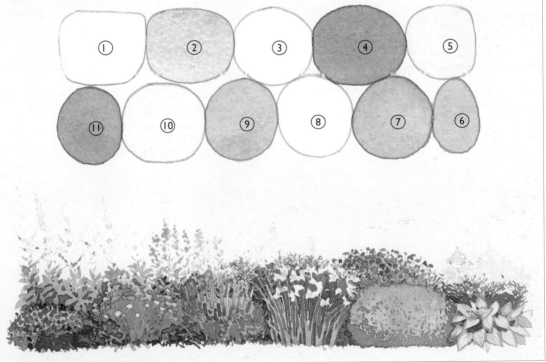

Water-loving perennials

Some plants thrive in very moist soil or with their feet in water itself. A few are actually aquatic plants, floating in deep water. It is important to ensure that the plants are grown in appropriate conditions if they are to survive. Some prefer full sun; others will cope well with partial shade, and while some are frost hardy, others, such as the big-leaved gunneras are not. Ideally a pond needs a range of water-loving perennials: a couple of deep water plants, a few in the shallow margins of the pond, and some which enjoy moist soil alongside the pond's edges.

Astilbe x *arendsii* 'Rotlicht'

Astilboides tabularis

ASTILBE X ARENDSII
H 50–120cm (1¾–4ft) ★★★★
Grown for its elegant plumes of tiny flowers in shades of white to red in summer. The dissected, mainly basal leaves are mid-green, sometimes bronze-tinted and coarsely fern-like. Grow in moist to wet soil in sun or partial shade. Propagate by division in autumn or early spring. 'Bressingham Beauty', H 90cm (3ft), has bronze-flushed leaves and bright pink flowers. 'Deutschland', H 50cm (1¾ft), has bright green leaves and pure white flowers.

ASTILBOIDES TABULARIS
H 90–120cm (3–4ft) ★★★★
Handsome, clump-forming, herbaceous perennial with thick rhizomes and large, stiff, but open clusters of numerous tiny white flowers in early to midsummer. The large, oval, softly hairy leaves are deeply veined and a shiny, deep green. Grow in permanently wet soil at the edge of a pond or watercourse in sun or partial shade. Propagate by division in autumn or early spring.

CALTHA PALUSTRIS
H 25–45cm (10–18in) ★★★★
Cheerful, herbaceous perennial, also known as Marsh Marigold, grown for its bowl-shaped, 5-petalled, bright yellow flowers in spring. The long-stalked, heart- to kidney-shaped leaves are toothed and rich, lustrous green. Grow in wet soil at the edge of a pond or watercourse in sun or partial shade. Propagate by division in early autumn or very early spring. Var. *alba* has white flowers, 'Flore Pleno' has double ones.

EUPHORBIA PALUSTRIS
H 70–90cm (2¼–3ft) ★★★★
Useful, clump-forming herbaceous perennial with erect, unbranched stems, topped by clusters of small, deep yellow flowers in late spring and surrounded by larger, paler, leaf-like bracts.

The entirely stem-borne leaves are oblong to elliptic, bright green, with orange and yellow tones in autumn. Grow in any permanently moist soil or pond margins in a sunny position. Propagate by division in late winter or early spring or sow seeds when ripe in a cold frame.

GUNNERA MANICATA
H 2–2.5m (6½–8ft) or more ★★
Statuesque, half-hardy, herbaceous perennial forming loose clumps from large rhizomes. Grown for its huge, deeply-lobed, rounded, deep green leaves on robust, erect, prickly stalks. Grow in wet soil at the edge of a pond in sun or partial shade. Propagate by division, separating the rhizomes in spring, or sow seeds as soon as ripe in wet soil in a cold frame.

IRIS ENSATA (I. KAEMPFERI)
H 75–90cm (2½–3ft) ★★★★
Beautiful, herbaceous perennial forming loose clumps with large, round-petalled flowers in shades of purple, in summer. The erect, sword-like leaves are mid- to bright green. Grow in any permanently moist soil or pond margins in sun. Propagate by division in early spring or sow seeds when ripe, in wet soil in a cold frame. 'Alba' has white flowers. 'Moonlight Waves' has white flowers with lime-green centres. 'Rose Queen' is soft pink, 'Variegata' has green and white striped leaves and purple flowers. *I. laevigata* has

Caltha palustris 'Flore Pleno'

Gunnera manicata

Iris ensata **Higo Hybrids**

smaller, narrower-petalled flowers produced in larger numbers. *I. pseudacorus*, Yellow Flag, is very vigorous, forming wide clumps up to 1m (3ft) tall and has yellow flowers with violet to brownish markings. Variety *bastardii* has sulphur-yellow flowers.

LYSICHITON AMERICANUS
H 60–90cm (2–3ft) ★★★
Distinctive, herbaceous perennial, also known as Skunk Cabbage, grown for its large, hooded, bright yellow, arum-like, flowering spathes which appear in early spring before the leaves. The mature leaves are large, oval to oblong, boldly-veined, glossy mid- to deep green. Grow in wet soil at the edge of a pond or watercourse in sun or partial shade. Propagate by offsets in spring or by seed sown as soon as ripe in wet soil in a cold frame. *L. camtschatcensis* is slightly smaller with pure white flowering spathes.

LYTHRUM SALICARIA
H 90–120cm (3–4ft) ★★★★
An excellent, self-supporting perennial, also known as Purple Loosestrife, for moist soils with close spikes of rose-purple flowers from summer to early autumn. Leaves are mid- to deep green and lance-shaped. Grow in moist to wet soil in sun or partial shade. Propagate by division in early spring or basal cuttings in late spring. 'Feuerkerze' ('Firecandle') is intense rose-red. 'Robert' is bright pink.

MYOSOTIS SCORPIOIDES (M.PALUSTRIS)
H 15–30cm (6–12in) ★★★★
One of the few, true blue-flowered aquatics, Water Forget-me-not is a colony-former, producing a profusion of bright blue, rounded, 5-petalled flowers from early to late summer. The oblong to narrowly oval, mid-green leaves have bristly hairs.

Grow in permanently wet soil, planted either above or below shallow water, in sun or partial shade. Propagate by division in spring or seed when ripe in wet soil in a cold frame. 'Mermaid' is more erect and compact with darker green leaves.

PETASITES JAPONICUS
H 60–90cm (2–3ft) ★★★★
Colony-forming, herbaceous perennial spreading by thick rhizomes. The dense-clusters of white, groundsel-like flowerheads in early spring are surrounded by large, lime-green leaf-like bracts. The large, long-stalked, kidney-shaped, entirely basal leaves are bright to mid-green and arise after the flowers. Grow in damp soil in sun or partial shade. Can become invasive.

PONTEDERIA CORDATA
H 75–90cm (2½–3ft) or more ★★★
Attractive, dense, colony-forming, herbaceous perennial known as Pickerel Weed, slowly spreading by rhizomes and producing spikes of blue, tubular flowers in late summer. The long-stalked leaves, some of which may be floating when grown in water, are oval to triangular and a glossy, rich green. Grow in shallow water, rooted in the soil or in baskets, in sun or partial shade. Propagate by division in spring.

PRIMULA FLORINDAE
H 90–120cm (3–4ft) ★★★★
A splendid giant cowslip for permanently wet or moist soil with large, terminal clusters of nodding, yellow bell-flowers in summer. The entirely basal leaves are oval to oblong, bright green and long stalked. Grow in moist soil in sun or partial shade. Propagate by seed sown when ripe or in spring in a cold frame. *P. pulverulenta* has deep red or red-purple flowers, *P. japonica* is similar

but has green stems, larger leaves and magenta flowers. *P. denticulata* has tubular to trumpet- or bell-shaped, purple flowers with yellow eyes.

ZANTEDESCHIA AETHIOPICA
H 60–90cm (2–3ft) ★★★
Dramatic, tuberous-rooted perennial, also known as Arum Lily, with large, waxy white, erect, trumpet-shaped, flowering spathes, each with a central yellow spike which appear in summer. The long-stalked, arrowhead-shaped leaves are glossy, bright green. This plant will survive most winters if planted in at least 15cm (6in) of water. It prefers full sun. Propagate by removing offsets when dormant, or by division of large clumps in spring. 'Crowborough' is reputedly hardier than the ordinary species. 'Green Goddess' has green and white spathes and matt green leaves.

Lysichiton americanus

Petasites japonicus

Pontederia cordata

Primula denticulata

Zantedeschia aethiopica

Plants for sunny corners and containers

Plants from hotter, drier regions of the world, such as the Mediterranean, do well in warm, sunny parts of the garden. They are particularly suited to the drier conditions of containers, as they are drought tolerant, and will thrive in relatively poor soils. These sun-loving plants give exciting displays of colourful flowers and, sometimes, foliage. Those that are not frost-hardy should be brought indoors in winter in cold climates. Annuals will need to be planted from seed each spring.

Abutilon 'Kentish Belle'

Browallia speciosa

Plants listed below need more-or-less frost-free conditions in winter.

ABUTILON PICTUM (A. STRIATUM)
H 3–5m (10–15ft) ★★

Attractive, evergreen shrub with long-stalked, maple-like mid- to deep green leaves and bell-shaped, yellow to orange flowers on slender stalks from late spring to autumn. Grow in fertile, well-drained soil in sun or partial shade. Propagate by greenwood cuttings in summer. *A.* x *hybridum* is similar but with more rounded, bell-shaped flowers in shades of yellow, red, orange and white. *A. megapotamicum* is smaller with slender, arching stems and bi-coloured flowers with a large, bright red calyx from which protrudes a short skirt of yellow petals and a tuft of purple stamens. 'Kentish Belle' has pendent, bell-shaped apricot-yellow flowers and purple stamens protruding from red calyces.

BEGONIA X TUBERHYBRIDA
H 60cm (2ft) or more ★

Colourful, tuberous-rooted perennial with thick, erect, mainly unbranched stems, topped by fully double, rose-like, male flowers in shades of white, pink, red, yellow and bi-colours. The large, basically oval, lop-sided leaves are mid- to deep glossy green. The Pendula Group is similar but with slimmer, arching to pendulous stems and smaller flowers. Grow in humus-rich, moist but well-drained soil in partial shade. Good for hanging baskets. Propagate by basal cuttings in spring or by seed in late winter.

BROWALLIA SPECIOSA
H 45–60cm (1½–2ft) ★

Charming, bushy, woody-based perennial, clad with oval to elliptic, veined, matt green leaves which are slightly sticky. The tubular-based, 5-petalled, pansy-like flowers in shades of violet-blue are freely borne in summer. Grow in fertile, moist but well-drained soil in sun or partial shade. Propagate by seed sown in warmth in early spring or late summer. *B.s.* 'Blue Troll' does not exceed 25cm (10in). *B.s.* 'Heavenly Bells' has pale blue flowers.

BRUGMANSIA X CANDIDA (DATURA X CANDIDA)
H 2–5m (6½–15ft) ★★

Spectacular shrub, also known as Angels' Trumpets, with robust, sparingly branched stems and large, oval to elliptic, sometimes toothed, mid- to deep green leaves. The 25–30cm (10–12in) long, pendent, trumpet-shaped flowers are white to soft yellow, or (rarely) pink, from summer to autumn. Grow in fertile, moist, but well-drained soil in sun or partial shade. Propagate by semi-hardwood cuttings in summer. *B.*x *c.* 'Grand Marnier' has apricot flowers. *B.*x *c.* 'Knightii' has semi-double white ones.

CANNA X GENERALIS
H 1.5–2m (5–6½ft) ★

This magnificent, clump-forming, rhizomatous perennial bears terminal spikes of orchid-like flowers in shades of red, orange, yellow and pink, sometimes bi-coloured or picotee. The handsome, stem-borne leaves are oval to elliptic, mid- to deep green, in some cultivars flushed with purple. Grow in fertile, moist soil in sun. Propagate by dividing established clumps or removing short sections of rhizome, in spring.

Canna 'General Eisenhower'

Cordyline australis

Felicia amelloides

Heliotropium arborescens 'Marine'

CORDYLINE AUSTRALIS
H 2–5m (6½–15ft) ✱✱

Also known as the New Zealand Cabbage Palm. An erect, sparingly branched tree, the stem tips bearing a palm-like head of lance-shaped, light- to mid-green leaves which may reach 1m (3ft) in length. Mature specimens bear huge, airy clusters of tiny, white, 6-petalled flowers followed by white or blue-tinted berries. Young plants make good non-flowering tub or pot plants. Grow in moist but well-drained soil in sun or partial shade. Propagate by seed in warmth or by removing rooted suckers, in spring. *C.a.* 'Purpurea' has its leaves heavily flushed with purple. *C.a.* 'Torbay Dazzler' has leaves striped with cream.

DIASCIA RIGESCENS
H 30cm (1ft) ✱✱

Delightful, bushy, erect to spreading, evergreen perennial with angular stems and heart-shaped, toothed, mid- to deep green leaves. Rich pink flowers are carried in dense, erect spikes throughout summer. Grow in fertile, well-drained soil in sun. Propagate by soft-wood cuttings in spring or late summer. *D. barberae* 'Ruby Field' is mat-forming, with heart-shaped leaves and salmon-pink flowers. *D.b.* 'Blackthorn Apricot' is similar with apricot flowers. *D.r.* 'Lilac Belle' is more compact with lilac-pink flowers.

FELICIA AMELLOIDES
H 35–45cm (14–18in) ✱✱

Dainty, bushy, semi-shrub with oval to narrow, spoon-shaped, deep green leaves and bright blue, yellow-centred, daisy flowers from summer to autumn. Grow in well-drained soil in sun. Propagate by seed in spring or softwood cuttings in summer. *F.a.* 'Read's Blue' is rich blue, *F.a.* 'Read's White' is white and *F.a.* 'Santa Anita Variegated' has white-patterned leaves.

LANTANA CAMARA
H 1m (3ft) or more ✱

Colourful, evergreen, some-what prickly-stemmed shrub with oval, finely corrugated, deep green leaves. The tubular flowers are freely produced in dense, rounded clusters in shades of purple, pink, yellow and white from late spring to autumn. Each flower opens paler and darkens with age, creating a bicoloured effect. Grow in ordinary, well-drained soil in sun. Propagate by semi-hardwood cuttings in summer or by seed in warmth in spring.

OSTEOSPERMUM JUCUNDUM (DIMORPHOTHECA BARBERAE)
H 30–60cm (1–2ft) ✱✱

Showy, mat-forming perennial with lance-shaped, somewhat greyish-green leaves. The daisy-like flower-heads are held well above the leaves in summer. Grow in well-drained soil in full sun. Propagate by soft cuttings in late summer. *O. ecklonis* has an erect habit to 60cm (2ft) or more, with white, blue-backed flowers. 'Pink Whirls' has spoon-shaped petals. 'Buttermilk' has yellow florets.

PELARGONIUM
H 30–75cm (1–2½ft) ✱✱

The most popular house and bedding geranium, an ever-green, shrubby perennial with fleshy, robust stems. In the Zonal Group, the long-stalked, rounded, shallowly-lobed, mid- to light green, aromatic leaves may have a ring-like bronze zone. The 5-petalled flowers, in shades of red, pink or white, are borne in dense, rounded clusters from spring to autumn. Hundreds of varieties are available in a wide colour range, some of them double or semi-double. Grow in well-drained soil in sun or partial shade. Propagate by stem-tip cuttings in summer. The Regal Group is similar but with toothed, rich green

leaves and larger flowers, often bicoloured, in shades of red, pink, purple, orange and white. The Ivy-leaved Group has flexible, trailing stems, fleshy leaves shaped like those of the ivy, and smaller clusters of single or double flowers in a similar colour range. From the Scented-leaved Group, *P.* 'Lady Plymouth' has eucalyptus scented leaves and lavender pink flowers.

STREPTOSOLEN JAMESONII
H 2–4m (6½–12ft) ✱

Dramatic, slender-stemmed shrub or semi-climber with elliptic, deep green leaves. The tubular flowers open yellow and turn bright orange and are carried in large, terminal clusters in profusion from spring to summer. Grow in fertile, moist but well-drained soil in sun or partial shade. May be kept to a smaller size by hard pruning after flowering. Propagate by softwood cuttings in early summer.

Lantana camara 'Mine d'Or'

Osteospermum 'Buttermilk'

Pelargonium 'Lady Plymouth'

Osteospermum 'Pink Whirls'

Regal Pelargonium

Streptosolen jamesonii

Large perennials

Aruncus dioicus

Campanula lactiflora

Crambe cordifolia

Euphorbia characias ssp. *wulfenii*

ARUNCUS DIOICUS (A. SYLVESTER)
H 1.5–2m (5–6½ft) ★★★★
Also known as Goatsbeard, this statuesque, self-support-ing perennial is grown for its large, frothy clusters of tiny, cream flowers from early to mid-summer. The large, fern-like leaves are composed of mid-green, toothed leaflets. Grow in moist garden soil in sun or partial shade. Propa-gate by division in autumn or early spring. *A.d.* 'Kneiffii' is smaller in all its parts with more finely divided leaves.

CAMPANULA LACTIFLORA
H 1.5–1.8m (5–6ft) ★★★★
Herbaceous perennial pro-ducing wide clusters of 5-petalled, upward-facing bells in shades of lavender-blue to lilac blue. The entirely stem-borne leaves are oval to oblong, toothed, mid- to light green. Grow in fertile, moisture-retentive soil in sun or partial shade. Propagate by division in autumn or early spring. *C.l.* 'Alba' is pure white. *C.l.* 'Loddon Anna' is lilac-pink.

CIMICIFUGA RACEMOSA
H 1.5–2.2m (5–7ft) ★★★★
Imposing, herbaceous peren-nial, also known as Black Snakeroot, with strong, wind-firm stems branching above and bearing numerous slender, tapered spikes of small, fluffy white flowers in summer. The broad leaves are dissected into oval, toothed, dark green leaflets. Grow in fertile, moist but well-drained soil in sun or partial shade. Propagate by seed when ripe in a cold frame or by division in early spring.

CRAMBE CORDIFOLIA
H 2–2.5m (6½–8ft) ★★★★
Striking, robust, herbaceous perennial with widely branching, erect stems bear-ing a profusion of tiny, 4-petalled, white flowers in early summer. The mainly basal leaves are large, long-stalked, kidney-shaped, dark green and often puckered and toothed. Grow in fertile, moist but well-drained and, ideally limy, soil in a sunny site. Propagate by division in early spring or by root cut-tings in early winter.

DELPHINIUM HYBRIDS
H 2m (6½ft) or more ★★★★
Beautiful, herbaceous peren-nials bearing long, tapering spires of bowl-shaped flowers in shades of blue, purple and white, rarely pink, pale yel-low and red. The long-stalked, rounded leaves are deeply cleft into several mid-green, toothed lobes. Grow in fertile, moist but well-drained soil in a sunny site.

Delphinium 'Carl Topping'

Propagate by basal cuttings in spring or by seed sown in warmth in early spring. A wide variety of cultivars is available.

ECHINOPS SPHAEROCEPHALUS
H 2m (6½ft or more) ★★★★
Striking, herbaceous perenni-al, also known as Globe Thistle, bearing large, globu-lar heads of small, 5-petalled, tubular silvery blue flowers in late summer. The entirely stem-borne leaves are irregu-larly cut into jagged lobes, deep green above and grey beneath. Grow in any fertile, moist but well-drained soil in a sunny position. Propagate by division in autumn to spring or by seed in a seed-bed in spring. *E. ritro* is simi-lar but smaller, H 1.2m (4ft), with bright blue flowerheads.

EUPHORBIA CHARACIAS
H 1.2m (4ft) ★★★
This handsome, evergreen perennial (sometimes classed as a shrub) has large spread-ing mounds of bottle brush-like stems covered with long, slim, grey-green, waxy leaves. At their tips are borne green-ish flower bracts with brown centres from spring to early summer. Prefers well-drained soil in full sun. Propagate by division in spring. The sub-species *wulfenii* has green flower centres.

FILIPENDULA CAMTSCHATICA
H 2–3m (6½–10ft) ★★★★
Imposing, clump-forming perennial with strong, wind-proof stems and long leaves divided into several, rounded to oval, mid-green, toothed leaflets. From late summer to early autumn, tiny, fragrant white or pale pink flowers are carried in large, flattish, terminal heads. Grow in moist, fertile soil in sun or partial shade. Propagate by

division in winter and early spring. *F. rubra*, Queen of the Prairies, is a little shorter, with pink flowers and rounded leaflets.

HELIANTHUS SALICIFOLIUS
H 2–2.5m (6½–8ft) ★★★★
This striking, herbaceous perennial has daisy-like flowerheads with golden yellow petals and a brown, central disk from late summer to mid-autumn. The leaves are narrow, willow-shaped, deep green and arching. Grow in fertile, moist but well-drained soil in sun. Propagate by division in winter and early spring. *H.* x *laetiflorus* is shorter, with larger, entirely bright yellow flowers. *H.* x *l.* 'Miss Mellish' is semi-double and orange-yellow.

INULA MAGNIFICA
H 1.5–1.8m (5–6ft) ★★★★
This bold, self-supporting perennial bears large, golden yellow daisies in terminal clusters, in late summer. The basal and stem leaves are large, elliptic to oval, dark green and softly hairy beneath. Needs fertile, reasonably moist soil and sun or partial shade. Propagate by division in autumn or spring, or by seed sown in a cold frame in early spring.

LIGULARIA PRZEWALSKII
H 2m (6½ft) or more ★★★★
Dramatic, herbaceous perennial with clumps of purple-brown stems bearing airy spikes of small, bright yellow, daisy flowers from mid- to late summer. The basal and stem leaves are rounded, mid-green, deeply cut into long, jaggedly toothed lobes. Grow in moist, fertile soil in sun or partial shade. Propagate by division in early spring. *L. stenocephala* 'The Rocket' is slightly shorter with oval to triangular leaves bearing many large teeth and slightly darker yellow flowers. *L.* 'Gregynog Gold', with lighter green, heart-shaped leaves

and shorter, pyramidal spikes of larger, deep yellow flowers. *L. dentata* 'Desdemona' is smaller, H 1m (3ft), with deep orange flowers and rounded, brownish leaves.

MACLEAYA CORDATA (BOCCONIA CORDATA)
H 2.5m (8ft) ★★★★
A graceful, herbaceous perennial, known as Plume Poppy, with stems topped by large, airy plumes of tiny, creamy white flowers with many stamens from mid- to late summer. The long-stalked, rounded leaves are olive green above and downy white beneath. It prefers fertile, moist but well-drained soil in sun or partial shade. Propagate by division in winter to early spring. *M. microcarpa* 'Kelway's Coral Plume' has buff pink to coral-pink flowers.

PENSTEMON BARBATUS
H 1.2–1.8m (4–6ft) ★★★★
Grown for its wand-like spikes of tubular red flowers from summer to early autumn. The basal and stem leaves are lance- to strap-shaped, pointed, mid-green or slightly blue-tinted. Grow in well-drained, fertile soil in full sun. Propagate by softwood cuttings in early summer or division in spring.

RHEUM PALMATUM
H 2m (6½ft) or more ★★★★
Self-supporting perennial, also known as Chinese Rhubarb, with cream to red plumes of tiny flowers in summer and large, long-stalked, deep green leaves Grow in moist soil in sun or partial shade. Propagate by division in early spring or by seed when ripe. 'Bowles' Crimson', has dark red flowers and leaves which are flushed crimson beneath.

RODGERSIA AESCULIFOLIA
H 1.8m–2m (6–6½ft) or more ★★★
An impressive, widely clumpforming herbaceous perennial spreading by thick rhi-

Inula magnifica

Ligularia 'The Rocket'

Macleaya microcarpa

zomes. The mainly basal leaves are large, long-stalked and rounded, bronze-flushed when young, then mid- to deep green. The tiny, white or pink flowers form fluffy, loose or pyramidal clusters in summer. Grow in moist, fertile soil in partial shade. Propagate by division in early autumn. *R. podophylla* has broader, jaggedly lobed, red-bronze leaflets and creamy white flowers.

THALICTRUM FLAVUM SSP. GLAUCUM (T. SPECIOSISSIMUM)
H 2m (6½ft) ★★★★
Charming, clump-forming, herbaceous perennial with airy clusters of tiny, bright yellow, many-stamened flowers in summer and rounded leaves cut into small, blue-grey leaflets. Grow in fertile, moist soil in sun. Propagate by division in early spring. *T. chelidonii* has clusters of fewer, larger purple-mauve flowers.

Rheum palmatum

Rodgersia aesculifolia

Medium perennials

Agapanthus hybrid

AGAPANTHUS HEADBOURNE HYBRIDS
H 60–120cm (2–4ft) ✱✱✱

Striking, herbaceous perennial, also known as African Lily, bearing large, globular heads of 6-petalled, funnel-shaped flowers in shades of blue, purple and white. The strap-shaped leaves are mid- to deep green. Grow in fertile, moist but well-drained soil in sun or partial shade. Propagate by seeds sown when ripe or in spring in a cold frame, planting out when at least two years old, or by division in spring.

ANCHUSA AZUREA (A. ITALICA)
H 90–150cm (3–5ft) ✱✱✱✱

Grown for its 5-petalled, gentian blue flowers in long, erect, loose sprays in early to mid-summer. The basal and stem-leaves are lance-shaped, mid- to deep green and coarsely hairy. Grow in fertile, moist but well-drained soil in a sunny position. Propagate by seed in spring or root cuttings in winter. 'Little John', H 40cm (16in), stays at this height, 'Loddon Royalist', H 90cm (3ft), seldom needs staking.

ANEMONE X HYBRIDA (A. JAPONICA OF GARDENS)
H 1–1.5m (3–5ft) ✱✱✱✱

Outstanding, autumn-flowering perennial, also known as Japanese anemone, with bowl-shaped flowers ranging from white to shades of pink. The mainly basal leaves are divided into three broad leaflets, mid-green above and softly hairy beneath. Grow in moist soil in partial shade. Propagate by division in late autumn. 'Honorine Jobert' has pure white flowers with golden stamens.

DICENTRA SPECTABILIS
H 60–75cm (2–2½ft) ✱✱✱✱

Also known as Bleeding Heart, or Dutchman's Breeches, this intriguing plant has unique heart-shaped, pendent flowers produced in arching sprays in early summer. The leaves are large, pale green and cut into many small leaflets creating a fern-like effect. Grow in moist but well-drained soil in sun or partial shade. Propagate by division in early autumn. 'Alba' produces pure white flowers.

DICTAMNUS ALBUS
H 60–90cm (2–3ft) ✱✱✱✱

Handsome, self-supporting perennial known also as Burning Bush or Dittany, grown for its fragrance and irregularly 5-petalled, white or pink summer flowers borne in stiff spikes. The stem-borne leaves are divided into leathery, mid- to deep-green, lemon-scented leaflets. Grow in ordinary soil in a sunny site. Propagate by seed when ripe, or by division in autumn or spring.

HELENIUM AUTUMNALE
H 90–150cm (3–5ft) ✱✱✱✱

Showy, clump-forming, herbaceous perennial, also known as Sneezeweed, freely producing large, terminal clusters of yellow daisy flowers with brown centres. The narrowly oval to lance-shaped, toothed leaves are mid-green. Grow in a fertile, moist but well-drained soil in a sunny position. Propagate by division in late winter to early spring. Several cultivars are available and are more popular than the species, being sturdier with flowers in shades of yellow to crimson.

LEUCANTHEMUM X SUPERBUM (C. MAXIMUM)
H 75–90cm (2½–3ft) ✱✱✱✱

Also known as Shasta Daisy, the most striking of the garden daisies has large, single or double flowers in shades of white to pale yellow from early summer to early autumn. Stem-borne leaves are narrow, toothed and deep green. Grow in moist, fertile soil in a sunny site. Propagate by division in autumn or early spring, or by seed sown in spring. 'Wirral Pride' has white flower-heads with double centres.

Dicentra spectabilis 'Alba'

Dictamnus albus

Helenium 'Gartensonne'

LUPINUS POLYPHYLLUS HYBRIDS
H 60–90cm (2–3ft) ★★★★

Essential border perennial, also known as Russell Lupins, grown for its bold, colourful spikes of pea flowers in early to midsummer, occurring in a wide range of self and bicolours. The long-stalked stem and basal leaves are mid-green, circular, divided into several lance-shaped leaflets. Grow in good garden soil in a sunny position. Propagate by seed, sown in spring or autumn, or by basal cuttings in a cold frame in spring. The following cultivars are recommended: 'My Castle', deep rose-pink, 'The Chatelaine', bicoloured, pink and white, 'The Governor', blue and white.

MONARDA DIDYMA
II 75–90cm (2½–3ft) ★★★★

An intriguing, self-supporting aromatic perennial, also known as Bee Balm, or Oswego Tea, with whorls of slender, tubular, 2-lipped flowers and red-tinted bracts in mid- to late summer. The leaves are oval to lance-shaped, mid-green, toothed and hairy beneath. Grow in reasonably moist garden soil in sun or partial shade. Propagate by division in spring. 'Mahogany' has wine-red flowers with brownish bracts. The hybrid 'Prärienacht' ('Prairie Night') has purple-lilac flowers with green, red-tinted bracts, hybrid 'Schneewittchen' ('Snow White') has white flowers with green bracts.

PAEONIA LACTIFLORA (P. ALBIFLORA) ★★★★
H 55–75cm (1¾–2½ft)

Grown for its large, handsome bowl-shaped flowers in shades of pink and white in summer. The entirely stem leaves are mid- to deep green divided into several lance-shaped leaflets. Grow in moist, but well-drained, fertile soil in full sun.

Propagate by division in late winter. Cultivars include 'Globe of Light', which has fragrant, anemone-centred rose-pink flowers with yellow petaloids. 'Defender' is a hybrid, with deep crimson flowers and golden stamens.

PAPAVER ORIENTALE
H 60–90cm (2–3ft) ★★★★

This striking perennial is also known as Oriental Poppy, and has huge poppy flowers in mid-summer in shades of red and orange, often with a black basal blotch. The stems and rich green leaves are prominently bristly. Grow in ordinary soil in full sun. Propagate by division in early spring or by root cuttings in early winter. 'Allegro' has bright orange-scarlet flowers with black basal marks. 'Perry's White' has white flowers with maroon blotches.

PHLOX PANICULATA
H 90–120cm (3–4ft) ★★★★

A showy, attractive, self-supporting perennial which bears a profusion of fragrant flowers in a wide variety of colours. The leaves are lance-shaped, pointed and mid- to bright green. Grow in moist, reasonably fertile soil in either sun or partial shade. Propagate by division in autumn or spring or by root cuttings in winter. 'Balmoral' has large trusses of pink flowers, 'Eventide' has lavender-blue flowers. 'Harlequin' has ivory-white margined leaves and reddish-purple flowers, and 'Prince of Orange' has orange-red flowers.

POLYGONATUM X HYBRIDUM
H 90–120cm (3–4ft) ★★★★

Elegant, self-supporting perennial with arching stems and small, pendent green and white bells in spring. The oval- to broadly lance-shaped leaves are prominently ribbed and mid- to grey-

ish green. Grow in ordinary soil. Propagate by division of the rhizomes in winter. 'Striatum' has the leaves boldly striped with cream.

SIDALCEA MALVIFLORA
H 90–120cm (3–4ft) ★★★★

An elegant, usually self-supporting perennial, also known as Prairie Mallow, with erect spires of pink to lilac silky textured, bowl-shaped, 5-petalled flowers in summer. The basal leaves are rounded to kidney-shaped and long stalked, the stem leaves are deeply lobed and short stalked. Grow in well-drained soil in full sun. Propagate by division in autumn or by seed in spring. 'Puck' has deep pink flowers on 40cm (1¼ft) stems. 'Sussex Beauty' has satin-textured, clear pink flowers on 90cm (3ft) stems.

VERBASCUM PHOENICEUM
H 90–120cm (3–4ft) ★★★★

Also known as Purple Mullein, this striking, short-lived perennial has long spires of bowl-shaped flowers in shades of white, pink and purple in early summer. The basal leaves are large, oval, wrinkled and deep green, the stem leaves are smaller and narrower. Grow in ordinary soil in a sunny site. Propagate by sowing seed in spring. Among hybrid cultivars is the striking 'Pink Domino' with deep rose-pink flowers on 1.2m (4ft) stems.

Leucanthemum x superbum
'Esther Read'

Paeonia lactiflora
'Bowl of Beauty'

Papaver orientale

Verbascum **hybrid**

Small perennials

Alyssum spinosum

Arenaria montana

Armeria maritima

Aubrieta hybrid

Campanula carpatica

Erigeron karvinskianus

ACHILLEA CLAVENNAE
H 15–20cm (6–8in) ★★★★
This handsome, silvery, hairy mat-former is usually grown for its flat clusters of small, white, daisy flowers, in summer. Leaves are narrowly spoon-shaped, usually toothed or lobed, silvery grey-green. Grow in well-drained soil in full sun. Propagate by division in late winter or soft cuttings in late spring.

ALCHEMILLA CONJUNCTA
H 15–25cm (6–10in) or more ★★★★
Useful, clump- and mat-forming perennial, also known as Lady's Mantle, with frothy clusters of tiny, greenish-yellow flowers in summer. The long-stalked, rounded leaves are dissected into 7 to 9 finger-shaped lobes, which are dark green above, silvery haired beneath. Grow in ordinary soil in sun or partial shade. Propagate by division in autumn or early spring.

ALYSSUM SPINOSUM (PTILOTRICHUM SPINOSUM)
H 10–15cm (4–6in) ★★★
Loosely hummock-forming, shrubby perennial with dense, wiry, sometimes spine-tipped stems and a profusion of small, 4-petalled, white to pink flowers in late spring. The tiny leaves are grey and oval to spoon-shaped. Grow in well-drained, ideally limy, soil in full sun. Propagate by greenwood cuttings in summer or seed in autumn or spring in a cold frame. The best forms of var. *roseum* have deep pink flowers.

ARENARIA BALEARICA
H 1–2cm (³⁄₈–³⁄₄in) ★★★
Charming Lilliputian carpeter, also known as Balearic Sandwort, with starry white flowers from late spring to late summer. The minute leaves are oval and light green. Grow in moist garden soil in partial shade. Propagate by division in spring. *A. montana* differs, being loosely mat-forming, H 10cm (4in) or more, with larger, white flowers and much larger, lance-shaped, dark greyish-green leaves. Best in a sunny site.

ARMERIA JUNIPERIFOLIA (A. CAESPITOSA)
H 5–8cm (2–3¹⁄₄in) ★★★
A delightful, small, evergreen hummock-former, also known as Thrift, which is freely studded with globular pink to purple-pink flower-heads in spring and early summer. The grey-green leaves are short and bristle-like. Grow in well-drained soil in a sunny position. Propagate by semi-ripe cuttings in late summer. *A. maritima*, the Common Thrift, H 15–20cm (6–8in), is larger in all its parts with a 20–30cm (8–12in) spread. The grassy foliage is mid- to deep green. 'Bloodstone' is rich red and 'Vindictive' is rose pink.

AUBRIETA HYBRIDS
H 5–10cm (2–4in) ★★★★
Showy, mat-forming perennial producing abundant clusters of 4-petalled flowers in shades of mauve and purple in spring. The small, crowded leaves are oblong to spoon-shaped, mid- to deep green. Grow in well-drained, ideally limy soil in full sun. Propagate by seed in autumn or spring or by softwood cuttings in summer. *A.* 'Bressingham Pink' is double pink. *A.* 'Greencourt Purple' is rich purple.

AURINIA SAXATILIS (ALYSSUM SAXATILE)
H 15–25cm (6–10in) ★★★★
This plant is grown for its spectacular blaze of golden yellow, crowded clusters of small flowers in spring. The densely borne, grey-green, spoon-shaped leaves form low hummocks. Grow in well-drained, ideally limy soil in full sun. Propagate by seed in autumn or spring or softwood cuttings in summer. 'Citrina' has lemon-yellow flowers. 'Dudley Nevill' has yellowish-buff flowers. 'Variegata' bears leaves with irregularly cream margins.

CAMPANULA CARPATICA
H 30cm (12in) ★★★★
Beautiful clump-forming perennial grown for its profusion of large, upturned, bell flowers in shades of purple, blue and white. The basal leaves are heart-shaped, toothed and mid-green, the stem leaves somewhat smaller and narrower. Grow in well-drained soil in full sun. Propagate by seeds in a cold frame when ripe, or by

division in autumn or early spring. Var. *turbinata* has pale lavender-blue flowers on 10-15cm (3-4in) stems. *C. cochleariifolia*, Fairies' Thimbles, is creeping and tufted, H 8-10cm (4-6in), with small, thimble-shaped bells of white, lavender or slate blue. *C. glomerata*, Clustered Bell-flower, H 40cm (16in) or more, is a vigorous perennial with clusters of violet to pur-ple-blue bells in summer.

DIANTHUS DELTOIDES
H 20–25cm (8–10in) or more ★★★★

Attractive, mat-forming perennial, also called Maiden Pink, with a profusion of miniature 'pinks' in shades of white, pink to red, often with a darker eye. Leaves are small, narrow, deep green and densely borne. Grow in well-drained soil in sun. Propagate by seed in spring or by cut-tings in summer. *D. superbus* is a taller, tufted plant H 20-30cm (8-12in), spread with large, rose-purple flowers with more deeply fringed petals and mid-green leaves.

EPIMEDIUM GRANDIFLORUM
H 20–30cm (8–12in) or more ★★★★

Shade-tolerant perennial with white, pink or purple flowers, like tiny columbines, carried in short, arching spikes. Light green leaves, bronze-flushed when young, are divided into heart-shaped leaflets. Grow in moist but well-drained soil. Propagate by division in autumn or after flowering. 'White Queen' has pure white flowers. 'Rose Queen' has darker, bronze-green leaves and rose pink flowers.

ERIGERON AURANTIACUS
H 20–30cm (8–12in) ★★★★

Clump-forming perennial with bright orange, daisy-like flowerheads in summer. The basal, mid- to deep green leaves are elliptic to spoon-shaped, the velvety downed stem leaves are smaller and

narrower. Grow in ordinary soil in full sun. Propagate by division or basal cuttings in spring. *E. karvinskianus (E. mucronatus)* H 15-20cm (6-8in), is similar, with smaller flowerheads opening white and aging to pink and purple.

GENTIANA ACAULIS
H 7–10cm (2¾–4in) ★★★★

Perhaps the best-loved of the gentians, with large, trumpet-shaped flowers of pure deep blue, spotted green, in spring. The small, mid- to deep-green, lance-shaped, ever-green leaves are borne in dense hummocks. Grow in moist garden soil in sun or partial shade. Propagate by division in late winter or off-sets in spring. *G. verna* is like a miniature *G. acaulis* with broad, spreading lobes to its brilliant blue flowers.

GERANIUM X MAGNIFICUM
H 45–60cm (1½–2ft) ★★★★

Handsome and vigorous clump-forming perennial, also known as Cranesbill, with large, saucer-shaped, rich vio-let-blue flowers freely pro-duced in summer. The long-stalked, rounded, broadly-lobed leaves are downy, and colour well in autumn. Grow in ordinary soil in sun or par-tial shade. Propagate by divi-sion from autumn to early spring or by seed when ripe. *G. sanguineum* is a clump-forming perennial with saucer-shaped, magenta pink flowers in summer.

GEUM CHILOENSE (G. COCCINEUM)
H 40–60cm (16–24in) ★★★★

Valuable front of the border plant with saucer-shaped, 5-petalled, scarlet flowers from early to late summer. The mainly basal leaves are divided into heart to kidney-shaped, toothed, mid-green leaflets. Grow in moist, well-drained garden soil in sun or partial shade. Propagate by division in autumn or early spring or by seed sown in a cold frame

when ripe. *G. rivale* is similar to *G. chiloense* but of rather spreading habit with bell-shaped, nodding flowers of pink to orange-red. Of the hybrids, 'Fire Opal' has semi-double orange flowers. 'Lady Stratheden' has semi-double, rich yellow flowers.

HELICHRYSUM BELLIDIOIDES
H 10–15cm (4–6in) ★★★

Pleasant, evergreen mat-forming perennial with white-hairy stems and white, papery, daisy-like flowerheads in late spring and summer. The tiny, oval to spoon-shaped leaves are mid-green above and white felted beneath. Grow in any well drained soil. Propagate by careful division in spring or cuttings in summer.

HELLEBORUS NIGER
H 30–40cm (12–16in) ★★★★

Beautiful, winter-flowering, evergreen perennial, also known as Christmas Rose, bearing bowl-shaped white

Epimedium grandiflorum 'Rose Queen'

Geranium x *magnificum*

Geranium sanguineum

Geum 'Lady Stratheden'

Helleborus niger

Helleborus orientalis hybrid

Hosta fortunei **var.** *albopicta*

Lewisia cotyledon **hybrids**

Phlox subulata **'Scarlet Flame'**

flowers from early winter to early spring. The leathery, deep green leaves are composed of lance-shaped leaflets. Grow in moist but well drained soil in partial shade. Propagate by division after flowering or in late summer. Pink-flushed cultivars are available. *H. orientalis* hybrids, H45cm (18in), are more robust and free-flowering with nodding flowers in shades of white, pink and purple, often with darker spotting. *H. argutifolius* (*H. corsicus*), H 90cm (3ft), has biennial stems which bear large, dark green, trifoliate leaves. The bright yellow-green flowers are carried in trusses in late winter.

HOSTA FORTUNEI
H 50–60cm (20–24in) ★★★★

Handsome, long-lived perennial grown for its narrow, trumpet-shaped mauve flowers carried in loose spikes above the leaves. The leaves are heart-shaped, long-stalked and deep green. Grow in fertile soil in partial shade.

'Albomarginata' has the leaves edged with cream to white. *H. sieboldiana* is larger, H 1m (3ft), with rounded to heart-shaped, grey-green, strongly ribbed leaves. Flowers are lilac-grey, fading with age. Var. *elegans* has strongly blue-grey leaves.

LEWISIA COTYLEDON
H 25–30cm (10–12in) ★★★★

Attractive perennial grown for its freely produced showers of shallowly funnel-shaped flowers in shades of pink to purple or white, usually with darker stripes. The entirely basal leaves are fleshy and narrowly oblong, mid- to deep green. Best grown against a dry wall, it prefers a well-drained, humus-rich soil and thrives in either sun or partial shade. Propagate by seed sown when ripe in a cold frame or offsets as cuttings in late spring. The popular *L. cotyledon* hybrids are more robust and come in a wide colour range.

PHLOX DOUGLASII
H 8–12cm (3–5in) ★★★★

This evergreen mat-former produces many starry flowers in white to blue and pink. Its crowded, tiny, leaves are dark green. Grow in well-drained soil in sun. Propagate by softwood or semi-hardwood cuttings in summer. 'Iceberg' is white, 'Red Admiral' is crimson and 'Violet Queen' has violet-purple flowers. *P. subulata* is similar, but has a larger, looser habit, longer leaves and flowers in a wider variety of colours.

PRIMULA VULGARIS
H 15cm (6in) ★★★★

Also known as Primrose, this rosette and clump forming perennial has a profusion of circular, 5-petalled single and double flowers in pinks, yellows and white. The semi-evergreen, corrugated leaves are lance-shaped, mid- to deep green. Cultivars and hybrids are available in many

colours from purple-blue and red to pale cream. Grow in moist soil in partial shade. Propagate by seed when ripe, or in spring in a cold frame, or by division after flowering. *P. auricula* is distinctive, having short, wrinkled stems that bear clusters of deep-yellow, white-mealy flowers, often with banded petals, and spoon-shaped, pale to grey-green leaves in rosettes.

PULSATILLA VULGARIS
H 10–20cm (4–8in) ★★★★

This beautiful clump-forming perennial is also known as Pasque Flower. It is grown for its erect to nodding, 6-petalled, bell-shaped, purple flowers and its finely dissected, fern-like foliage. Grow in ordinary, preferably limy, soil in full sun. Propagate by seed when ripe or root cuttings in winter. 'Alba' is white, 'Eva Constance' is red, opening wide. Var. *rubra* is similar but with more bell-shaped, rich red flowers.

RUDBECKIA FULGIDA
H 60–90cm (2–3ft) ★★★★

Long-lived, clump-forming perennial, also known as Black-eyed Susan, with a profusion of bright orange-yellow, black-brown centred daisies from late summer to mid-autumn. The stalked, basal leaves are lance-shaped, toothed and veined. Grow in ordinary soil in sun or partial shade. Propagate by division in autumn or early spring. *R.f.* var. *deamii* is one of the best-known and most freely flowering forms, with hairy stems and long pointed leaves.

SAXIFRAGA X ANGLICA
H 2–5cm (¾–2in) ★★★★

One of the best of the silver-encrusted saxifrages, *S. x a.* 'Cranbourne' forms firm, low hummocks and bears many cup-shaped, deep rose-pink flowers in early spring. The narrow, grey-green, white-dotted leaves are borne in tiny rosettes. Grow in well-drained, limy soil in full sun. Propagate by single rosettes taken as cuttings in late spring or early summer. *S. x apiculata* 'Gregor Mendel' has larger hummocks and many clusters of starry, light yellow flowers. *S. fortunei* is a clump-forming, herbaceous perennial with slender stems to 30cm (12in) tall bearing loose clusters of white flowers with petals of irregular sizes in autumn.

SEDUM
H 10cm (4in) ★★★★
Huge genus of mostly mat- or hummock forming perennials, also known as Stonecrop, some of which are evergreen. They have rosettes of basal leaves and small, starry flowers. Grow in well-drained soil in full sun. Propagate by division in spring or cuttings in summer. *S. spurium* has reddish stems bearing flattened clusters of star-shaped, pinkish-purple flowers in late summer. 'Schorbuser Blut' ('Dragon's Blood') has deep reddish-pink flowers and purple-tinted leaves. *S. kamtschaticum* forms low clumps of deep golden yellow flowers. *S. kamtschaticum* 'Variegatum' has pink-tinted leaves with cream margins. *S. spectabile*, Ice Plant, a clump-forming, herbaceous perennial, H 45cm (18in), has large, flattened heads of starry, pink flowers in late summer.

SEMPERVIVUM TECTORUM
H 15–25cm (6–10in) ★★★
Popular hardy, succulent perennial grown for its handsome rosettes with a bonus of pink to red-purple star-shaped flowers in summer. The narrowly oblong, slender-pointed leaves are mid- to blue-green, often tipped with red-purple. Grow in well-drained soil in full sun. Propagate by offsets in spring or summer. *S. ciliosum* has smaller, hairy rosettes

with incurved leaves and green-yellow flowers. *S. arachnoideum* has even smaller rosettes, green to purple-flushed leaves tipped with long, white hairs that form a cobweb over the rosette and reddish-pink flowers.

THYMUS
H 3–20cm (1–8in) ★★★
Aromatic, mat-forming evergreen perennial, also known as Thyme, thickly set with dense heads of tiny, tubular, purple flowers in summer. The tiny leaves are hairy and mid-green. Grow in well-drained, ideally limy, soil in full sun. Propagate by cuttings in mid- to late summer or by division in spring. *T serpyllum* var. *coccineus* ('Coccineus') has red flowers and 'Pink Chintz' has pink flowers and grey-green leaves. *T. x citriodorus*, lemon-scented thyme, forms low, bushy plants bearing lavender-pink flowers and lemon-scented leaves. 'Aureus' has gold-dappled leaves. 'Golden King' is more erect with gold-margined leaves. 'Silver Queen' has creamy white variegated leaves.

VERONICA SPICATA
H 30–40cm (12–16in) ★★★
Colourful, clump- or mat-forming perennial bearing numerous, erect, slender dense spikes of small flowers in shades of blue in summer. The leaves are oval to oblong, toothed, mid- to bright green. Grow in ordinary, ideally limy, soil in full sun. Propagate by division in autumn or early spring or by seed when ripe. The cultivar 'Heidekind' has pink flowers and grey leaves, ssp. *incana* has silvery-grey leaves and rich purple-blue flowers, and 'Rotfuchs' ('Red Fox') has red flowers. 'Shirley Blue' bears vivid blue flowers, *V. prostrata* forms wide mats bearing short spikes of blue flowers in early summer.

Saxifraga x apiculata **'Gregor Mendel'**

Saxifraga fortunei

VIOLA ODORATA
H 10cm (4in) ★★★★
This well-loved perennial is also known as Sweet Violet. It forms wide, loose clumps or mats bearing scented, purple-blue, 5-petalled flowers. The long-stalked leaves are heart-shaped and mid- to bright green. Grow in ordinary garden soil in a sunny position or in partial shade. Propagate by seed when ripe or by division in autumn or early spring. Forms in other shades of purple-blue, pink, red, apricot and white are grown. *V. riviniana* 'Purpurea' (*V. labradorica* of gardens) is like a less robust *odorata* with smaller, smooth leaves that are heavily flushed with purple. *V. cornuta*, Horned Violet, is a tufted to clump-forming perennial, H 15cm (6in), with long-spurred, purple-blue flowers from spring to autumn. Lilac and white forms are also grown.

Sempervivum

Thymus doerfleri **'Bressingham'**

Viola cornuta

Bamboos, grasses and ferns

These plants are used, primarily, for the contribution that their foliage brings to the garden. Ferns do not flower, bamboos (which are giant grasses) effectively do not, whereas the flowers of grasses often have considerable ornamental value, but for their form rather than their colour. Generally, grasses prefer drier soil and sunnier conditions. Bamboos cope well with more moist soil, and bamboos and ferns generally do best in partial shade but will cope with some sun as well.

Phyllostachys aurea

Phyllostachys nigra

Pseudosasa japonica

Hakonechloa macra 'Aureola'

Bamboos

FARGESIA MURIELIAE (ARUNDINARIA MURIELIAE)
H 3–4m (10–12ft) ★★★★

Graceful, densely clump-forming bamboo with many slender, erect then arching, yellow-green stems and very slender branches with small, lance-shaped, bright green leaves. Grow in ordinary garden soil in sun or partial shade. Propagate by division in spring.

PHYLLOSTACHYS AUREA
H 4–10m (12–30ft) ★★★★

Colourful, clump-forming bamboo, also known as Golden or Fishpole Bamboo, with stiffly erect, grooved canes which are bright green at first, then brownish-yellow. The branchlets bear narrowly lance-shaped, yellowish to golden green leaves. Grow in ordinary soil in sun or partial shade, sheltered from freezing winds. Propagate by division in spring. *P. nigra*, Black Bamboo, has more slender green canes that turn lustrous black in their second or third year.

PSEUDOSASA JAPONICA (ARUNDINARIA JAPONICA)
H 4–6m (12–20ft) ★★★

Very hardy bamboo, eventually forming thickets of erect, olive-green stems which mature to pale brown. The dark green, oblong to lance-shaped leaves are 30cm (12in) or more in length. Grow in moist soil in sun or partial shade. Propagate by division or by separating rooted canes in spring.

SASA PALMATA
H 2m (6½ft) or more ★★★

Handsome but vigorous bamboo which spreads widely by woody rhizomes and bears erect to slightly arching, green canes, sometimes purple streaked. The large, broadly elliptic leaves are glossy, bright, rich green with paler midribs. The leaf tips may turn brown in severe winters. Grow in ordinary, preferably moist, garden soil in either sun or shade. Propagate by division or by separating rooted canes in spring. *S. veitchii* has scarious, parchment-coloured leaves giving the effect of variegation.

YUSHANIA ANCEPS (ARUNDINARIA ANCEPS)
H 3–4m (10–12ft) ★★★★

Elegant, colony-forming bamboo with glossy, dark green canes, erect then arching. The slender branches bear numerous narrow, lance-shaped, mid-green leaves. Grow in ordinary garden soil in either sun or partial shade, ideally sheltered from freezing winds. Propagate by division or by separating individual, rooted canes in spring.

Grasses

CAREX ELATA 'AUREA'
H 60–70cm (2–2½ft) ★★★★

Attractive, clump-forming perennial, also known as Bowles' Golden Sedge, with arching, slender, yellow leaves and short, contrasting brown flower spikes in summer. Grow in ordinary, ideally moist soil in sun. Propagate by division in spring.

CORTADERIA SELLOANA
H 2.5–3m (8–10ft) ★★★

Familiar, spectacular evergreen, known as Pampas Grass. This is densely clump-forming, with arching mid- to grey-green, rough-edged leaves and erect stems bearing large, fluffy plumes of numerous, silvery florets in late summer to autumn. Grow in well-drained soil in sun. Propagate by division in spring. *C.s.* 'Pumila' H 1.5m (5ft) is much smaller. *C.s.* 'Rendatleri' has pinkish-purple florets.

HAKONECHLOA MACRA
H 30–40cm(1–1½ft) ★★★★

Striking, tufted to mound-forming, herbaceous grass with densely borne, arching, mid- to bright-green leaves. Pale green florets are carried in sparse, slender plumes in summer. Grow in ordinary, ideally moist, soil in sun or partial shade. Propagate by division in spring. Represented in gardens by one of its variegated forms, *H.m.* 'Albo-aurea', with leaves striped white and gold, and *H.m.* 'Aureola' with yellow leaves narrowly striped with green.

MISCANTHUS SINENSIS
H 2m (6½ft) ★★★★

Handsome, ornamental, clump-forming herbaceous perennial bearing arching, narrow, matt to slightly bluish-green leaves topped by silk-haired, greyish florets in a sheaf of slender spikes which arch with age. Grow in ordinary, ideally moist, soil in sun. Propagate by division in spring. *M.s.* 'Silberfeder' ('Silver Feather') is a reliable, free-flowering cultivar. *M.s.* 'Zebrinus' has broader leaves with zones of white to cream and green.

MOLINIA CAERULEA
H 60–90cm (2–3ft) ★★★★
Also known as Purple Moor Grass, this densely tufted, herbaceous perennial has slender, arching, mid-green leaves and erect, yellow-flushed flowering stems bearing loose, narrow heads of tiny, purplish florets. Grow in moist soil in sun or partial shade. Propagate by division in spring.

STIPA ARUNDINACEA
H 1m (3ft) ★★★★
Elegant, tufted, evergreen also known as Pheasant's-tail Grass, producing slender, arching, dark green leaves turning orange-brown in autumn. The large, airy, flowering plumes are formed of many, purplish-green florets. Grow in well-drained soil in sun. Propagate by division in spring. *S. calamagrostis* has bluish green leaves and smaller, more compact, floral plumes of purple-tinted to buff spikelets. *S. gigantea* is a fine, large specimen grass, H 2m (6½ft) or more, with robust, erect stems bearing huge, loose plumes of purplish green florets which turn corn yellow when ripe.

Ferns

ADIANTUM PEDATUM
H 30–40cm (1–1¼ft) ★★★★
Also known as Maidenhair Fern, this elegant, herbaceous, clump-former has slender, purple-black leaf stalks and hand-shaped fronds made up of triangular to diamond-shaped leaflets, bright green, darkening with age. Grow in ordinary, ideally humus-rich, soil in partial shade. Propagate by division in early spring. *A. pedatum* var. *subpumilum* (*A. aleuticum*), H 20–30cm (8–12in), has tighter clumps of congested fronds. *A. venustum*, Himalayan Maidenhair, is a widely spreading fern with triangular, lacy fronds of small, fan-shaped leaflets which emerge bright bronze-pink and age to mid-green. The hardiest true Maidenhair Fern.

ASPLENIUM SCOLOPENDRIUM (PHYLITTIS SCOLOPENDRIUM)
H 40–60cm (1¼–2ft) ★★★★
Distinctive, evergreen, clump-former, also known as Hart's Tongue Fern, with leathery, bright green, strap-shaped fronds which have a heart-shaped base and a pointed tip. Grow in ordinary soil. Propagate by division in early spring. *A.s.* Crispum Group has boldly crimped leaves. *A.s.* Undulatum Group has less strong undulations.

DRYOPTERIS FILIX-MAS
H 60–90cm (2–3ft) ★★★★
The most familiar shuttlecock fern, also known as Male Fern, with lance-shaped, semi-evergreen fronds dissected into oblong leaflets. Grow in moist, well-drained soil in full or partial shade. Propagate by division in early spring. *D. affinis (D. borreri)*, Golden-scaled Male Fern, is larger and more erect, its leaf stalks and midribs covered in golden brown scales. *D. erythrosora*, H 60cm (24in), has coppery red fronds when young, aging to lustrous, deep green.

MATTEUCCIA STRUTHIOPTERIS
H 1.2m (4ft) – single rosette ★★★★
Handsome, colony-forming, herbaceous fern, also known as Ostrich Plume Fern, with shuttlecock-shaped rosettes of lance-shaped, bright green leaves The dark brown, fertile fronds are much shorter and borne in the centre of the rosette. As this fern can spread 1m (3ft) a year, it is only for large gardens or where roots can be restricted. Grow in moist soil in sun to full shade. Propagate by separating individual rosettes in late winter.

Miscanthus sinensis 'Silberspinne'

Stipa gigantea

Asplenium scolopendrium

POLYPODIUM VULGARE
H 30–40cm (12–16in) ★★★★
Decorative, evergreen fern with narrowly triangular to lance-shaped fronds, deeply dissected into bright green lobes. Grow in well-drained soil in sun or partial shade. Propagate by division in spring or early summer. *P. interjectum* is very similar. The vigorous 'Cornubiense' makes good ground cover.

POLYSTICHUM SETIFERUM
H 45–75cm (18–30in) ★★★★
Attractive, evergreen, clump-forming fern, also known as Soft Shield Fern, with low arching, soft-textured, lance-shaped fronds dissected into tiny, oval, toothed leaflets. Grow in well-drained soil in partial to full shade. Propagate by division in spring or by detaching plantlets from old fronds. Divisilobum Group includes cultivars with feathery, finely dissected fronds.

Polypodium interjectum

Polystichum setiferum

Using ground cover

Shady places
Ferns, bamboos and grasses are ideal choices for shady areas of the garden as they provide dense, weed-suppressing cover in low light conditions.

The most familiar ground cover, lawn grass, is very dependent upon regular mowing and irrigation. Unfortunately, not all of us have the time to mow grass and water is in increasingly short supply. There are also areas where grass does not do well, notably in shade. Although paving is sometimes used as an alternative, its hard surface detracts from the idea most of us have of a garden, and you cannot pave slopes.

Ground cover plants are another, more attractive, low-maintenance alternative to lawn grass, and their development and use is one of the fastest growing areas of horticulture. There are some that can even be walked upon, although none will stand as much foot traffic as lawn grass. One of these is chamomile, which has been used as a lawn plant for centuries, another is yarrow (*Achillea millefolium*). The majority, however, are decorative ground covers only.

Since the object is to cover the ground, plants used are invariably evergreen, most commonly those which develop quite a dense foliage canopy which protects the ground underneath from erosion and suppresses weeds.

Types of ground cover

It is conventional to use only one kind of ground cover in any area, but there is no reason to restrict them in this way. Taller plants, such as bergenias and alchemilla, with more distinctive foliage can be used amongst lower growing, more undisciplined, creeping species, like ajuga and *Lysimachia nummularia*. In this way, the number of more-expensive, slower growing plants is minimized.

Ground cover plants can create excitingly different textures and colours when planted in distinct shapes, either geometrical, or 'organic' and curved. The only proviso here is that it will be necessary to separate the groups of plants, otherwise they will begin to merge with each other and blur the boundaries.

An unorthodox, but often successful, method of creating ground cover is to use climbers, allowing them to trail over the ground. Ivy (*Hedera* spp.) is one plant that in nature seems as happy to trail as to climb. Honeysuckles (*Lonicera* spp.) make good, strong-growing ground cover. It is even possible to use clematis.

Ribbon planting
Ferns (above and right) are an excellent choice for ground cover for the area at the foot of a wall or fence, as they are among the few plants that flourish in the low light levels.

Planting ground cover

When selecting plants for ground cover, check they will thrive in the conditions in which you plan to plant them. The most useful types are those that spread rapidly by creeping stems or runners.

The best way to plant ground cover is through black plastic, as this keeps weeds down until the plants are established. A large area may need a lot of plants, which can be prohibitively expensive. One answer is to propagate your own.

1 *Peg down black, plastic sheeting across the area to be planted. Then cut crosses in the black plastic to create planting holes for the plants at appropriate distances apart.*

2 *Dig planting holes through the cut areas of the plastic. Carefully insert the plant through the sheeting and backfill the hole. Water in well and keep watered in dry weather.*

3 *To disguise the black plastic, cover it with a layer of coarse bark chippings. Once the ground cover is well established and serving its purpose, you can remove the plastic sheeting.*

Places for ground cover

It is possible to use ground cover plants in a naturalistic way, intermingling them so that the end result resembles wild vegetation growing on a woodland floor. It is important, though, that plants of fairly equal vigour are chosen. Putting a rampant spreader like *Lamium galeobdolon* next to a less speedy grower like bergenia is asking for trouble. It will soon be swamped.

Most of the ground covers that are commonly used are for planting in shade, where grass does not flourish and where there is often little incentive to grow flowering plants. Some, like *Ajuga reptans*, grow relatively low and because of their habit of rooting from the base of their spreading stems, can be used to cover an area quite rapidly. Others like the bergenias, are considerably taller – up to 30 cms (12in) – and much more slow growing. Some of these larger plants have considerable decorative value, as they are evergreen, have attractive foliage and good flowers. Before planting ground

Ground cover carpet

A great advantage of ground cover is that it is very low maintenance. Plants like Pachysandra terminalis *and* Trillium luteum, *are ideal for shady conditions.*

cover, ensure all perennial weeds have been destroyed, as it will be difficult to remove them later. Weeds growing in between a smooth planting of ground cover will mar its otherwise regular appearance.

In some parts of the garden, particularly under the canopies of evergreen trees, very little will grow. *Hedera hibernia* or *H. colchica* are among the candidates for this kind of deep shade. There are many different species of ivy with markedly different sizes and shapes of leaf, so you could grow more than one kind to add interest.

Woodland garden

Primulas, meconopsis and ferns are intermingled to produce a carpet of flowers and foliage that resembles the wild vegetation of a woodland floor.

Ground cover

Ajuga reptans

Alchemilla mollis

Heuchera micrantha
'Palace Purple'

AJUGA REPTANS
H 15–20cm (6–8in)
S 60cm (2ft) or more ★★★★
Vigorous, evergreen perennial, also called Bugle, with erect stems of tubular, deep blue flowers in late spring and summer. The dense, basal leaves are oblong to spoonshaped, rich green and semiglossy. Grow in ordinary soil in sun to full shade. Propagate by division in autumn to spring. A.r. 'Multicolor' ('Rainbow') has bronze green leaves marked cream and pink, 'Variegata' has greygreen leaves edged and splashed with creamy white.

ALCHEMILLA MOLLIS
H 40–60cm (1½–2ft)
S 60–75cm (2–2½ft) ★★★★
Also called Lady's Mantle, this plant has rounded, shallowly lobed, softly hairy, light green leaves to 15cm (6in) across that die down in late autumn and lime green clusters of tiny flowers in summer. Grow in ordinary soil in sun or partial shade. Propagate by division from autumn to late winter. Selfsown seedlings often occur.

BERGENIA CORDIFOLIA
H 45–60cm (1½–2ft)
S 75–90cm (2½–3ft) ★★★★
A valuable, evergreen perennial, also known as Elephant's Ears, forming spreading

clumps from thick rhizomes which produce clusters of pink to red, 5-petalled, bellshaped flowers in early spring. The large, rounded to heart-shaped mid- to deep green leaves are often purpletinted in winter. Grow in well-drained, ideally humusrich soil in sun or partial shade. Propagate by division in autumn. B.c. 'Purpurea' has red-purple flowers and redder winter leaves. B. crassifolia has narrower, paddle-shaped leaves and pink flowers.

BRUNNERA MACROPHYLLA (SYN. ANCHUSA MYOSOTIDIFLORA) ★★★★
H 45cm (18in) S 60cm (2ft)
Sprays of blue, forget-menot-like flowers are produced from spring to early summer. The mainly basal leaves are bold, heart-shaped and mid- to deep green. Grow in ordinary soil in sun or partial shade. Propagate by division from late autumn to early spring or root cuttings in winter. B.m. 'Hadspen Cream' has leaves irregularly variegated with creamy white. B.m. 'Langtrees' has leaves spotted with silvery grey.

HEDERA HELIX
H 10m (30ft) S indefinite
★★★★
This self-clinging climber or trailing perennial is also known as Common Ivy. It has broadly oval to triangular, glossy dark green leaves. There are many variants and cultivars, which are more commonly grown. 'Angularis Aurea' has shallowly lobed, glossy mid-green leaves, becoming suffused and variegated with yellow as they age.

HEUCHERA SANGUINEA
H & S 30cm (12in) ★★★★
Dainty, clump-forming, evergreen perennial, known as Coral Bells, grown for its clouds of tiny, red, pink or

white bells. The leaves are rounded to kidney-shaped, toothed, deep green, sometimes with paler marbling. Grow in ordinary soil in sun or partial shade. Propagate by seed when ripe or by division in autumn. Hybrids are H. 'Red Spangles' with crimsonscarlet flowers and H. 'Pearl Drops', pink tinged with white. H. micrantha 'Palace Purple' has jagged, bronzered leaves and greenish cream flowers with red anthers.

LAMIUM MACULATUM
H 15–20cm (6–8in)
S 60–90cm (2–3ft) ★★★★
Attractive, evergreen perennial with pink to red-purple, tubular, hooded flowers in early summer. The broadly oval to triangular leaves bear a central silvery-white zone. Grow in ordinary soil in sun or partial shade. Propagate by division in early spring or in autumn. L.m. 'Album' has white flowers. L.m. 'Aureum' has yellow-suffused leaves. L.m. 'White Nancy' has pure white flowers above silver green margined leaves.

LYSIMACHIA NUMMULARIA
H 3–5cm (1¼–2in)
S 45–60cm (1½–2ft) ★★★★
Also known as Creeping Jenny, this vigorous, evergreen perennial bears cupshaped, 5-petalled flowers in summer. The broadly oval to rounded leaves are mid- to deep green. Grow in ordinary, ideally moist, soil in sun or partial shade. Propagate by division in autumn or spring. L.n. 'Aurea', Golden Creeping Jenny, has leaves suffused with golden yellow.

PACHYPHRAGMA MACROPHYLLUM
H 25–35cm (10–14in)
S 60cm (2ft) or more ★★★★
Cheerful, evergreen to semievergreen perennial producing spikes of pure white,

Lamium maculatum and L.m. 'Album'

4-petalled flowers from late winter to late spring. The oval to rounded, irregularly scalloped leaves are mid- to deep green. Grow in moisture-retentive, fertile soil in sun or partial shade. Propagate by division in autumn or early spring or sow seeds when ripe.

PACHYSANDRA TERMINALIS
H 15–20cm (6–8in)
S 45–90cm (1½–3ft) ★★★★
Useful, strong-growing evergreen perennial with glossy, deep green, coarsely toothed, spoon-shaped leaves. Petalless, white-stamened flowers are produced in short, terminal spikes in early summer. Grow in ordinary soil in sun or partial shade. Propagate by division in spring or softwood cuttings in summer. *P.t.* 'Variegata' has cream- to white-margined leaves and is less vigorous.

PULMONARIA SACCHARATA
H 30cm (12in) S 45–60cm (1½–2ft) ★★★★
This early-flowering perennial bears funnel-shaped, violet flowers from reddish buds in spring. Leaves large, evergreen, elliptic and silvery spotted. Plants of the Argentea Group have entirely silvered leaves. Grow in ordinary soil in partial shade. Propagate by division after flowering or by seed when ripe. *P. officinalis* differs in having heart-shaped leaves and violet to blue flowers. *P.o.* 'Sissinghurst White' has pure white flowers. *P.o.* 'Cambridge Blue' has pale blue flowers. *P. longifolia* has funnel-shaped, blue-purple flowers.

SAXIFRAGA X URBIUM
H 30cm (12in) or more
S 40–60cm (1¼–2ft) ★★★★
Vigorous, evergreen perennial, known as London Pride, with slender, erect, reddish stems and airy clusters of tiny, star-shaped, pink-flushed, white flowers from late spring to summer. Spoon-shaped, toothed, mid- to deep green leaves are produced in neat, round rosettes. Grow in ordinary, even poor, garden soil in sun or partial shade. Propagate by division in autumn.

STACHYS BYZANTINA (S. LANATA)
H 40–50cm (16–20in)
S 60cm (2ft) or more ★★★★
Also known as Lambs' Ears, this evergreen mat-former has densely grey-white, woolly, elliptic leaves. The small, tubular, two-lipped, purplish-pink flowers are borne in leafy spikes in summer. Grow in ordinary soil in sun. Propagate by division in autumn or spring. *S.b.* 'Cotton Boll' has flower clusters like cotton-wool balls. 'Silver Carpet' H15cm (6in) rarely flowers. *S.b.* 'Primrose Heron' has leaves suffused with yellow.

SYMPHYTUM IBERICUM (S. GRANDIFLORUM)
H 25cm (10in) or more
S 60cm (2ft) or more ★★★★
Fast-growing evergreen perennial, known as Comfrey, bearing narrowly bell-shaped, white to cream flowers from red-tipped buds. Elliptic to oval leaves are mid- to deep green. Grow in ordinary soil in sun or partial shade. Propagate by division in early spring. Large hybrids include *S.* 'Hidcote Blue' with pale blue flowers and *S.* 'Hidcote Pink', pale pink and white. *S. officinale* has purple-violet, pink or creamy yellow flowers.

TIARELLA CORDIFOLIA
H 20–30cm (8–12in)
S 40–60cm (1¼–2ft) or more ★★★★
Delightful, evergreen perennial, also known as Foam Flower, producing many slender stems which bear a foam-like mass of tiny, creamy white flowers in summer. The hairy, maple-like, 3 to 5-lobed leaves are light green, often with a flush or pattern of bronze. Grow in ordinary, ideally humus-enriched, soil in partial shade. Propagate by division in early spring. *T. wherryi* (*T. cordifolia* var. *collina*) is compact-growing, rarely spreading beyond 30cm (12in) across with mainly 3-lobed, maroon-patterned leaves. Flowers are sometimes pink tinted. Best in moist shade.

TRACHYSTEMON ORIENTALIS
H 45–60cm (1½–2ft)
S 1m (3ft) ★★★★
Robust, herbaceous groundcover for the larger garden with long-stalked, oval to heart-shaped, coarse-textured, deep green leaves. The star-shaped, blue-purple flowers are borne in pendent clusters in spring. Grow in ordinary, ideally moist, soil in partial shade. Propagate by division in early spring. Will tolerate dry shade.

Lysimachia nummularia

Pulmonaria longifolia

Pulmonaria saccharata 'Dora Bielefeld'

Stachys byzantina 'Silver Carpet'

Symphytum ibericum

Using bulbs

Bulbs are nature's form of instant gardening, neatly packaged and able to spring to life within months. Plants have tended to evolve the bulb form as a way of surviving adverse conditions – they can either grow rapidly in spring, before trees overhead have sprouted leaves, or they can grow in hot, dry climates or mountain areas that have short growing seasons. Many bulbs are still dug up from their native countries, resulting in losses and local extinction. Rarely do they do as well as cultivated ones, so ensure you buy from companies who can assure you that all their bulbs are cultivated and propagated in nurseries. Bulbs are invaluable for bringing spring colour to gardens and are very easy to combine with other plants. Plan ahead and you can have bulbs all year round!

Spring colour
By planting bulbs, you can look forward to a flowering display within months. Here, plants including the distinctive orange Fritillaria imperialis, *grape hyacinth (*Muscari*) and tulips provide a show of colour.*

Bulbs for all seasons

The bulb year starts with snowdrops, aconites and crocuses which may be grown under trees or in grass.

Daffodils and narcissi come next, available in a great many varieties, both 'normal' size and dwarf. The larger daffodils are useful for 'naturalizing' in grass. Bluebells, scillas and chionodoxas, most of which flourish in sun or light shade, can all be naturalized, too.

Wonderful shades of blue are very much a feature of spring bulbs. For example, grape hyacinths (*Muscari* spp.) are among those that come in good blues, although they prefer sunnier conditions. Tulips tend to flower later, as spring turns into summer. As well as the vast range of brightly coloured, stiffly upright hybrids, there are a large number of 'species' tulips, which are the wild ancestors of the hybrids. These are much smaller and more informal in habit, but just as cheerfully coloured. Lilies (*Lilium* spp.) are probably the best-known summer bulbs, but there are others, such as the rather statuesque *Galtonia candicans* and the robustly majestic *Crinum* x *powellii*, with its large, pink trumpets.

At the end of the year, the smaller bulbs come into their own again, with cyclamen flowering beneath trees and the 'autumn crocuses', which produce flowers before they grow leaves.

Seasonal flowering
Lilium regale *(above) is one of the best-known summer bulbs, while tulips, such as* Tulipa *'Blizzard' (left), are a popular choice for a late spring border.*

Planting a bulb

Bulbs need to be planted at roughly twice their own depth. A bulb 5cm (2in) deep should be planted at a depth of 10cm (4in). The depth is important, because if bulbs are planted too close to the soil surface, or too deep, it will affect their flowering performance and/or their form.

Tulips planted too close to the soil surface, for example, tend to flop unattractively. Spring-flowering bulbs are generally planted in the autumn, and summer- and autumn-flowering bulbs in early spring.

Bulbs are also very successful container plants, and can be grown in any good potting compost. They must be well-watered, including during the period after flowering when next year's storage system for flowering is being built up.

If you plant bulbs in containers, remember to label the containers after planting. It is only too easy to forget precisely what you have planted!

1 *Fill the container to the appropriate level with compost (using a layer of stones as drainage at the base) and place the bulbs growing point upwards on top.*

2 *Top up with compost to within 2.5cm (1in) of the container rim. Water and keep moist, but not wet, throughout the growing period, and after flowering.*

Places for bulbs

Bulbs can be planted underneath deciduous shrubs or around summer flowering perennials to bring colour to what would otherwise be bare ground. Try combining them with early perennials like primulas, pulmonarias and hellebores.

It is important, though, not to plant them in places where they might get dug up accidentally during the summer. Smaller bulbs can be interplanted with dwarf shrubs and alpines in rockeries. Species tulips make excellent rockery plants, and are good to combine with alpines in containers, too.

Buying bulbs

Buying bulbs is more fraught with problems than almost any other plant purchase. They are easily muddled for one thing, which makes buying them in pre-packs from garden centres the most reliable way of getting what you want. These, however, often contain sub-standard bulbs. The punier the bulb, the less well it will flower. The best way of buying them is from a reputable mail-order company that specializes in bulbs.

Many of the smaller bulbs need high summer temperatures to repeat flower, so they should not be grown where they can get covered by the growth of other plants that would insulate them from the sun's heat.

Bulbs easily become naturalized given the right conditions, which means that they spread themselves over the years. When they are grown in a lawn, it is important that the grass is not cut until the leaves have died back, otherwise they will not be able to build up enough food reserves to flower the year after.

Bulbs that are good for this kind of situation are daffodils and narcissi, snowdrops, crocuses, and small fritillaries, like the snakeshead fritillary (*Fritillaria meleagris*). You can plant bulbs directly into grassed areas with the help of a special bulb planter, which cuts through tough grass easily to create a planting hole. For shady borders, bluebells (*Hyacinthoides non-scripta*) or lily-of-the-valley (*Convallaria majalis*) are ideal.

Nearly all tulips need hot, dry conditions in summer to encourage them to flower again the next year. This does not pose too much of a problem with the species tulips

Bulbs for all situations

Chionodoxa *and* narcissus, *(above) easily become naturalised in grass, while many bulbs, such as* Hyacinthus *and* Viola *(right) make excellent spring or summer bedding plants.*

that thrive in rockeries, but many of the hybrids rarely get enough sun unless they are dug up and stored in a warm, dry place over the summer. Alternatively, they can be treated as annuals.

Bulbs

Allium karavatiense

Anemone coronaria

Colchicum speciosum
'Album'

ALLIUM CHRISTOPHII
(A. ALBOPILOSUM)
H to 60cm (2ft) ★★★★

Intriguing, ornamental onion
with erect, ribbed stems
topped by airy, globular clusters to 20cm (8in) across,
formed of numerous star-
shaped, metallic, pinkish purple flowers in early summer.
The entirely basal leaves are
grey green and strap-shaped.
Grow in ordinary soil in full
sun. Propagate by seeds sown
when ripe or in spring, in a
cold frame or by removing
offsets when dormant. *A. hol-
landicum* is a little taller with
smaller, denser heads of
brighter, rose-purple flowers.
A. karavatiense has pairs of
elliptic, red-margined, grey-
green or grey-purple leaves
and star-shaped, pale mauve
flowers with purple mid-ribs.

ANEMONE BLANDA
H 15cm (6in) ★★★★

Charming, clump-forming
perennial with comparatively
large, saucer-shaped, deep
purple-blue flowers in
spring. The mainly basal
leaves are divided into three,
mid- to deep green, irregularly lobed and toothed
leaflets. Grow in ordinary,
ideally humus-rich soil in
sun or partial shade.
Propagate by dividing the
tubers when dormant. *A.b.*
'Atrocaerulea' is deep blue,
A.b. 'Charmer', deep pink,
and *A.b.* 'White Splendour'
has large, white flowers. *A.
nemorosa*, Wood Anemone,
with white, often pink-
backed or blue flowers, is
similar but spreads more
widely. *A. ranunculoides* is
similar in habit but has bright
yellow single or double flowers. *A. coronaria* has showy,
single flowers in red, blue or
white, in spring.

CHIONODOXA SARDENSIS
H to 10cm (4in) ★★★★

Delightful, easy-going plant,
also known as Glory of the
Snow, with small clusters of
6-petalled, star-shaped, rich
blue flowers with a white eye
appearing in early spring. The
few, entirely basal leaves are
mid-green and strap-shaped.
Grow in ordinary garden soil
in sun or partial shade.
Propagate by offsets removed
when dormant or by seed
sown when ripe, ideally *in
situ*. Will self-sow when happily situated. *C. luciliae* is
somewhat larger in all its
parts with lighter blue flowers
having larger white centres.

COLCHICUM SPECIOSUM
H to 30cm (12in) ★★★★

Indispensible for the autumn
garden, autumn crocus produces sturdy, goblet-shaped
flowers up to 20cm (8in) long
in shades of pale to deep rose-
purple, often with white

throats before the leaves. The
spring-maturing leaves are
glossy, mid- to deep green,
lance-shaped to oblong, in
sheafs of three or four, fading
by midsummer. Grow in
moist, well-drained soil in sun
or partial shade. Propagate by
removing offsets when dormant. *C.s.* 'Album' has shapely, pure white, firm-textured
flowers. Several cultivars are
derived from this species, like
'The Giant' with larger, violet-purple flowers and
'Waterlily' which has fully
double, lilac-pink flowers.

CRINUM X POWELLII
H 1–1.5m (3–5ft) ★★★

Striking, lily-like plant with
strong, erect stems bearing
clusters of nodding, 5-
petalled, trumpet-shaped, fragrant flowers in shades of
pink and white. The entirely
basal, mid-green, deciduous
leaves are strap shaped and
arching. Grow in fertile, well-
drained soil in sun, best at
the foot of a sheltered wall as
not fully frost-hardy.
Propagate by separating offsets in spring before growth
starts. *C. x p.* 'Album' has
pure white blooms.

CROCUS VERNUS
H 12–20cm (5–8in) ★★★★

Cheerful harbingers of spring
with shapely, 6-petalled, goblet-shaped flowers in shades
of lilac and purple. The
entirely basal leaves are narrowly strap-shaped, mid- to
deep green with a narrow,
central silvery stripe. Grow in
ordinary, well-drained soil in
a sunny position. Propagate
by separating offsets when
dormant. *C.v.* 'Jeanne d'Arc'
is white with deep purple
base, *C.v.* 'Pickwick', purple
and white striped and *C.v.*
'Purpureus Grandiflorus' rich
violet with a dark base. *C.
tommasinianus* is smaller and
more slender, the silvery lilac
to reddish-purple flowers

Crinum powellii

appearing in late winter; it is good for naturalizing. *C. chrysanthus* flower at the same time but have broader petals in shades of cream to orange or golden yellow; outstanding is *C. x luteus* 'Golden Yellow'. Hybrids such as 'Blue Bird' or 'Blue Pearl' are shaded or marked with blue. *C. speciosus* has larger flowers in shades of purple-blue and white appearing in autumn before the leaves.

CYCLAMEN HEDERIFOLIUM (C. NEAPOLITANUM)
H 10–12cm (4–5in) ★★★★
Dainty, smaller version of the familiar pot-plant producing 5-petalled, shuttlecock-shaped flowers in shades of pink or white from late summer to late autumn, often before the leaves. The entirely basal, long-stalked, triangular to heart shaped, mid to deep green leaves bear silver markings. Grow in ordinary, ideally humus-rich, well-drained soil in partial shade. Propagate by seed sown when ripe in a cold frame or *in situ*; it sometimes self-sows. *C. coum* is smaller with rounded leaves, sometimes unmarked and with more rounded flowers in shades of pink to red or white in winter to early spring.

ERANTHIS HYEMALIS
H 10cm (4in) or more ★★★★
Cheerful, winter-flowering, clump former, also known as Winter Aconite, with erect stems topped by a ruff of bright green dissected leaves centred by 6-petalled, buttercup-like, bright yellow flowers. Grow in ordinary, ideally humus-rich, soil in partial shade. Propagate by dividing the tubers when dormant or by sowing seeds when ripe in a cold frame. Often self-sows when happily situated.

ERYTHRONIUM DENS-CANIS
H 10–15cm (4–6in) ★★★★
Also known as Dog's Tooth Violet, charming, modestly clump-forming herbaceous, bulbous perennial bearing 6-petalled flowers in spring in shades of pink, white or lilac which are star-shaped at first, then reflex into a Turk's-cap shape. The entirely basal, oblong to elliptic leaves are attractively marbled with purplish-brown. Grow in moist but well-drained, humus-rich soil in partial shade. Propagate by division of established clumps when dormant. 'White Splendour' is white with a brown eye. 'Pagoda', a hybrid cultivar, is a little taller and stronger growing with several light yellow flowers; in 'Kondo' these are darker.

FRITILLARIA IMPERIALIS
H 1–1.5m (3–5ft) ★★★★
Dramatic, robust bulb, also known as Crown Imperial, producing dark, erect stems thickly set with lance shaped, glossy bright green leaves and topped by a cluster of large, pendent, orange to red, 6-petalled bells, each cluster crowned with a tuft of narrower leaves. Grow in fertile, well-drained soil in sun or partial shade. Propagate by separating offsets when dormant. *F.i.* 'Lutea' has bright yellow flowers and is easier to grow. *F. meleagris* H 30cm (12in) is very different, with a slender stem sparingly set with narrow leaves and topped by one or rarely two, large, chequered bells in shades of purple to white.

GALANTHUS NIVALIS
H 8–12cm (3¼–4½in) ★★★★
Also known as Snowdrop, this winter-flowering clump-former has pure white, bell-shaped, pendent flowers formed of three larger outer petals and three, much smaller, green-marked inner ones. The entirely basal leaves are narrowly strap-shaped and grey-green. Grow in moisture-retentive but well-drained soil in sun or partial shade. Propagate by separating clumps or by removing off-

Crocus x luteus 'Golden Yellow'

Cyclamen hederifolium

Eranthis hyemalis

sets when in leaf. Several variants are grown, including 'Flore Pleno', which has double flowers.

GALTONIA CANDICANS
H 1–1.2m (3–4ft) ★★★
Elegant, robust herbaceous plant, also called Summer Hyacinth, with sturdy, erect stems topped by a spire of white, 6-petalled, bell-shaped flowers which dangle from slender, green stalks in late summer. The entirely basal leaves are strap-shaped and grey-green. Grow in moist, well-drained soil in sun. Propagate by removing off-sets when dormant.

GLADIOLUS COMMUNIS SSP. BYZANTINUS (G. BYZANTINUS)
H. 60–75cm (2–2½ft) ★★★
Showy clump-former producing stiff, one-sided spikes of curved, funnel-shaped magenta flowers with paler markings in the centre from

Erythronium 'Pagoda'

Galanthus nivalis

Gladiolus communis ssp. *byzantinus*

Iris danfordiae

Muscari armeniacum

Narcissus 'Peeping Tom'

late spring to early summer. The mid-green, sword-shaped leaves are arranged in a flattened sheaf. Grow in well-drained garden soil in a sunny position. Propagate by separating established clumps or by removing offsets when dormant. A wide range of hybrid cultivars in all colours of the rainbow is freely available.

HYACINTHUS ORIENTALIS
H 20–30cm (8–12in) ★★★★
Indispensible for the spring garden, producing erect, thick, fleshy stems topped by a dense spike of tubular, six-petalled, starry, highly blue to blue-purple fragrant flowers. The entirely basal, bright green glossy leaves are strap-shaped and slightly incurved. Many cultivars are available in shades of blue, pink, red, orange, yellow and white. Grow in fertile, moist but well-drained soil in sun or partial shade. Propagate by offsets when dormant.

IRIS XIPHIUM
H 40–60cm (1¼–2ft) ★★★★
Beautiful, herbaceous plant, also known as Spanish Iris, with a slender, wind-firm stem topped in early summer by several large, 6-petalled flowers in shades of blue and violet, rarely white or yellow, with an orange blotch at the tip of each of the three larger petals (falls). The arching, grassy, grey-green leaves have upturned edges. Grow in fertile, well-drained soil in sun. Propagate by offsets when dormant. Best-known as the parent of the similar but more sturdy Dutch iris that is available in a greater colour range. Very different are the dwarf, winter-flowering irises with erect, rush-like leaves and smaller flowers. *I. unguicularis* H 20cm (8in) has larger, scented, lilac flowers. *I. reticulata* H 10–15cm (4–6in) has flowers in shades of purple to blue. *I. histrioides* is purple-blue and *I. danfordiae* is yellow.

LEUCOJUM VERNUM
H 20–30cm (8–12in) ★★★★
This clump-forming, charming harbinger of spring is also known as Spring Snowflake. It has, in late winter and early spring, an erect stem bearing one or two, white, green-tipped bells like snowdrops but with six petals all the same size. The entirely basal leaves are strap-shaped, glossy deep green. Grow in ordinary soil, moist during the growing season. It prefers partial shade. Propagate by dividing clumps or by separating offsets when dormant. *L. aestivum*, Summer Snowflake, H up to 60cm (2ft), has clusters of flowers to each stem later in spring.

LILIUM REGALE
H 1–1.5m (3–5ft) ★★★★
Superb, popular, summer-flowering trumpet-lily with terminal clusters of large, fragrant, white flowers with yellow centres and stamens from

brown-purple flushed buds. The leaves are narrowly lance-shaped and deep green. Grow in fertile, ideally humus-rich, moist but well-drained soil in sun or partial shade. Propagate by seed as soon as ripe or in spring in a cold frame. This is a classic trumpet-shaped lily, typical of a large group of species and hybrids which vary in height and flower colour and include the well-known pure-white *L. candidum*. Equally popular are species and hybrids with petals creating a Turk's-cap shaped flower, for example, *L. martagon* which has spikes of purplish-red to pink or white flowers. Also recommended are the Asiatic hybrids which have less recurved petals and larger flowers in many colours.

MUSCARI ARMENIACUM
H 15–20cm (6–8in) ★★★★
The most popular clump-forming grape hyacinth with smooth, erect stems topped by dense, oval spikes of small, bright blue bells with constricted white mouths. The entirely basal leaves are narrowly strap-shaped, grooved, bright to mid-green. Grow in well-drained soil in sun or partial shade. Propagate by dividing established clumps or by removing the freely produced bulblets when dormant. *M. comosum*, Tassel Hyacinth, is a little taller with loose spikes of fertile, brownish white flowers at the base and smaller, sterile, bright blue-violet ones in a tassel at the top. 'Plumosum' has airy spikes entirely formed of purple-blue, tassel-like flowers.

NARCISSUS PSEUDONARCISSUS
H 15–30cm (6–12in) ★★★★
The best known of the truly wild trumpet daffodils, each erect stem bearing six, creamy yellow outer petals and a darker shaded trumpet. The entirely basal, strap-shaped leaves are mid- to

grey-green. Good for naturalizing. Grow in ordinary soil, ideally moist during the growing season. Propagate by separating clumps or removing offsets when dormant. Many hybrid cultivars are available, from white to yellow with contrastingly coloured trumpets, a few of them fully double. There are also cultivars with shorter trumpets (cups) which are generally known as narcissus, these also have a wide colour range and are freely available. *N. triandrus* H 25cm (10in) is very different, bearing two to six, small, short-cupped yellow to white flowers on each stem. There are many taller hybrid cultivars with this form of growth with larger flowers in shades of yellow to white, some of them with red to orange cups. These are better garden plants. 'Peeping Tom', H 30cm (12in), is a small, dainty bulb which is particularly good for naturalizing.

NERINE BOWDENII
H 45–60cm (1¼–2ft) ★★★
Striking, robust plant with erect stems topped with rounded clusters of 6-petalled, somewhat lily-like flowers formed of six narrow, arching, wavy, pink petals which open in autumn as the leaves die down. The entirely basal, strap-shaped leaves are mid- to bright green. Grow in well-drained soil in a sunny position. Propagate by separating offsets when dormant. *N.b.* 'Mark Fenwick' is a recommended cultivar with rich pink flowers on dark stems.

ORNITHOGALUM UMBELLATUM
H 15–25cm (6–8in) ★★★
Attractive clump-former, also known as Star of Bethlehem, producing slim, erect stems topped by clusters of erect, 6-petalled, starry, pure white flowers from green buds in late spring. The entirely basal leaves are very narrowly strap-shaped with a silvery, central vein and wither just before or at flowering time. Grow in well-drained soil either in sun or partial shade. Propagate by dividing clumps or by separating the freely borne off-sets. In light soils this plant can be invasive. *O. nutans*, Drooping Star-of-Bethlehem, differs mainly in that it bears spikes of nodding green and silvery white bells.

SCILLA SIBERICA
H 10–20cm (4–8in) ★★★★
Pretty, dwarf clump-former, also known as Siberian Squill, each bulb producing several erect stems topped by 3 to 5 bell-shaped, 6-petalled, bright blue or white flowers in spring. The entirely basal leaves are strap-shaped and glossy, mid- to deep green. Grow in moist but well-drained soil in sun or partial shade. Propagate by dividing clumps or by separating offsets when dormant. 'Spring Beauty' ('Atrocaerulea'), is the most reliable cultivar with deep blue flowers. *S. mistschenkoana* (*S. tubergeniana*) blooms a little earlier with slightly larger, white, blue-striped flowers. *S. bifolia* has upward-facing, star-shaped deep blue flowers.

TULIPA KAUFMANNIANA
H 15–30cm (6–12in) ★★★★
Decorative, dwarf tulip, also called Water-lily Tulip, with long-tapered, pink-flushed, urn-shaped buds which open out flat in the sun to disclose the petals' yellow inner faces. Leaves are lance-shaped, smooth and grey-green. Of similar size is *T. clusiana*, having white petals striped deep pink. *T.* 'Giuseppe Verde' has golden yellow petals striped red. Grow in well-drained, garden soil in a sunny position. Propagate by removing offsets when dormant. Several hybrid cultivars are available, usually in a variety of striking bicolours, some with purple-striped leaves. There are many other hybrid groups of tulips which vary in flowering time, shape, height and come in a wide colour range. Cultivars of the Single Early Group produce large, cup-shaped flowers from early to mid-spring, the Double Earlies have fully double flowers. Plants of the Lily-flowered Group have pointed-petalled, goblet-shaped flowers in late spring and those of the Parrot Group have large, cup-shaped flowers, the petals sometimes striped or blotched with other colours. Tallest is the Darwin Hybrid Group with large, deep cup-shaped flowers in a range of bright colours from early to mid-spring.

Narcissus pseudonarcissus

Nerine bowdenii

Scilla siberica

Tulipa clusiana

Tulipa 'Giuseppe Verde'

Using annuals and biennials

Annuals are plants that complete their life cycle within one year – germinating, flowering, setting seed and dying. Hardy annuals can withstand late frosts and so can be sown in the ground in spring without danger. Half-hardy annuals are frost-sensitive, so are usually started off inside and planted out after the frosts. These include a certain number of plants, such as ageratum and antirrhinum, that are, in fact, perennials in frost-free climates. They are grown as annuals in cooler climes, as it is possible to bring them to flower from seed in only a few months. The half-hardies are often referred to as bedding plants. Biennials are plants that are started off as seed one year, to flower the next, either dying after flowering or being discarded. Hollyhocks (*Alcea* spp.) are an example.

Shade-loving biennials

Although we often think of annuals and biennials as being plants for sunny corners of the garden only, some, like the biennial foxglove (Digitalis) do best in partial shade and are ideal for adding colour to a shady spot in the garden or for woodland planting.

Fillers and bedding

The speed with which annuals grow and the intensity of their colours are the main reason for their popularity with gardeners. They usually start to flower in mid-summer, after the perennials of early summer but before the profusion of late-season perennials has started. For people wanting a practically instant garden, annuals are just what is needed.

Annuals are particularly useful in new gardens where there are considerable gaps between young plants. They provide temporary cover while you make your mind up about permanent plans.

In established gardens, annuals of either kind are ideal for combining with other plants as gap fillers among shrubs and perennials. They provide colour long after these bedfellows have finished flowering, or, in the case of late perennials, before they have got into their stride. They can even be grown over dormant spring bulbs, so long as there is no risk of the bulbs being uprooted when the annuals are removed at the end of the year.

While there are no true spring-flowering annuals available for gardens, there are certain plants, usually short-lived perennials, or biennials, that take their place

Border colour

Wallflowers and tulips (above) are excellent for spring bedding, while plants such as dahlias, salvia, pelargonium and petunias (right) are combined to provide a spectacular burst of colour in early autumn.

as spring bedding, being discarded after they flower. These are generally started off as young plants, from seed, the year before and planted out in autumn or late winter. Wallflowers (*Erysimum cheiri* varieties) and pansies (*Viola* hybrids) are the best known.

Formal versus informal

There are two traditions of annual growing. One is the formal one, familiar from public parks the world over, with the emphasis on strong, contrasting colours and geometrical layouts, using a lot of half-hardy annuals. The other is the informal, cottage-garden tradition, which relies on cheaper hardy annuals that are sown where they are to grow. Here, the colours are more muted, many are fragrant and a certain amount of untidiness is acceptable. Both traditions are currently undergoing changes as both are now using a much wider range of plants than formerly.

French marigolds (*Tagetes* spp.) and petunias are typical of the first tradition, while cornflowers (*Centaurea cyanus*) and Pot Marigolds (*Calendula officinalis*) are cottage garden staples. Formal planting also, increasingly, makes use of the kind of plants discussed under 'Perennials for sunny corners and containers'.

Planting contrasts
Formal borders (above) empha-size regular, tidy patterns and contrasting colours, while in informal borders (right) the colours are muted and plants are allowed to grow as they will.

Annuals in containers

Annuals, or plants grown as annuals, are a favourite for use in containers. Hanging baskets, tubs and windowboxes are the most usual, but there is nothing to stop those imaginative people who make use of practically anything that holds soil. Given that most have been bred for compactness and a long flowering season, it is the half-hardy annuals, like petunias, lobelias, impatiens and pelargoniums, that often find their way into containers.

Just as foliage plants are used in the perennial border, so they can be used among annuals, too. Silver helichrysum species are often found in hanging baskets, their foliage forming an attractive counterpoint to the flowers.

Long-lasting displays
Annuals, especially those that are half-hardy, are favourites for window-boxes (left) and containers (right) because many have been bred for their compactness and long flowering seasons.

Effective containers have a lot of plants packed into them, which means that the compost used must be very fertile. The best way to make sure that the plants never run short of nutrients is to use slow-release fertilizer pellets, which will gradually release nutrients over the whole summer. Plentiful and regular watering is essential too.

When it comes to designing container plantings, a few plants widely used have more impact than trying to use as many as possible. The same 'rules' that apply to mixing colours and using structural plants in borders can be applied to containers too.

Annuals and biennials

Ageratum houstonanium
'Blue Danube'

AGERATUM HOUSTONIANUM
H 15-45cm (6-18in) ⋆
Pretty, half-hardy annual with tiny, blue, powder-puff shaped flowerheads in dense terminal clusters in summer to autumn. The oval to heart-shaped, downy leaves are mid- to bright green. Grow in fertile, ideally moist soil. Propagate by seed sown in warmth in spring. Usually represented in gardens by the dwarf cultivars such as 'Adriatic', H 15-20cm (6-8in), which is mid-blue, and 'Bavaria', blue and white. 'Blue Danube' is lavender-blue and weather-resistant. 'Blue Mink', H 20-30cm (8-12in), is extra-vigorous and powder blue. 'Hawaii White', H 15cm (6in), is white. 'Blue Horizon' bears purple-blue flowers on long stems.

ALCEA ROSEA (ALTHAEA ROSEA)
H 2–3m (6½–10ft) ⋆⋆⋆⋆
Statuesque, short-lived, hardy perennial, also known as Hollyhock, grown as an annual and biennial for its shallowly funnel-shaped, 5-petalled flowers in a variety of colours. The mid- to light green, rounded leaves are shallowly 3 to 7-lobed and roughly hairy. Grow in fertile soil in sun. Propagate as annuals by sowing seed in warmth in late winter and as biennials or perennials *in situ* in late spring. Chater's Double Group has fully double, pom-pon-like flowers in shades of pink, red, yellow, lavender, purple and white. 'Nigra' has deep chocolate-maroon, single flowers. Summer Carnival Group has double flowers in a wide colour range.

ANTIRRHINUM MAJUS
H to 1.2m (4ft) or more ⋆⋆⋆
Colourful, short-lived perennial, also called Snapdragon, usually grown as an annual with spikes of tubular, broadly two-lipped flowers in shades of yellow, red, pink, purple, bronze and white from summer to autumn. The leaves are lance-shaped, glossy mid- to dark green. Grow in ordinary, fertile soil in sun. Propagate as annuals by sowing seed in warmth in late winter. Many cultivars are available in mixed or single colours. The Tahiti Series are dwarf and rust-resistant.

BEGONIA X CARRIEREI (B. SEMPERFLORENS)
H 20–30cm (8–12in)
Showy, tender, evergreen perennials usually grown as annuals, bearing a profusion of waxy, 4-petalled flowers in shades of red, pink and white in mid- to late summer. The lopsidedly oval leaves are slightly fleshy and bright glossy green, flushed with reddish-bronze in some cultivars. Grow in fertile soil in sun or partial shade. Propagate by seed sown in late winter in warmth or by cuttings of non-flowering shoots in late summer. The Cocktail Series is a good, weather-resistant strain in a wide range of shades. 'Organdy' has a mixture of white, pink and red flowers and green and bronze leaves.

BELLIS PERENNIS
H 10–15cm (4–6in) ⋆⋆⋆⋆
Also known as Daisy, this perennial is grown as a biennial for its pompon-like, fully double daisies in shades of red, pink and white from late winter to late summer. The spoon-shaped, glossy leaves are mid- to bright green. Grow in ordinary soil in sun or partial shade. Propagate by seed sown in a nursery bed outside in summer or in warmth in late winter. Can be divided in autumn, early spring or after flowering. Habanera Series bears large flowerheads. Roggli Series produces semi-double flowers. Tasso Series has large flowerheads of quilled petals.

CALENDULA OFFICINALIS
H 30–60cm (1–2ft) ⋆⋆
Also known as Pot Marigold, these popular, hardy, orange and yellow daisies are produced over a long period in

Begonia semperflorens

Bellis perennis

Antirrhinum

summer to autumn. Spoon-shaped to oblong leaves are softly hairy, somewhat aromatic and mid-green. Grow in ordinary soil in sun. Propagate by seed sown *in situ* in spring or autumn. 'Orange King' is double, deep orange. Pacific Series has double flowers in shades of orange, yellow and cream and bicolours. 'Indian Prince' is taller and dark orange.

CAMPANULA MEDIUM
H 60–90cm (2–3ft) ★★★
Handsome biennial, also known as Canterbury Bells, producing substantial spikes of large, bellflowers in shades of blue, pink and white. The mainly basal, lance-shaped leaves are mid-green and hairy and arranged in a neat rosette. Grow in fertile soil in sun or partial shade. Propagate by seed sown in late spring in a nursery bed or in boxes. 'Bells of Holland' H 45cm (18in) does not grow any taller and 'Calycanthema', Cup and Saucer Canterbury Bells, has the bell sitting in a colourful, saucer-like calyx.

CENTAUREA CYANUS
H 30–75cm (1–2½ft) ★★★
Well-known, hardy annual, also known as Cornflower, grown for its pompon-like blue flowers in summer. The narrowly lance-shaped, sometimes lobed leaves are deep green and woolly haired beneath. Grow in fertile soil in sun. Propagate by seed sown *in situ* in spring. Cultivars are available in shades of pink, blue and white. The Florence Series are compact and well-branched to 35cm (14in). Baby Series are dwarf plants to 30cm (12in).

CHEIRANTHUS CHEIRI
(ERYSIMUM)
H 30–60cm (1–2ft) ★★★
Also known as Wallflower, this short-lived, hardy perennial grown as a biennial for its fragrant, colourful, 4-petalled flowers borne in

bold, terminal spikes in a variety of colours. The lance-shaped leaves are mid- to deep green and crowded along the stems. Grow in well-drained, ideally limy soil in sun. Propagate by seed sown in a nursery bed in late spring. 'Blood Red', deep red, 'Ivory White, creamy white. 'Harlequin' is a mixed strain in shades of red, orange, cream and bicolours.

CLARKIA ELEGANS
(C. UNGUICULATA)
H 30–90cm (2–3ft) ★★★
Popular, erect, self-supporting, hardy annual bearing spikes of 4-petalled flowers in shades of pink, red, lavender and white in summer. The oval to lance-shaped leaves are mid-green. Grow in fertile soil in sun. Propagate by seed sown *in situ* in autumn or spring. In cold areas, protect autumn-sown seedlings with cloches. Single and double-flowered cultivars and several colour mixes are available of which the dwarf ones such as *C.e.* 'Royal Bouquet' H 30cm (1ft) has particularly valuable double flowers. *C. amoena*, also known as godetia, is an erect, hardy, branching annual bearing clusters of cup-shaped, 4-petalled flowers. Single or double, tall and dwarf cultivars are available in single or mixed colours.

COSMOS BIPINNATUS
H 60–150cm (2–5ft) ★
Elegant, half-hardy, erect annual bearing large, daisy-like flowers with broad, notched-tipped petals in shades of red, pink and white in summer to autumn. The mid- to deep green leaves are finely cut into many filament-like segments. Grow in well-drained, fertile soil in sun. Propagate by seed sown in early to mid-spring in warmth or *in situ* in late spring. There are cultivars in a variety of colours and mixes, from *C.* 'Sensation',

H90cm (3ft) varying from bright pink to white, to dwarfs at 30cm (1ft). *C. sulphureus* has more coarsely cut leaves and slightly smaller, orange to yellow flowers.

DIANTHUS BARBATUS
H 45–60cm (1½–2ft) ★★★★
A hardy cottage garden plant, also known as Sweet William. It is a short-lived perennial grown as a biennial or annual bearing broad heads of small, 5-petalled, strongly fragrant flowers in shades of red, pink and white, often bicoloured. The mid- to deep green leaves are oval to lance-shaped. Grow in fertile soil in sun. Propagate as a biennial by sowing seed in a nursery bed in spring or as an annual. Several cultivars are available in single or mixed colours, some with bronze or purple-tinted foliage, others dwarf, such as 'Wee Willie', H 15cm (6in).

DIGITALIS PURPUREA
H 1–2m (3–6½ft) ★★★★
Unmistakable, hardy biennial, also known as Foxglove, grown for its long, one-sided spires of thimble-shaped bells in shades of rose-purple to white in early to mid-summer, often with darker spotting within. The large leaves are oval to lance-shaped, toothed and deep green, forming a handsome rosette the first year. Grow in ordinary soil in sun or shade. Propagate by seed sown in a nursery bed in late spring.

Calendula officinalis

Erysismum x allionii

Cosmos 'Sensation Mixed'

Dianthus barbatus 'Harbinger Mixed'

Digitalis purpurea Excelsior Group

Eschscholzia californica

Iberis umbellata 'Fairyland'

Impatiens 'Accent Salmon'

Several cultivars in single or mixed colours are available, some more dwarf, e.g. Foxy H 1.2m (4ft). The Excelsior Group have flowers arranged in cylindrical spikes.

ESCHSCHOLZIA CALIFORNICA
H 25–35cm (10–14in) ★★
Showy, hardy annual, also called Californian Poppy, grown for its brilliant orange, poppy-like flowers which open in long succession in summer. The grey-green leaves are cut into slender segments. Grow in well-drained soil in sun. Propagate by sowing seeds *in situ* in spring or autumn. Several cultivars are available in single colours or in mixtures in shades of reds, pinks and orange. 'Ballerina' has semi-double flowers.

GYPSOPHILA ELEGANS
H 45–60cm (1½–2ft) ★★★
Dainty, hardy annual grown for its large, airy clusters of small, 5-petalled, starry white to pink flowers in summer. The narrowly lance-shaped, pointed leaves are grey-green. Grow in well-drained, preferably limy soil in sun. Propagate by seeds sown *in situ* in spring. A useful flower for cutting. Cultivars are available in shades of pink, carmine and white.

HELICHRYSUM BRACTEATUM (BRACHTEANTHA BRACTEATA)
H 60–90cm (2–3ft) ★★
Distinctive, short-lived, half-hardy perennial, also known as Strawflower, grown as an annual for its daisy-like flowers with yellow, pink or red petals. The broadly lance-shaped leaves are mid- to grey-green. Grow in well-drained soil in sun. Propagate by seed sown in warmth in mid-spring. Cultivars come in single and mixed colours. The Monstrosa Series bear huge fully double flower-heads. Bikini Series, H 30cm (1ft), has papery, pink, orange or white flowers.

IBERIS AMARA
H 30–45cm (1–1½ft) ★★★
Bright, erect, hardy annual, also known as Candytuft, grown for its dense, rounded to shortly cylindrical clusters of 4-petalled white to purple-tinted, fragrant flowers in summer. The entirely stem-borne, lance-shaped to narrowly spoon-shaped leaves are mid- to deep green. Grow in fertile, well-drained soil in sun. Propagate by sowing seeds *in situ* in spring or autumn. *I. umbellata*, Common Candytuft, rarely exceeds 30cm and is more freely branching with smaller, clusters of white, lavender, pink, purple or crimson flowers. Several cultivars are available in the 15–23cm (6–9in) height range in a variety of mixed colours.

IMPATIENS WALLERIANA
H 40–60cm (1¼–2ft) ★
Showy, bushy, tender perennial, also called Busy Lizzie, grown as an annual producing a long succession of rounded, 5-petalled flowers in shades of pink, red, orange, purple, white and bicolours. The elliptic to lance-shaped, toothed leaves are bright green. Grow in fertile soil in sun or partial shade. Propagate by seeds sown in warmth in early

spring. Numerous cultivars are available in a range of colours, most of them dwarf and compact and very free flowering, such as 'Florette Stars', H 15–20cm (6–8in).

LATHYRUS ODORATUS
H 2–2.5m (6½–8ft) ★★★★
Also known as Sweet Pea, this well-loved, hardy, climbing annual is grown for its rounded, very fragrant pea-shaped flowers in shades of red, pink, purple, lavender and white, sometimes bicoloured with picotee margins to the petals. The mid- to deep green leaves are formed of two oval leaflets and branched tendril by which the plant clings to its support. Grow in moist but well drained soil in sun. A support of netting, trellis or tall pea sticks is required. Propagate by seeds, ideally first soaked, sown in a cold frame in early spring.

LAVATERA TRIMESTRIS
H 90–120cm (3–4ft) ★★★
Decorative, erect, bushy, hardy annual grown for its profusion of large, shallowly funnel-shaped 5-petalled flowers in shades of luminous pink and white. The softly hairy, mid- to deep green, rounded leaves have three to five or sometimes seven lobes. Grow in fertile soil in sun. Propagate by sowing seeds *in situ* in mid-spring. *L.t.* 'Loveliness' is deep pink, *L.t.* 'Mont Blanc' is white. *L.t.* 'Ruby Regis' is reddish-pink.

LIMNANTHES DOUGLASII
H 10–15cm (4–6in) ★★★
Colourful, hardy annual, also known as Poached Egg Plant, grown for its mass of shallowly cup-shaped, 5-petalled flowers which are bright yellow with white edges. The dissected, finely toothed leaves are somewhat fleshy and bright yellow-green. Grow in ordinary soil in sun. Propagate by seed sown *in situ* in autumn or mid-spring.

LOBULARIA MARITIMA
H 10–20cm (4–8in) ★★★

Useful, low-growing, hardy bushy annual, also known as Sweet Alison, producing a profusion of tiny, 4-petalled, scented, white to purple flowers throughout the summer. The narrowly lance-shaped leaves are mid- to greyish green. Grow in ordinary soil in sun. Propagate by sowing seed *in situ* in mid- to late spring. 'Carpet of Snow' H 10cm (4in) has white flowers, 'New Purple' is very compact with purple flowers. Several cultivars are available.

MATTHIOLA INCANA
H 30–75cm (12–30in) ★★★★

Pretty, woody-based perennial, also called Stock, grown as annuals or biennials, with erect spikes of scented, 4-petalled flowers in shades of purple, pink and white. The white-hairy to grey-green leaves are lance-shaped to narrowly spoon-shaped. Grow in well-drained, ideally limy soil in sun. Propagate by seed. For growing as an annual sow in warmth in early spring, as a biennial sow in summer and over-winter in a frame or *in situ*. A variety of cultivars in mixed and single colours is available.

MYOSOTIS SYLVATICA
H 15–30cm (6–12in) ★★★★

Forget-me-not, perhaps the best known of all hardy biennial bedding plants, produces a profusion of a small, bright blue 5-petalled flowers from spring to midsummer. The oval to lance-shaped, coarsely hairy leaves are mid- to deep green. Grow in ordinary garden soil in sun or partial shade. Propagate by sowing seeds in summer in a seed bed. Several cultivars are available, some of them of hybrid origin, with *M. alpestris* smaller and more compact, like Ball Series, H 15cm (6in). Pink and white cultivars are also available.

NEMESIA STRUMOSA
H 20–30cm (8–12in) ★

Dainty, erect, branching, half-hardy annual bearing terminal spikes of two-lipped flowers in shades of pink, blue, purple, yellow, red and white, sometimes bicoloured. The lance-shaped leaves may be toothed or smooth-edged, mid- to bright green. Grow in fertile, well-drained soil in sun. Propagate by sowing seeds in warmth in early to mid-spring. Several cultivars in single and mixed colours are available, mostly under 20cm (8in) in height.

PETUNIA HYBRIDS
H 15–30cm (6–12in) ★

Popular, colourful annual grown for its long succession of funnel-shaped flowers in shades of pink, red, purple, yellow and white, some bicoloured and frilled. The oval to lance-shaped leaves are mid-green and sticky. Many cultivars in single and mixed shades are available, some are dwarf and compact, e.g. the Celebrity and Merlin Series, H 23cm (9in), others have a more spreading growth habit, e.g. the Super Cascade Series, which have branches up to 45cm (1½ft) long and are good for hanging baskets.

TAGETES ERECTA
H 45cm (1½ft) ★

Brilliantly coloured, half-hardy, erect annual, also known as African Marigold, bearing large, often double, daisy-like flowers with broad petals in shades of yellow and orange. The mid-to bright green leaves are cut into several lobes. Grow in ordinary soil in full sun. Propagate by sowing seed in early spring in warmth or late spring *in situ*. Many cultivars are available, e.g. the Lady Series, H 40–45cm (16–18in), in orange, primrose and golden yellow shades. *T. patula*, French Marigold, H 30cm (1ft), is smaller, sometimes with red-brown petals or

bicoloured. Cultivars of the Boy Series, H 15cm (6in), are compact with double flower-heads in shades of yellow, orange and mahogany, often bicoloured. 'Lemon Gem' has lemon-yellow flowerheads.

TROPAEOLUM MAJUS
H 30cm–2m (1–6½ft)

Striking, colourful, tender annual, known as Nasturtium, with large, 5-petalled, spurred flowers in shades of red, orange and yellow throughout summer. Smooth, rounded leaves are bright green. Grow in ordinary soil in sun. The normal species is a climbing plant, needing support. More popular are the bushy, non-climbing cultivars like Jewel Series. Propagate by sowing seed in mid-spring in warmth or late spring *in situ*.

VIOLA x WITTROCKIANA
H 10–25cm (4–10in) ★★★★

This short-lived, hardy ever-green perennial, also known as Garden Pansy, is often grown as an annual. It has the typical 5-petalled, flat, pansy flower in shades of purple, blue, yellow, red and white, often with a dark, face-like pattern in the centre. The oval, scalloped leaves are mid- to deep green. Grow in fertile soil in sun or partial shade. Propagate by seeds sown in spring or early autumn in a nursery bed or frame. Cultivars are available in single and mixed colours, e.g. the Clear Crystal Series which have self-coloured flowers with no markings.

Lavatera 'Parade'

Nemesia 'Carnival'

Petunia 'Vogue'

Tagetes 'Lemon Gem'

VEGETABLES, FRUIT AND HERBS

For many gardeners, being able to sample the freshness and taste of home-grown produce is hugely satisfying. The quest for maximum flavour, size, juiciness, sweetness or crispness, however, is not without its pitfalls, which makes this section of the book essential reading for the less-experienced grower! Explaining just how simple it can be to reap a sensational harvest, all year round, it tells you how to organize and maintain your plot to grow crops efficiently and keep them healthy and productive. A second section is dedicated to step-by-step instructions on how to sow, cultivate and harvest a wide range of vegetables, fruit and herbs. From crisp mangetouts and succulent Brussels sprouts to curly endive, juicy tomatoes and ripe raspberries, each entry is colourfully illustrated and easy to follow. And if you can save room for a few herbs, there is also all you need to know about how to grow and use them.

Getting started

Gardeners want to grow their own fruit, vegetables and herbs for a variety of reasons. You may, for example, wish to control what you eat, which means growing produce organically and avoiding the use of potentially harmful chemicals and fertilizers necessary for higher yields of commercial production. There is also the pleasure of eating garden-fresh produce, which has a fullness of flavour that is lost in shop-bought food. Another attraction is the opportunity to experiment by growing more exotic and unusual fruit and vegetables that are either not available in most shops or are expensive.

Growing your own
Fruit, vegetables and herbs not only taste good, they can also look good if they are well laid-out.

The ornamental potager

There is no reason why your vegetable garden should be any less attractive than the flower garden. A mixture of fruit, vegetables and herbs, laid out in a square design, with perhaps an edging of clipped box, will turn the edible garden into an object of beauty. You can make a very simple square design with just a few rows of vegetables or opt for a series of squares, with brick paths in between each square, to make a more elaborate potager. Herbs are ideally suited to this kind of design, and your potager could devote one or two squares to them. Site such a potager near the house, to make access easier. Soft fruit, like gooseberries, can be trained as ornamental standards, and tree fruit can be fan-trained on wire supports, taking up minimal space and adding to the attraction of the garden.

Planning an attractive kitchen garden
Growing edible crops can be as satisfying visually as it is in culinary terms, as this elegant kitchen garden demonstrates.

Room for all
A neatly laid-out herb garden can succeed in the tiniest of areas.

Good planning
Close cultivation of vegetables makes the best use of space.

Growing edible plants

The earliest gardens evolved out of a purely functional need to have useful plants (those needed for food and medicines) close at hand, rather than having to search and scavenge for them far and wide.

Today, a huge range of vegetables, fruit and herbs can be grown. New and vastly improved cultivars are continually being introduced by gardeners and plant breeders who have selected plants with qualities that gardeners desire. The parsnip cultivar 'Avonresister', for example, can tolerate canker disease, to which parsnips are vulnerable. Other vegetables have been bred and

introduced for their improved performance or yield, such as the Brussels sprout cultivar 'Peer Gynt', which has the ability to develop all its sprouts to an even size over a short period of time; or there are dwarfing cultivars that are ideal for growing in small spaces, such as the sweet pepper 'Baby Belle'. Cultivars are also chosen for their qualities of long storage life, flavour, or rapid maturity.

Many of today's vegetables are hybrids that are bred for a specific purpose. They are called F1 hybrids. F2 hybrids are the result of either cross-pollination or self-pollination of F1-hybrid parents.

Growing in containers

Vegetables, fruit and herbs can be grown in containers in the most unlikely of places – on patios, balconies, fire escapes and landings, or on any small plot of ground where the light is good.

Although you will want to choose the most attractive container, for successful results the container's appearance is not as important as the contents. You need to fill it with fresh, well-balanced potting compost and a base dressing of fertilizer, adding further top-dressings of fertilizer throughout the growing

season. Long-rooted vegetables such as carrots and parsnips need deep containers (at least 45cm/18in deep) to grow well.

Tall crops tend to become unstable, especially if grown in small pots, and can blow over in strong winds, so protect these with stones or netting. Container-grown crops need to be watered frequently during warm or dry weather.

Vegetables in containers
You can grow vegetables in containers or growbags on any small plot where the light is good.

Keeping crops healthy

It is important to ensure that your crops are not damaged or reduced by pests and diseases. To do this you can use either chemical or organic methods.

Chemical methods

These can be very effective in pest and disease control, as long as they are used strictly according to the instructions on the container and are applied thoroughly. Their main drawbacks are:
• Some chemicals may kill beneficial insects as well as harmful ones.
• Certain chemicals are very long-lasting.
• Chemicals may taint the produce with residue.

Organic methods

Reaching for a chemical is not the only solution to an outbreak of pests or disease; there are many other preventive measures that can be

taken. The first step is to grow healthy, vigorous plants as these seem less susceptible to attack, especially when there is also good garden hygiene, and crop rotation is carried out (see p.70).

Physical barriers can be put in place to deny pests access to the crop: for example, lay mats around the bases of brassicas to keep cabbage root fly at bay, or cover your crops with fine nets, the edges of which should be buried in the soil to deter flying pests.

Traps of shallow dishes containing cola or beer can also be laid to entice crawling pests into them so they can be easily disposed of.

Organic sprays based on natural substances, such as derris, pyrethrum, insecticidal soaps and sulphur, are useful and very effective controls against a variety of pests and diseases.

Organic sprays
Brassica plants are treated with a solution of insecticidal soap to kill aphids.

Protective barriers
A layer of netting protects succulent young vegetable plants from marauding birds.

Baited traps
Fill a sunken dish with beer to catch slugs and snails. The sticks help any beetles to escape.

Wasp traps
Hanging from a plum tree, this jar full of sweet-smelling liquid attracts wasps.

Growing vegetables

Vegetables tend to be relatively short-term crops, because most grow rapidly and are harvested before they reach maturity. The ideal soil for growing vegetables is a loam (a mixture of clay, sand and silt in more or less equal proportions) containing humus and with a pH preferably between 6.5 and 7.0. Soils that vary from this ideal – that is, they are more sandy, or have little humus – may need more cultivation. Soil also needs to be fertile, which usually means adding fertilizers or well-rotted manure before sowing or planting.

Growing vegetables
Vegetables and herbs, like these cabbages, lettuces, chives and fennel, can be grown even in small gardens, packed a little tighter than usual.

Crop rotation

When groups of related vegetables are grown on a different plot from year to year, this is called crop rotation. One reason for moving crops from one part of the plot to another is to avoid the build-up of diseases and pests in the soil. Another benefit is that the soil's fertility can be improved by growing crops that add nitrogen, such as peas and most beans.

Start by making a list of the various vegetables you intend to grow, and then classify them into groups based on their needs and growth patterns (see p.75).

Allocate each rotation group to a plot of land, and draw up a month-by-month cropping timetable. This will keep the land fully occupied and provide continuity. For example, after Brussels sprouts and leeks are finished in early spring, follow with sowings of peas, carrots, lettuces or salad onions.

If you prefer, the vegetables can be from different crop groupings, which means that the rotation from one plot to another is a gradual process, rather than a wholesale changeover on a certain date.

If there is not enough space in a small garden to rotate entire blocks of crops, you could grow the plants in narrow strips and swop the groups between the strips.

Grouping the different types of vegetables together makes crop management easier. Leave at least two years before planting any vegetable from the same group on the same ground.

Watering

Plants, whether they are seed-germinating or fruit-developing, must have water for growth. Vegetables will grow well only if they have enough water to replace that lost from the leaves. Most plants have critical periods when water is especially vital, so the skill in providing an optimum water supply is to know when and how to apply the water:
• At the seed and seedling stage, to aid establishment. Water the seed drills with a fine-rosed watering can until they have developed a deep root system.
• After transplanting, to aid re-establishment. Leave a slight depression in the soil at the base of each stem, then fill it with water.
• To produce crops. Fruiting crops such tomatoes and runner beans most need water while flowering and when the fruit starts to swell. Leafy crops need heavy watering about 15 days before harvesting. Root crops should have a steady supply of water from sowing through to cropping.

The best times to water are early mornings or evenings when the sun is less intense, reducing the amount of moisture lost to evaporation.

Crop rotation groups
This plot is divided into three groups: peas and beans (left), brassicas and leafy crops (middle) and roots and stems (right). A fourth, permanent, plot can be created for crops that are not shifted, such as asparagus (see p.146). Each group is moved each year onto a new strip of land.

Feeding the soil

Soil that is intensively cultivated needs generous feeding for optimum results. This can be provided with organic or inorganic fertilizers. A great advantage of organic manures and fertilizers is that they encourage worm activity, which in turn aids soil fertility. Soil that has had no organic matter added is likely to have a worm count of 100–300 per sq m (sq yd) in the top 30cm (12in) of soil. This figure often increases to around 400–500 per sq m (sq yd) if organic matter is added on a regular basis.

Although quite adequate crops of vegetables can be grown in soils where only organic manure and fertilizers are used, higher yields are usually achieved where inorganic, 'chemical' fertilizers are incorporated. The amount of fertilizer needed will depend on the soil type, because light, sandy soils lose fertilizer quickly, whereas clay soils will hold nutrients for much longer. It is also affected by the kind of crop being grown: leafy crops, such as cabbages, need plenty of nitrogen, with one-third of this being provided when they are planted and the remaining two-thirds supplied while the plants are growing.

Vegetable crops growing through winter should get most of their nitrogen in spring rather than autumn, because nitrogen encourages soft growth and if large quantities of nitrogen are added in autumn, this could lead to the soft growth being killed by frost. Therefore, overwintering crops should be given a balanced fertilizer to toughen the leaves and stems. Fruiting crops such as tomatoes and peppers need regular feeding with phosphate and potash fertilizers as soon as the plants start to flower in order to encourage good flower and fruit development.

Preparing the soil

The aim of tasks such as digging and raking the soil is to get the soil into the best condition possible for growing vegetables. Digging is the most important of these operations, because it allows air into the soil. This encourages the biological activity so essential for soil fertility, as well as raising clods of earth so that they can be broken up by frost.

No-dig method
Growing methods involving little or no cultivation are very popular, especially on light soils where the soil structure is easily damaged or where natural fertility is low. The no-dig, or 'zero-cultivation', technique uses the resident worm population to cultivate the soil; layers of well-rotted organic matter are spread over the soil as a mulch and the worms incorporate this into the soil. Thus no digging is needed. Crop plants are inserted through the mulch, and when they have matured, the stalks are cut off at soil level and the new crop is planted between the rows of the previous crops, while the roots rot *in situ*.

Deep-dig method
The deep-digging method of soil preparation involves incorporating large amounts of compost or manure while double-digging a plot. This creates a deep, fertile rooting zone for the plants. Further dressings of organic matter are added at regular intervals, but there is no need for additional digging.

Difficult soils
The no-dig and deep-dig methods are ideal if you have a heavy soil that suffers from compaction when cultivated in wet conditions (although this problem may be overcome by working on wooden boards laid on the soil) or a light, sandy soil needing humus and fertility. These soils benefit from the lack of cultivation and the large amount of organic matter that is added.

Crops such as onions and lettuce, which can be planted close together, will usually do particularly well when they are cultivated in these kinds of soil.

Preparing a seedbed
Digging alone would leave the soil too uneven for growing most vegetables, so further cultivation is needed to produce a fine crumb structure, or 'tilth', on the soil surface. This usually involves raking the soil several times to break down any lumps, and removing any stones you find, to create a fairly level, even surface.

The no-dig method
Young plants should be inserted into the soil through a thick layer of well-rotted organic matter.

The deep-dig method
1 *Spread a thick layer of well-rotted organic matter on to the soil surface.*

2 *Dig the bed, incorporating the manure. The final bed should have a slightly domed surface.*

Well-raked seedbed
Seeds germinate more evenly in soil that has fine particles.

Getting the most from your plot

Many people grow vegetables only if they can find some spare room in the garden, while for others the challenge is to produce a year-round supply of home-grown food. The planning and layout of a vegetable plot and the types of vegetable chosen will be influenced by the number of people who want to eat home-grown vegetables, and the vegetables they like the most. It should be possible to keep a family of three supplied with vegetables all-year-round from a plot 7m x 4m (21ft x 12ft), but a good supply of produce can be grown on an area much smaller than this. Where space is limited, greater yields can be produced by plants that grow vertically rather than those that spread sideways.

Making the best use of available space
Summer and winter cabbages are interspersed in rows. As one row is harvested before the other, there is room for the remainder to grow on.

Planning the vegetable plot

It is important that you organize your vegetable plot as efficiently as possible, to ensure that the crops are rotated correctly (see p.70) and that you make the maximum use of the available sun and shelter.

Plant the tallest crops (such as Jerusalem artichokes or runner beans) so that they do not block the light from the smaller-growing vegetables. Use the walls or fences for shelter, and for supports for beans, peas, or cordon or espalier fruit trees.

Remember to leave yourself ample space to walk between the blocks or rows of vegetables. Trampling on the soil will destroy its structure, and reduce its potential yield.

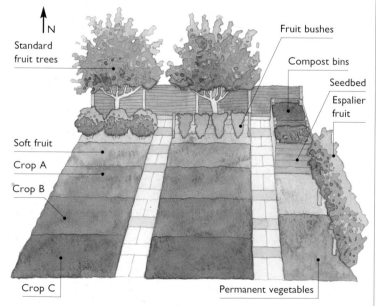

Designing your vegetable garden
An efficient vegetable garden should be planned to make the best use of sun, shelter and space. The vegetables should be planted in rotation groups (see p.144) to ensure pests do not build up.

Choosing a suitable site

The ideal site in which to grow vegetables is one that is warm and sunny during the growing season, and has plenty of light and good air circulation, while being sheltered from strong winds (as wind exposure can reduce plant growth by up to 30 per cent). The air flow is particularly important for wind-pollinated crops, such as sweetcorn, and to reduce the incidence of pests and diseases, which is worse in still air conditions. A gently sloping, sunny site is perfect for an early start in spring, because it will warm up slightly quicker than other aspects. On steeper slopes, plant across the slope rather than down it, as this will reduce soil erosion during heavy rain.

Hedging as a shelter
The hedge surrounding this vegetable plot protects it from the prevailing winds.

Spacing

Where space is limited, a special, multi-row bed system can be introduced. This has more, narrower beds than a conventional plot, and several rows of plants are grown more closely together than usual.

With this multi-row system, the beds are only 0.9–1.5m (3–5ft) wide and the centre of the bed can be reached from a path, so there is no need to walk on the soil and possibly crush it when tending plants. For several rows the plants are grown close together, with the distance between the rows being the same as the distance between the plants.

With such close spacing more plants can be grown per square metre (square yard) than by using a conventional system, where plants are usually grown 45–60cm (1–2ft) apart. In the multi-row system the pathways, at 60–75cm (2–2½ft) across, are slightly wider than those on the conventional system, which are generally about 45cm (1½ft) across.

By growing plants closer together, the competition for space between plants can be used to restrict the ultimate size of the individual vegetables. This can mean that having a small vegetable plot works as an advantage, and often the close spacing of plants reduces the amount of weeding necessary because the weeds are smothered.

However, such close planting does not work with all vegetables: lettuces, for example, will not form good hearts if grown at close spacings, unless a naturally small cultivar is chosen.

Extending the season

By making the most of your plot you can harvest crops all year round. This can be achieved by careful planning and successional sowings (see p.75), growing several types of the same crop and protecting the plants from frost. If protection is used, the growing season can be advanced in spring or run into autumn and winter.

For raising young plants, a cold frame with a glass or plastic top can be used to acclimatize them before they are planted out. Plastic sheeting, polytunnels and cloches warm the soil before planting and are invaluable for protecting young or overwintering plants. Floating mulches, such as fleece, laid over the crop or suspended on hoops will also protect early crops.

Forcing crops
Tuck in plastic sheeting with an edging iron over soil that needs warming before planting.

Hardening young plants
Gradually open the cold frame lid to harden off young plants.

Overwintering
Protect overwintering plants, such as broad beans, with a plastic tunnel in very cold weather.

Growing under glass

To establish early crops, a large number of vegetables, such as leeks and brassicas, can be sown in containers in a greenhouse. Other crops, like cucumbers and melons, need such a frost-free environment at all times.

Plants dislike very hot temperatures, so apply a shading paint to the glass in late spring and always ensure that the greenhouse is well ventilated during the day. Plants will require copious watering.

Intercropping

The space between crops that are slow-growing or need a wide spacing can be used to grow quick-maturing crops such as radishes, salad onions or turnips, which are harvested before the main crop is large enough to fill its allotted space.

Such gaps between crops within a bed can also prove invaluable as seedbeds for other vegetables, which will later need to be transplanted into permanent positions at much wider spacings elsewhere in the garden.

Maximum yields
Radishes and turnips make excellent catch crops when planted at the same time as later-maturing brassicas.

Planning through the year

How long crops take to grow, whether continuity is required, how much time is available and the skill of the gardener are all major considerations when planning a garden, as these will influence the time needed to tend the plot. Inexperienced gardeners should try not to be too ambitious at first and thus risk disappointment; they should start with fast-maturing salad crops, and gradually experiment with vegetables that are more difficult to grow as they gain more skill and experience. One advantage of short-term crops is that they often allow several cropping cycles in each year, which is a quick way to gain tangible results – and if something does go wrong, the mistakes will have no long-term implications.

Successional sowings

Some crops, particularly the short-term salad crops, are the most susceptible to gluts and gaps, but this can be avoided to a large extent by sowing batches of seed on a planned basis. Timing of sowings can be difficult to gauge, but a good guide is to choose the date when you hope to harvest the crop and count back from there the number of weeks needed for the plants to grow. Most of the information for this simple exercise will be given on the back of the seed packet.

To make the maximum use of the available soil, some vegetables, such as cabbages, cauliflowers and leeks, can be grown in a seedbed until they are large enough to transplant, and then they can be planted out into their cropping area. This is a very helpful technique that can be introduced on a wide range of vegetables, and is invaluable for plants that would otherwise occupy the ground for a long period of time at a wide plant spacing. The disadvantage of transplanting young plants is that the disruption may check their growth unless they are kept well watered so that they establish and grow quickly. This is particularly critical where the transplants are dug up from a seedbed and replanted; some roots will always be damaged by this process, and a good supply of water is essential to help these plants recover. If they are short of water, many vegetables will 'bolt': that is the plant will stop growing leaves and develop instead a flower-bearing stem in an attempt to produce seeds.

A timing guide to successional sowings is to make the next sowing when the previous sowing has germinated and emerged through the soil.

Fast-growing crops
Quick-maturing carrots and beetroot allow you to re-use the space within one growing year.

Slow-growing crops
Slower-maturing maincrop potatoes and onions occupy a section of the plot for most of the year.

Harvesting and storage

When to harvest vegetables and how to store them will depend on a number of factors, including the time of year and the type of storage organ that the vegetable consists of. Most vegetables are harvested when fully mature, but a few such as spinach can be cropped repeatedly as a cut-and-come-again crop.

Leafy vegetables, such as Brussels sprouts, are quite hardy and will survive outdoors in temperatures well below freezing point. Many root vegetables, however, have a high moisture content and are easily damaged in winter, even if left in the soil. Exceptions to this are carrots, parsnips and swedes, which are particularly hardy and can be allowed to overwinter in the ground until they are required for consumption.

The main causes of deterioration during storage are moisture loss from the plant tissue (with beetroot and carrots in particular drying out very quickly), or infection and rotting of damaged tissue caused by rough handling when the vegetables were being harvested. Onions and potatoes both tend to bruise particularly easily.

Some vegetables such as onions, chillis, peas, beans and garlic will keep quite well if stored in a dry condition. If they are not to deteriorate, they must be allowed to

Drying chillis
Bulbous vegetables and chillis should be hung up in an airy, frost-free place to dry.

dehydrate slowly in a cool dry place. Once dry, store beans and peas in airtight containers. Garlic, chillis and onions can be hung up in an airy place. Any storage area must be frost free.

Many vegetables also freeze well (see p.90). These should be blanched before being cooled rapidly and frozen in sealed, airtight boxes or bags.

Harvesting parsnips
Parsnips can be left to overwinter in the soil and dug up as required.

Vegetable chart

The chart below shows which conditions each vegetable needs and how long it is likely to occupy the ground.

	Crop rotation group	Ease of growing	pH range	Suitable for freezing	Length of growing season	Yield (kg per sq.m)	Tolerates frost
Asparagus (p.100)		D	6.0-7.5	✓	52	1.5	✓
Asparagus peas (p.77)	1	M	6.0-7.0	✗	16	1.0	✗
Aubergines (p.95)	3	D	5.5-6.5	✓	30	5.0	✗
Beetroot (p.90)	3	M	6.5-7.5	✓	26	2.0	✓
Broad beans (p.79)	1	M	6.5-7.5	✓	28	4.0	✓
Broccoli (p.83)	2	M	6.0-7.0	✓	45	2.0	✓
Brussels sprouts (p.81)	2	E	6.0-7.5	✓	52	1.5	✓
Cabbages (p.80)	2	E	6.5-7.5	✓	24	4.0	✓
Calabrese (p.82)	2	M	6.5-7.5	✓	45	2.0	✗
Carrots (p.88)	3	M	6.0-7.5	✓	36	2.0	✓
Cauliflowers (p.82)	2	D	7.0-7.5	✓	24	4.5	✓
Celeriac (p.99)	3	M	6.5-7.5	✓	28	3.0	✓
Celery (p.99)	3	D	6.5-7.5	✓	36	4.0	✓
Chicory (p.85)	2	D	6.5-7.5	✗	40	0.4	✓
Chinese cabbage (p.81)	2	E	6.5-7.5	✓	16	1.5	✗
Courgettes (p.96)	3	M	5.5-6.5	✓	20	2.0	✗
Cucumbers (p.96)	3	M	5.5-6.5	✗	20	3.0	✗
Dwarf beans (p.78)	1	D	6.5-7.5	✗	20	2.0	✗
Endive (p.85)	2	M	6.5-7.5	✗	12	1.5	✓
Florence fennel (p.100)	3	D	6.0-7.5	✗	16	3.0	✓
Garlic (p.93)	3	M	6.5-7.5	✗	40	2.0	✓
Globe artichokes (p.98)	3	D	6.5-7.5	✓	52	1.5	✓
Jerusalem artichokes (p.89)	3	E	6.5-7.5	✗	52	2.5	✓
Kale (p.81)	2	M	6.5-7.5	✓	40	1.5	✓
Kohl rabi (p.100)	2	M	6.5-7.0	✓	24	2.5	✓
Lamb's lettuces (p.85)	2	E	6.5-7.5	✗	24	1.0	✓
Leeks (p.101)	3	M	6.5-7.5	✓	36	1.5	✓
Lettuces (p.84)	2	E	6.5-7.5	✗	16	1.0	✗
Lima beans (p.79)	1	E	6.5-7.0	✓	20	2.5	✗
Mangetouts (p.77)	1	M	6.0-7.0	✗	20	1.5	✗
Marrows (p.96)	3	M	5.5-6.5	✓	20	2.0	✗
Melons (p.97)	3	D	5.5-6.5	✗	28	1.5	✗
Okra (p.77)	1	M	6.5-7.0	✗	16	2.0	✗
Onions (p.92)	3	M	6.5-7.5	✓	32	1.5	✗
Parsnips (p.89)	3	M	6.5-7.5	✓	40	1.5	✓
Peas (p.76)	1	E	6.0-7.0	✓	28	3.0	✗
Peppers (p.95)	3	M	5.5-6.5	✓	28	1.5	✗
Potatoes (p.87)	3	E	5.5-6.5	✗	32	3.0	✗
Pumpkins (p.97)	3	E	5.5-6.5	✓	20	3.0	✗
Radishes (p.91)	3	E	6.0-7.0	✗	6	0.4	✓
Rocket (p.84)	2	E	6.5-7.5	✗	24	0.5	✓
Runner beans (p.78)	1	D	6.5-7.5	✓	20	4.0	✗
Salsify (p.90)	3	M	6.5-7.5	✗	40	1.5	✓
Scorzonera (p.91)	3	M	6.5-7.5	✗	40	2.0	✓
Shallots (p.93)	3	M	6.5-7.5	✗	40	2.0	✗
Sorrel (p.85)	2	E	6.5-7.5	✗	24	0.5	✓
Spinach (p.86)	2	M	6.5-7.5	✓	36	1.5	✓
Squashes (p.97)	3	M	5.5-6.5	✗	20	2.0	✗
Swedes (p.89)	3	E	6.0-7.0	✓	28	2.0	✓
Sweetcorn (p.98)	3	D	6.0-7.0	✓	20	0.5	✗
Swiss chard (p.86)	2	E	6.5-7.5	✗	40	1.0	✓
Tomatoes (p.94)	3	M	5.5-6.5	✓	24	2.5	✗
Turnips (p.88)	3	E	6.0-7.0	✓	30	1.5	✗

Crop rotation group = 1 Peas and beans, 2 Leaves and flowerheads, 3 Roots, stems and fruiting vegetables

Ease of growing = D difficult, M moderate, E easy

pH range = Preferred pH

Suitable for freezing = ✓ yes, ✗ no

Length of growing season in weeks

Yield = kilograms per square metre (double poundage for square yards)

Tolerates frost = ✓ yes, ✗ no

Pods and beans

These vegetables are grown for their succulent seedpods or seeds, although they can also be attractive plants in the border. Some, such as broad beans and peas, like cool temperatures, others including French beans and lima beans need high temperatures. All prefer soil that has previously been manured but they require no extra nitrogen during their growing season. Once the pods are forming, do not allow these plants to dry out: ensure they have good supplies of water – about 22 litres/sq m (5 gallons/sq yd) if conditions are dry.

Peas

Pisum sativum

Garden peas are grown for their sweet-tasting edible seeds, which are produced in green or (in a few cultivars) purple pods. The peas are generally round with a wrinkled or smooth skin, and can be eaten fresh – either cooked, or raw in salads – or dried and stored for use later.

Garden peas vary in height: the more recent, dwarf cultivars are only 18in (45cm) high,while the traditional types can grow to 5ft (1.5m). They are divided into three groups, according to when the peas are mature enough to eat, called earlies, second earlies and maincrop; the maincrop cultivars bear the heaviest crops and the earliest the lightest.

The time from sowing to harvesting varies with each type. If you sow early crop peas in mid-spring, they will be ready to harvest 12 weeks later in midsummer. Crops of

P.s. 'Holiday'

second early and maincrop cultivars will be ready to harvest about 10–12 weeks after sowing.

Sowing Sow seed in flat-bottomed drills 3–5cm (1–2in) deep. String foil across the rows to deter birds from taking the seeds or attacking the seedlings.

Cultivation The crop will be larger when the plants are supported by canes, sticks, or plastic or wire mesh. This is introduced as soon as two pairs of 'true' leaves develop.

If you are using a tent-like structure, a wide mesh will allow you to reach through to the pods. Keep the plants well watered from soon after flowering starts because this increases your yield appreciably, particularly with maincrop cultivars.

Harvesting Start harvesting the pods when they are well developed but before they become too tightly packed with peas. Keep picking regularly to encourage further flowering and the production of more pods.

Tip

The pods develop on the plant from the base up, so the bottom ones will be ready for harvesting first.

Peas have delicate rooting systems and, if you are not careful, you may pull up the whole plant by mistake if you tug at the pea pods when harvesting them, or you could break or damage the main stem. This will greatly reduce the available crop.

To avoid damaging the plant, hold the stem with one hand and the pod with the other, and gently pull the pod downwards and away from the stem.

Station sowing

First of all prepare the soil, removing large stones and raking it to a fine tilth. As a guide, for a cultivar growing to 60–75cm (24–30in), make the drills 60cm (24in) apart and 20cm (8in) wide, and scatter the seeds along them so that the seeds are spaced about 6cm (2½in) apart. Return the soil to the drills, covering the seeds, but do not firm it. Keep the seeds well-watered; do not let them dry out.

1 *Rake the soil to a fine tilth, then use a draw hoe to make a wide, flat seed drill in which to place the seeds.*

2 *Sow seeds at set spacings along the drill to produce a broad band of plants which are easier to support.*

Mangetouts
Pisum sativum var. *macrocarpon*

P.s. var. *macrocarpon*

Also known as sugar snap peas, sugar or snow peas, mangetouts are grown for their delicate, sweet-tasting pods, which are eaten young and whole. Alternatively, the peas can be harvested later, in the same way as garden peas. Mangetouts are much easier to grow than garden peas because they need very little care after the seeds have germinated. They will be ready to harvest eight weeks after sowing.

Sowing Sow seeds from mid-spring onwards at three-week intervals to provide a succession of crops throughout the summer. Sow in flat-bottomed drills 4cm (1½in) wide and 15cm (6in) apart, with 10cm (4in) between the seeds. For cropping purposes, sow in blocks of three drills, which can be separated from the next block by a 45cm (18in) path.

Cultivation The crop is larger when the plants are supported by canes, sticks, or plastic or wire mesh. With the three-row system, arrange the support over the rows in a tent-like structure, about 45–60cm (18–24in) tall at its highest point.

Harvesting The perfect stage for picking is when the peas are just visibly swelling in the pods. Harvest the pods by tugging them gently from the stem.

Growing tall/short peas
While sticks are sufficient to support shorter plants, wire mesh may be needed for taller ones.

Asparagus peas
Psophocarpus tetragonolobus

P. tetragonolobus

Asparagus peas are grown for their decorative scarlet to chocolate-brown flowers, delicate bluish-green foliage and triangular 'winged' pods that have an asparagus-like flavour. They are eaten whole.

The pods will be ready for picking about eight weeks after sowing. Do not expect large quantities of pods though: even a heavy yield will be only about half that of garden peas.

The plants have a dense, compact habit, reaching 45cm (18in) high and up to 60cm (24in) across, giving an almost hedge-like appearance to the rows. They grow best in a sunny position in a well-drained soil.

Sowing Sow seed in mid- to late spring, in drills about 2–3cm (1in) deep and 30cm (12in) apart, with 30cm (12in) between the seeds.

Cultivation Support the plants with canes, sticks, or plastic or wire mesh, or they will produce very few pods. Protection from pigeons is essential: suspending nets on canes above the crop is the best method.

Harvesting The pods are ready for picking from midsummer until early autumn. For the best flavour, harvest the pods while they are still immature and about 3–5cm (1–2in) long. Pick regularly to encourage further flowering and the production of more pods.

Okra
Abelmoschus esculentus

A. esculentus

Grown for its elegant edible pods, okra is nicknamed 'lady's finger' because of its resemblance in shape. This tender vegetable must have as long a growing season as possible because it will take at least 16 weeks from sowing until harvesting the pods. It grows to a height of 60–90cm (24–35in) and prefers a sunny, sheltered site.

Sowing In mid-spring, sow three seeds per 7.5cm (3in) pot at a temperature of 18–24°C (65–75°F). Thin out the seedlings, removing the two smallest seedlings from the pot.

Cultivation The plants should be 15–20cm (6–8in) high before they are planted out, usually from early summer onwards when all danger of frost has passed. Cover the planting area with black plastic for at least three weeks to warm the soil and insert the young plants into the soil through the plastic. Space them at 35cm (14in) all round to encourage strong, bushy plants. They must be sheltered from wind for the first week after planting.

Harvesting From midsummer until early autumn, harvest the pods while they are still immature and before the seeds have developed fully. Cut them from the stem with a sharp knife. Harvest the pods as they form, to encourage the plant to produce more.

Runner beans
Phaseolus coccineus

These easy-to-grow climbing plants were originally introduced as ornamentals. There are cultivars with red, white or pink flowers, as well as red-and-white bicolours such as 'Painted Lady' which would not look out of place in the garden border. Today, they are grown mainly for their long, edible pods which are produced prolifically until the first frosts.

Grown as annuals, runner beans require a sturdy support system, as they can reach heights of 2.5–3m (8–10ft) in a relatively short growing season of 18–20 weeks.

Sowing Sow seeds in late spring or early summer – runner beans grow better in warm soil. Using a dibber, station-sow 5cm (2in) deep in a double row spaced 60cm (2ft) apart and with 15cm (6in) between the seeds, to give the plants plenty of room as they grow. In colder areas, sow the beans indoors, two or three to a 15cm (6in) pot. Transplant when about 10cm (4in) tall.

Cultivation Insert the supports when the plants are about 15cm (6in) high, just as the twining stem starts to develop in the tip of the plant. Sturdy 2.4m (8ft) bamboo canes are ideal, inserted just outside the row and angled to form a tent-like structure so the plants grow up it. Water the roots well from soon after flowering and continue throughout the harvesting period, as this can

P. coccineus

increase the crop appreciably. Spray plants with water to disturb the flowers and thus aid pollination.

Harvesting The pods will be ready for picking from midsummer onwards and harvesting can continue until the first frosts, when the plants are killed. Begin picking when the pods are well developed and about 15cm (6in) long, with the seeds just visible as swellings along the pods. Keep picking

Tip
For an early start, from mid-spring sow seeds individually in 7.5cm (3in) pots. Grow seedlings in a greenhouse or cold frame and plant out when the danger of frost is past.

them regularly (large pods become tough and stringy); this also encourages further flowering and the production of more pods.

Watering
While the flowers are setting, keep the plant well watered.

Bean supports
Canes can be used as supports, either in the form of a wigwam or in a double row; in each case tie the tops of the cones together firmly. Or grow them over a decorative metal arch.

Wigwam supports
These are ideal for climbing vegetables, where space is limited.

Arch support
Growing beans over an arch is both decorative and productive.

Dwarf beans
Phaseolus vulgaris

P. vulgaris

Also known as French, string or kidney beans, dwarf beans are grown for their curved, green pods which are eaten whole and for their partially developed seeds, better known as 'flageolets'. Bush forms will grow 40–45cm (16–18in) high and 30–45cm (12–18in) wide. Climbing cultivars can be grown up supports. Harvest 12–14 weeks after sowing.

Sowing Station-sow seeds at three-week intervals from late spring until midsummer 5cm (2in) deep in double rows spaced 20cm (8in) apart, with 15cm (6in) between seeds. Stagger them to give plenty of room.

Cultivation Keep plants well-watered once flowering starts to increase the crop and delay the onset of stringiness.

Harvesting Pick regularly once the pods are about 10cm (4in) long and will snap cleanly in half.

Under cloche
A late crop of dwarf beans is protected by a cloche.

Lima beans
Phaseolus lunatus

P. lunatus

Also known as the 'butter bean', this plant is grown for its large white seeds, although the young pods can be eaten whole about eight weeks after sowing. The plants prefer a warm climate, and a well-drained soil.

There are both bush and climbing forms of the lima bean, the latter being useful in small gardens where space is at a premium. The bush forms will reach about 75cm (30in) high but have a spreading habit, while the climbing forms get up to about 1.8m (6ft) if they are well supported. The beans will be ready to harvest 14 weeks after sowing.

Sowing Sow seeds from late spring onwards 7.5cm (3in) deep and 30–45cm (12–18in) apart. Allow 75cm (30in) between the rows for climbing cultivars, slightly less for bush forms.

Cultivation Provide climbing cultivars with canes at least 1.8m (6ft) tall for adequate support. Once the plants reach 30cm (12in) high, supply a proprietary liquid feed at two-week intervals to ensure growth, but stop feeding when the plants start to flower.

Harvesting The beans will be ready to harvest when the swollen seeds are visible in the pods. Pull pods gently to prevent damage to the stems.

Broad beans
Vicia faba

V.f. 'The Sutton'

Broad beans are very hardy plants, and will give a good crop with very little care and attention. They are grown mainly for their edible, greenish white seeds which develop inside thick, hairy pods, but the immature pods can be eaten when about 10cm (4in) long and the young shoots are also tasty. Those sown in autumn will take up to 24 weeks to harvest, spring-sown crops are ready in 16 weeks.

Sowing Sow in late autumn (this will discourage blackfly, to which broad beans are prone, since the plants will flower before the blackfly are out in force) or early spring, because the seeds germinate better at lower temperatures. Using a dibber, station-sow 5cm (2in) deep in a double row spaced at 30cm (12in), with 25cm (10in) between the seeds to give plenty of room.

Cultivation Most cultivars need support, and well-branched twigs 45cm (18in) tall will allow the plants to grow up through them. Insert the twigs after sowing to protect the seedlings from pigeons, especially if young plants are overwintered. Water the plants well once flowering starts and throughout harvest time.

Harvesting If you sow in autumn and spring, you should have broad beans for picking from late spring to mid-autumn. Begin picking when the swollen beans can be felt through the sides of the pods. Broad beans are delicious when young and tender, but as they age they become bitter and develop tough skins.

Tip
When the plants are in full flower, snap out the top 7.5cm (3in) to encourage the pods to develop and to discourage blackfly.

Types of bean
Grown for their pods, or the seeds inside them, or both, beans are in the main tender plants – broad beans being the exception.

Most beans are highly prized for their nutritious fibre and protein content, and many types have both bush and trailing forms to choose from.

Purple podded beans are coloured variants of French beans (*Phaseolus vulgaris*). They are available in both bush and climbing forms and can be eaten raw or cooked (when boiled the pod colour changes from purple to dark green). 'Royalty is a bush cultivar with a delicate flavour, and 'Climbing Purple' is a good climbing cultivar.

Bean varieties
French beans (left) including yellow and purple podded cultivars, broad bean (middle) and runner bean (right).

Bush forms
Broad bean 'Bonny Lad', 'Relon'
Dwarf bean 'Aramis', 'Tendergreen'
Lima bean 'Henderson', 'Fordhook'
Runner bean 'Gulliver', 'Pickwick'

Trailing forms
Dwarf bean 'Blue Lake', 'Purple Podded'
Lima bean 'Challenge', 'Florida Butter'
Runner bean 'Crusader', 'Liberty'

Leaves and flowerheads

Among vegetables grown for their leaves and flower-heads are brassicas (cabbages, cauliflowers, broccoli and calabrese), which prefer cool temperatures so are usually grown in winter and spring in warm regions. Brassicas must be planted in ground that has not been freshly manured as this promotes lush but easily damaged growth. Also grown for their leaves are lettuces, chicory, endive, and other salad vegetables. Most of these cannot tolerate consistently high temperatures – above 25°C (77°F) – without bolting (running to seed).

Cabbages

Brassica oleracea Capitata Group

The tightly packed leaves and growing point of the cabbage plant are often referred to as the 'head' or 'heart', and this varies in size and shape – from round, through pointed to almost flat – according to type and cultivar. Growing a selection of the many types on offer makes it possible to have fresh cabbage available to eat throughout the year, harvesting even through quite severe winter conditions.

All types of cabbage are cultivated in much the same way, with the timing of sowing and planting varying according to the season, the cultivars chosen and the time taken to reach maturity. The soil should be slightly alkaline to discourage a disease called club root, so apply lime if necessary (see p.157).

Sowing Sow seed thinly 2cm (¾in) deep in a well-

B.o. **'Red Drumhead'**

prepared seedbed outdoors from mid- to late spring through to midsummer, depending on the cabbage type. For many of the sowings, watering may be required to make sure the seedlings keep growing

B.o. **'Wheeler's Imperial**

rapidly. If cabbages dry out, they will produce 'hearts' too easily or 'bolt' to produce seed.

Cultivation Transplant the seedlings (see box). Firm the soil well by treading it down before planting to encourage a strong root system which will support the plants. Plant out spring cabbages at a spacing of 30cm (12in) all round, summer and autumn types at 40 x 45cm (16 x 18in), and hardy winter cabbages at a spacing of 50 x 50cm (20 x 20in) apart.

Harvesting When the cabbage has developed a good-sized, solid heart, it is ready for harvesting. Using a sharp knife, cut through the main stem to remove the entire heart and a few outer leaves, leaving the oldest leaves and the stem in the soil (see below).

How to transplant brassicas

When the seedlings are at the fourth 'true' leaf stage, they are ready for transplanting into rows of about 30cm (12in) apart, with 45cm (18in) between the plants.

This crop matures quite rapidly and can take as little as 10 weeks from germination to harvest. However, as it is shallow-rooted, it is very important to keep the plants well watered.

1 *Before transplanting, check that the growing point on a young plant is undamaged.*

2 *Embed the seedling to the depth of the lowest 'true' leaves to stabilize the plants.*

3 *The plant is firmly enough planted if a leaf snaps or tears when tugged.*

Tip
With many cabbages, cross-cutting the surface of the stem which has been exposed after harvesting will encourage more edible green leaves to develop close to the cuts.

Brussels sprouts

Brassica oleracea Gemmifera Group

B.o. 'Topline'

These very hardy vegetables are grown for their edible flower buds, which form small, tight, 'cabbage-like' sprouts in the leaf joints of the plant's main stem. Tall cultivars are ideal if space is limited as they can be grown close together and produce a good 'vertical' crop.

The soil for Brussels sprouts should be slightly alkaline to discourage club root disease, so apply lime if necessary (see p.157). They take about 20 weeks from sowing to harvesting.

Sowing Sow seed thinly into a seedbed outdoors in mid- to late spring. Some watering may be required to make sure that the seedlings keep growing rapidly.

Cultivation Firm the soil well by treading it down before planting to encourage a strong root system which will hold the plants erect. When the seedlings have developed four or five 'true' leaves, transplant them into their cropping site with the rows 60cm (2ft) apart and 60cm (2ft) between the plants, firming each plant well into the soil.

Harvesting The sprouts will be ready to harvest from early autumn through to mid-spring, depending on the cultivar. To pick, pull the individual sprouts downwards so they snap from the stem. As the season ends, the tops of the plants can be snapped off and eaten as spring greens.

Stripping lower leaves
This allows light to reach the developing Brussels sprouts.

Kale

Brassica oleracea
Acephala Group

B.o. 'Dwarf Green Curled'

This is the hardiest of annual winter vegetables. The soil for kale should be slightly alkaline to discourage club root, so apply lime if necessary (see p.157).

Sowing Sow seed in late spring outdoors in a seedbed. You may need to protect the seedlings against birds.

Cultivation When the seedlings have developed four 'true' leaves, transplant them into their cropping site, spacing the rows 60cm (2ft) apart, with 45cm (18in) between the plants. Water well until established.

Harvesting Harvest on a cut-and-come-again basis from mid-autumn to mid-spring by snapping off young leaves from all the plants. This will prevent any leaves from maturing and becoming tough and 'stringy'.

Hoeing between rows
Hoeing between kale plants controls weeds as they emerge.

Chinese cabbage

Brassica rapa Chinensis Group

B.r. 'Harmony'

This annual plant is grown for its crisp, delicately flavoured leaves with white midribs which are used fresh in salads. It is relatively fast-growing and may be ready to harvest as little as 10 weeks from germination.

Chinese cabbage resents root disturbance and is usually raised in pots. Transplant seedlings when three 'true' leaves are about 5cm (2in) high.

Sowing Sow seeds individually in plastic or peat pots 7.5cm (3in) square in mid-summer. Raise in a cold frame or unheated greenhouse as they need temperatures of 20–25°C (68–78°F) to germinate.

Cultivation When the seedlings have developed four 'true' leaves, transplant outdoors into rows about 30cm (12in) apart, with 45cm (18in) between the plants. Chinese cabbage is shallow-rooted and the plants must be kept well watered.

Harvesting Starting in late summer, harvesting can last for up to 14 weeks with successional sowings. Cut through the stem just above soil level to remove the heart. The remaining stalk will often sprout clusters of new leaves, which can be harvested later on.

Cauliflowers

Brassica oleracea Botrytis Group

Cauliflowers are grown for their edible flowerheads, which are harvested while they are in tight bud. Cauliflowers can be available for most of the year, and certainly from early spring through to midwinter. Autumn- and spring-heading cauliflowers are the easiest to grow, often producing curds (immature flowerheads) up to 30cm (1ft) across.

Cauliflowers are often judged on the whiteness and lack of blemishes on the curd – the 'yellow' curd types such as 'Marmalade' being the exception. There are also forms with green and purple heads, which have an outstanding flavour.

Cauliflowers are among the most difficult vegetables to grow well. They need plenty of water to ensure rapid growth and resent root disturbance, so should be transplanted as young as possible, certainly within six weeks of germination. If transplanted too late or allowed to dry out at this stage, they may produce small, premature, tight curds which are tough and woody.

The soil for cauliflowers should be slightly alkaline to discourage club root and because acid soils can

B.o. 'Idol'

promote some nutrient deficiencies, resulting in poor curds. (Apply lime if necessary; see opposite.)

Sowing Sow seed individually in plastic or peat pots 7.5cm (3in) square, and raise in a cold frame or unheated greenhouse. Sow early-summer cauliflowers in mid-autumn for harvest the following spring; autumn cauliflowers in late spring for harvest in autumn; winter cauliflowers in late spring for harvesting in winter the following year and sow spring cauliflowers in late spring for harvesting in early spring the following year.

Cultivation When the seedlings have developed four 'true' leaves, they are ready for transplanting to their cropping site. Spacing depends on the time of year: generally, the later the planting, the larger the cauliflower will grow and the greater the space needed for each plant. Early-summer cauliflowers, for example, should be planted at a spacing of 60 x 45cm (24 x 18in), winter cauliflowers at 75cm (30in) all round.

Harvesting When the covering leaves start to open and show the enclosed curd beneath, the cauliflower is ready to harvest. Using a sharp knife, cut through the main stem to remove the complete curd, together with a row of leaves around it to protect the curd from damage and marking.

Preparing the soil
Dig in plenty of well-rotted manure or compost in autumn to allow it to penetrate the soil.

Covering curds
Protect the curds from severe frost or sunlight by wrapping leaves over them.

Calabrese

Brassica oleracea Italica Group

Grown as an annual for its edible flowerheads, calabrese is similar to broccoli but less hardy, although it can be harvested in early spring if grown under protection. Many cultivars will mature within 12 weeks of sowing.

Well-grown calabrese is tasty eaten fresh and ideal for freezing, the main drawback being that the plant is very susceptible to mealy aphids, which are attracted to the flower spikes.

The soil for calabrese should be slightly alkaline in order to discourage club root, so apply lime if necessary. Calabrese resents root disturbance and often responds to transplanting by prematurely producing small, tight heads which can be tough and woody.

Sowing Sow seed thinly in drills 2.5cm (1in) deep and about 30cm (12in) apart, sowing three seeds 13mm (½in) apart in stations at 20cm (8in) intervals. Alternatively, sow seeds individually into 5cm (2in) diameter plastic or peat pots in a cold frame or unheated greenhouse if cold weather demands an earlier start.

Cultivation When the seedlings have developed three 'true' leaves, thin them to leave only the strongest and healthiest seedling at each station. Transplant pot-grown seedlings at this point. Watering is essential to keep the plants growing rapidly and to produce a good crop – critical times are the first month after sowing and the three-week period just before cropping commences.

Harvesting The main cropping season is from early summer to mid-autumn, but harvesting can continue until the plants are damaged by the first frosts. Cut the central spike first, before the flowers (usually yellow) start to open.

B.o. Italica Group

The slightly smaller spikes produced by the side shoots can be cut later. Main-season plantings will often yield up to four or five cuttings before the plants are discarded. (They make useful compost).

Transplanting seedlings
If transplanting peat pots, ensure the rim is just below ground level.

Applying lime
Lime can be applied at any time of year to raise the soil's pH but must be added alone, at least two to three months after manuring, or one month after fertilizing the soil. This is because lime and nitrogen react to release ammonia, which can harm plants.

If lime is used first however, fertilizers and manures can be added just one month later. It is also simpler to add lime before crops are sown or transplanted into the site. If lime is applied too often, plants may show signs of nutrient deficiency. Bear in mind that it is easier to raise the soil pH than it is to lower it.

Shattering stems
Bashing old brassica stems helps them rot and form compost.

Broccoli
Brassica oleracea Italica Group

B.o. 'Purple Sprouting'

Grown for its edible flower-heads, which are harvested while in tight bud, sprouting broccoli is a very hardy, biennial, winter vegetable. There are both white- and purple-flowered forms.

The soil for broccoli should be slightly alkaline in order to discourage club root, so apply lime if necessary.
Sowing Sow seeds individually in 5cm (2in) square plastic or peat pots, in a cold frame or unheated greenhouse in spring.

Cultivation Plant out in early summer with 60cm (2ft) between the plants all round. Water is essential to produce a good crop, the critical time being the first month after sowing.
Harvesting Broccoli can be harvested from late winter until late spring and has a natural cut-and-come again habit. Cut the central spike first, before the flowers start to open; side shoots will also try to flower and these smaller spikes can be cut later.

Cropping
Harvest broccoli spears by cutting them with a sharp knife.

Providing protection
Surround young stems with extra soil to reduce windrock.

Lettuces

Lactuca sativa

There are many forms of this annual vegetable, grown for its fresh leaves which are a mainstay of summer salads. For best results, grow several types, such as crisp cos, butterhead and loose-leaf lettuces. Loose-leaf types are less likely to run to seed, and are tolerant of most growing conditions. Leaf colour can vary from pale green to reddish brown, and cultivars such as 'Salad Bowl' and 'Valeria Red' are quite deep rooting, making them ideal for dry soils. Harvesting can begin about 12 weeks after planting.

Sowing Sow seed thinly in drills 15mm (½in) deep and 35cm (14in) apart. Sowing at regular intervals from early spring through until midsummer will provide a succession of lettuces from early summer through to mid-autumn. During hot weather, sow in the late afternoon and water well immediately afterwards, to reduce the chance of poor germination caused by high soil temperatures.

Cultivation When the seedlings have developed two 'true' leaves, thin to 30cm

L. sativa **Lobjoits Green**

(12in) apart. In dry weather, keep the plants well watered in the last two weeks before harvesting, when they make the most growth.

Harvesting Loose-leaf lettuces should be harvested by pulling away the outer rows of leaves from one or two large plants on a regular basis. Cut off the entire heads of other types.

L.s. **'Fortune'**

L.s. **'Salad Bowl'**

Rocket

Eruca sativa

E. sativa

This tender-looking plant is actually quite hardy and will survive winter temperatures down to just above freezing. The leaves have a strong, tangy flavour which increases in strength when the plant matures or is kept too dry. Rocket can be eaten raw or cooked, and grown as individual plants or harvested regularly as a cut-and-come again crop. It makes an excellent addition to other leafy vegetables in a mixed salad.

Sowing Sow seed in succession at three-week intervals from mid-spring to early summer. Sow in broad drills to create a band of plants about 30cm (1ft) wide. If sown in such broad drills, weeds will be unable to establish themselves owing to the density of the plants.

Cultivation Keep the plants well watered to promote rapid growth.

Harvesting Either remove individual leaves from the plants, or cut the seedlings down to about 2.5cm (1in) above ground level, and wait for them to resprout before cutting again.

Transplanting lettuces
Seed sown indoors can be planted out when all danger of frost is past. Seedlings should be big enough to handle, with five or six leaves. Space them 30cm (12in) apart and keep watered.

Ready to handle
Transplant seedlings once they have five to six leaves.

Protection from birds
Black cotton suspended over the plants prevents them being eaten.

Lamb's lettuces
Valeriana locusta

V. locusta

Also known as corn salad, this very hardy annual salad crop is grown for its mild-flavoured leaves and will survive winter temperatures down to just above freezing. The erect-growing 'French' cultivars are the hardiest; the 'Dutch' and 'English' forms have a much laxer growth habit, but are more productive. As it takes up very little room, lamb's lettuce is ideal for intercropping between slow-growing or tall vegetable crops. It will do well in most soils and is easy to grow.

Sowing Sow seed in summer in drills 15cm (6in) apart, with 2.5cm (1in) between the seeds. For all-year-round cropping, make an additional sowing in spring.

Cultivation After germination, thin the seedlings to 10cm (4in) apart, and keep the seedbed well watered until they are about 2.5cm (1in) high.

Harvesting Either remove individual leaves from the plants, or cut the whole head down to about 2.5cm (1in) above ground level to encourage fresh growth to be made, which can then be cut again for a further crop.

Endive
Cichorium endivia

C.e. 'Batavian'

This relative of the lettuce is a popular salad vegetable. The leaves have a piquant, slightly bitter taste which can be modified by blanching.

Endive relishes a rich, fertile, well-drained soil.

Sowing Sow seed thinly in drills 13mm (½in) deep and 30cm (12in) apart, from mid-spring onwards.

Cultivation When the seedlings are about 2.5cm (1in) high, thin them to 30cm (12in) apart. Once the plants reach about 25cm (10in) across, place an upturned plate on the centre of each to 'blanch' the heart. Water well in dry weather or the plants will bolt.

Harvesting The plants will be ready to harvest about three weeks after blanching. Cut off the heads just above ground level.

Blanching endive
Cover endive with a blanching cap. This makes it less bitter.

Chicory
Cichorium intybus

C.i. 'Elmo'

This hardy, winter salad vegetable has tight, conical buds ('chicons') of creamy white leaves with a distinctive, bitter flavour.

Sowing In early summer, sow seed in drills 13mm (½in) deep and 30cm (12in) apart, with 2.5cm (1in) between the seeds.

Cultivation Thin the seedlings to about 20cm (8in) apart, and keep the plants well watered until autumn. In late autumn, cut off the leaves to about 2.5cm (1in) above the neck and mound up earth evenly over the plants to a height of 15cm (6in), or cover with a black plastic bucket. This will force the shoots to grow up through the mound or inside the bucket.

Harvesting The forced spears of chicory will be ready to pick in mid-spring, when the creamy white spikes are about 15cm (6in) high or just emerging through the mound of soil. Cut off the heads about 2.5cm (1in) above the neck. If they are re-covered, the roots will often produce two or three smaller secondary spears, about 10cm (4in) tall. In order to prevent the harvested spears from turning green and developing a bitter taste, keep them in the dark until required.

Sorrel
Rumex acetosa

R. acetosa

This versatile plant is an incredibly hardy perennial which is also very easy to grow. The tasty leaves have a sharp flavour and can be used fresh in salads or as a flavouring for soups.

Sorrel will grow on a range of soils, but prefers well-drained yet moisture-retentive, fertile conditions.

Sowing In autumn or spring, sow seed in drills 13mm (½in) deep and 30–40cm (12–16in) apart.

Cultivation Thin the seedlings to 25–30cm (10–12in) apart. Remove any flowers or seed heads as soon as they are spotted – this will preserve the plants' energy for leaf production – and replace the plants themselves every 4–5 years as their productivity declines.

Harvesting Remove the outer leaves for use as they develop, and new leaves will continue to emerge from the centre of the plant.

Spinach
Spinacia oleracea

S.o. 'Triathlon'

This reasonably hardy vegetable is renowned for its strongly flavoured, dark green leaves, which are rich in iron and vitamins.

Spinach prefers a well-drained but moisture-retentive, fertile soil which is high in nitrogen. It will tolerate light shade. Although it is a perennial plant, it is best grown as an annual in order to produce the most vigorous leaves. The plants will often 'bolt' (run to seed) and produce seed in the first year, especially during periods of hot, dry weather.

Spinach is usually ready for eating about 10 weeks after sowing. Individual leaves can be removed, or the whole plant cut back to produce new leaves for cut-and-come-again harvesting.

Sowing For a continuous supply, sow seed at three-week intervals from early spring to midsummer. Sow seed thinly in drills 2cm (¾in) deep and 30cm (12in) apart.

Cultivation When the seedlings are about 2.5cm (1in) high, thin them to 15cm (6in) apart. For cut-and-come-again crops, thin to 5cm (2in).

Harvesting Harvest the larger plants grown at wide spacings by cutting off the outer leaves at soil level. For a cut-and-come-again crop, cut down the whole plant to 2.5cm (1in) above soil level, leaving the stubs to produce another crop of young leaves.

Preparing the drill
With a cane tip, draw a shallow line in a well-prepared bed.

Sowing the seed
Sprinkle the seed thinly along the drill in the seedbed.

Swiss chard
Beta vulgaris Cicla Group

B. vulgaris

This hardy vegetable is grown for its large, glossy, succulent leaves, which can be up to 45cm (18in) long and 20cm (8in) wide. The brightly coloured leaf stalks are red or white, and the leaves range in colour from the deep green of 'Fordhook Giant' to the lime-green of 'Lucullus' or copper-green of 'Rhubarb Chard'. The best-known is 'Rhubarb Chard', more commonly known as 'Ruby Chard, which is easy to grow but prone to bolting, especially in hot, dry weather.

Swiss chard prefers a fertile, well-drained but moisture-retentive soil. The crop is usually ready for cutting (either by removing individual leaves or on a cut-and-come-again basis) 12 weeks after sowing, although the plants can be harvested through the winter and will usually occupy the ground for almost a year.

Sowing Incorporate plenty of organic matter into the soil before sowing. Sow seed for new plants at any time from early spring to midsummer into drills 2cm (¾in) deep and 45cm (18in) apart, with 15cm (6in) between the seeds.

Harvesting ruby chard
Select the older leaves and cut off just a few at a time from the base of each plant.

Cultivation When the seedlings are about 5cm (2in) high, thin them to 30cm (12in) apart — as a long-term crop, the plants need plenty of room or mildew may attack them. For cut-and-come-again crops, thin to 7.5cm (3in) apart.

Harvesting Harvest the plants grown at wider spacings by cutting off the outer leaves at soil level. For a cut-and-come-again crop, cut the whole plant down to 2.5cm (1in) above soil level, leaving the stubs to produce another crop of young leaves.

Roots

Vegetables that are grown for their swollen roots or tubers include potatoes, carrots, turnips, swedes, Jerusalem artichokes, parsnips, beetroot, radishes, scorzonera and salsify. Onions and shallots, as well as garlic, are grown for their strong-flavoured bulbs. These groups prefer cool temperatures (18°C/64°F) but will tolerate up to 24°C/75°F, especially in the early stages of growth, and all store well during winter.

Potatoes

Solanum tuberosum

This versatile vegetable is divided into three main groups: early season (quicker-growing cultivars); maincrop (slower-growing cultivars, producing heavier crops); and second earlies, which mature between the other two. Most early-season potatoes are ready to harvest from early summer onwards, and do not store well. Maincrop potatoes are available from midsummer through into winter and can be stored.

Tuber shapes vary considerably between cultivars and sometimes even on the same plant. Flesh texture is either 'floury' (suitable for baking) or 'waxy' (suitable for boiling).

Sowing 'Seed' is the term used for young potato tubers which are planted to produce the next crop. Purchase good-quality 'seed' in late winter and arrange the tubers in shallow trays to chit (see below) in early spring.

Cultivation In most areas, planting can commence from

S. tuberosum

mid-spring onwards for earlies, finishing with the last of the maincrop tubers by early to midsummer. A few days before planting, incorporate a generous dressing of general fertilizer into the topsoil to encourage rapid growth. Plant the tubers 40cm (16in) apart, in rows 60cm (2ft) apart. Use a trowel to make holes about 20cm (8in) deep and carefully place a tuber in each one, with the 'rose' end uppermost and at least 5cm (2in) below the soil surface. Cover with soil, taking care not to damage the delicate new shoots.

To increase the number of tubers produced, when the potato stems are 20–25cm (8–10in) high, use a draw hoe to mound up loose soil over the bottom 10–12cm (4–5in) of each stem ('earthing up'). The top of the ridge should be flat to allow rainwater to soak into it rather than run down the sides.

Harvesting Early potatoes are ready for lifting when the flowers start to open. Two or three weeks before harvesting maincrop potatoes, cut off the tops ('haulms') and remove them from the site (if left, they will encourage slugs); this will allow you to see where the tubers are.

To harvest, use a garden fork to dig under the ridge of earth and ease the tubers from the soil to avoid 'stabbing' them. If the weather is dry, leave the potatoes on top for an hour or so to allow the skins to dry and harden; in damp conditions, spread out the tubers on a hessian sack or newspaper under cover and leave to dry overnight.

Store maincrop potatoes in a cool, dark, frost-free place. Some cultivars will keep well until the following summer.

Chitting potatoes

Arrange the tubers in boxes with the 'rose' end (the area with the most 'eyes', or dormant shoots) upwards. Cut large tubers into two or three sections, dip cut surfaces in dry sand to prevent excessive bleeding, and then treat the sections as individual tubers. Place the boxes in a light, frost-free environment. This process causes the tubers to produce shoots ('chit'). With early cultivars, allow three or four shoots to develop; with maincrop cultivars, the aim is to have as many shoots as possible.

Chitted 'earlies'
Once the chits develop, remove all but three or four.

Spacing tubers
Use a piece of cane to measure spacing between tubers accurately.

Earthing up
Draw the soil up around each stem to maximize yields.

Carrots

Daucus carota

D. carota

This popular root vegetable is usually classified according to the shape of its orange-coloured root, which can be eaten either raw in salads or as a cooked vegetable.

Carrots need a deep, stone-free, well-drained, fertile soil which is high in nitrogen. Do not manure the soil just before growing carrots or much of the crop will develop forked roots. Early-maturing cultivars will be ready to harvest 8 weeks after sowing, maincrop types after 10–12 weeks.

Sowing Sow seed thinly in drills 1.5cm ($\frac{1}{2}$in) deep and 15–20cm (6–8in) apart, from late spring to midsummer.

Cultivation Thin the seedlings to 4–7cm ($1\frac{1}{2}$–$2\frac{1}{2}$in) apart for medium-sized carrots, 7–10cm ($2\frac{1}{2}$–4in) for larger carrots suitable for storing through the winter. Thinning is best done in the evening or in cool, dull conditions to deter carrot root fly. Hoe between the rows until the foliage shades the soil and reduces weed seed germination.

Harvesting Early carrots can be eased out with a fork and then pulled by hand. Dig up maincrop carrots with a fork for immediate use, freezing or storing. Twist off and then discard the foliage.

Turnips

Brassica rapa Rapifera Group

B.r. 'Tokyo Cross'

Often regarded as winter vegetables, turnips can be available throughout the year if a range of cultivars are grown in succession. Some, such as 'Tokyo Cross', are large enough to eat within 6 weeks of sowing, others within 8–10 weeks. The strong-tasting flesh varies in colour from white through to yellow. Turnips require a neutral or slightly alkaline soil to discourage club root, so apply lime if necessary (see p.157). They prefer a light, fertile, well-drained but moisture-retentive soil which is high in nitrogen.

Sowing Sow seed thinly in drills 2cm ($\frac{3}{4}$in) deep and 25–30cm (10–12in) apart in a finely sieved, well-prepared seedbed and subsequently at three-week intervals from late spring until mid- to late summer.

Cultivation The soil should never be allowed to dry out, or much of the crop will develop forked roots and the plants may bolt. When seedlings are no higher than 2.5cm (1in), thin to 10cm (4in) apart for early-maturing cultivars, 15cm (6in) for later, hardy cultivars.

Harvesting Turnips will be ready to harvest from early to mid-autumn, but must be lifted by midwinter. (For storage tips see p.165.)

Thinning
Overcrowded plants will be weak, so allow plenty of space.

Digging carrots
Use a garden fork to reduce damage to the plants' roots.

Ridged beds
To grow vegetables on heavy soils, create a ridged bed.

Harvesting young turnips
Turnips can be harvested when about the size of a golf ball.

Swedes
Brassica napus Napobrassica Group

B. napus

This vegetable is one of the hardiest of all root crops and is grown for its mild, sweet-tasting flesh, which can be creamy white ('Lizzy') or yellow ('Marian').

Swedes require similar soil conditions to turnips (see left). The roots will be ready to harvest about 24 weeks after sowing.

Sowing Sow seed thinly in drills 2cm (¾in) deep and 40cm (16in) apart in a finely sieved, well-prepared seed bed, from late spring onwards.

Cultivation The soil should not be allowed to dry out at any stage, or a large proportion of the crop will develop forked roots and the plants may bolt. When the seedlings are about 2.5cm (1in) high, thin them to 7–10cm (3–4in) apart, and then thin again three weeks later to leave the plants 25cm (10in) apart.

Harvesting Swedes are usually ready to harvest from early to mid-autumn onwards. Although they survive well outdoors through the winter, the low temperatures often give the flesh a fibrous or woody texture. It is therefore advisable to lift them and store indoors.

Jerusalem artichokes
Helianthus tuberosus

H. tuberosus

Grown for its edible root, the hardy Jerusalem artichoke is also used to help clear rough ground. A vigorous perennial and relative of the sunflower, it can grow to a height of 3m (10ft), although the cultivar 'Dwarf Sunray' will only reach about 2m (6ft).

Sowing Plant purchased tubers in spring, 10–15cm (4–6in) deep in soil which has been deeply cultivated. Plant in rows 60cm (24in) apart, with 30cm (12in) between the tubers. Large tubers can be divided up so that each piece has a separate shoot, and the sections planted individually.

Cultivation When the plants are about 30cm (12in) high, mound up the soil 15cm (6in) high around the base to keep the plants stable. In summer, cut the stems down to 1.5m (5ft) to encourage tuber formation. In dry weather, irrigate to keep the tubers swelling.

Harvesting The tubers are ready from mid-autumn onwards and should be dug up with a garden fork. In well-drained soils, the tubers can be overwintered in the growing site. When harvesting, remove all parts of the tubers from the soil, or they will resprout next season.

Separating tubers
Use a sharp knife to divide large artichoke tubers.

Planting
Tubers should be planted into holes at least 10cm (4in) deep.

Parsnips
Pastinaca sativa

P. sativa

These winter vegetables have a very distinctive flavour and are hardy enough to over-winter in the soil. Parsnips prefer a deep, stone-free, well-drained, fertile soil, but on shallow soils shorter-rooted cultivars can be used.

Sowing Sow seed thinly in drills 1.5cm (½in) deep and 30cm (12in) apart, in early spring. Fresh seed gives the best results.

Cultivation When the seedlings are about 2.5cm (1in) high, thin them to 7–10cm (2½–4in) apart to produce large roots suitable for overwintering.

Harvesting The roots will be ready to be lifted from mid-autumn onwards. Dig them up with a fork.

Creating a fine tilth
Before sowing parsnips, form a tilth along a string-marked line.

Beetroot
Beta vulgaris

This useful root vegetable is a biennial plant which is grown as an annual, and can be used at just about any time of year either fresh, stored or pickled.

Although the round beet is the most common, other shapes such as oval, flat and oblong are also grown. There is also a wide variation in colour, red being the most popular, but golden forms such as 'Burpee's Golden', and white ones are available. The leaves are also edible, and taste similar to spinach.

Beetroot prefers a well-drained, fertile soil which is high in nitrogen.

Sowing Beetroot seed is either natural, which is a fruit containing two or three seeds in a cluster, or 'monogerm' in cultivars such as 'Cheltenham Mono' and 'Monopoly', which have been specially bred to produce one seedling only. Sow from mid-spring through to late summer. Soak the seed in warm water for half an hour before sowing to promote rapid germination, then sow thinly in drills 2cm (³⁄₄in) deep and 30cm (12in) apart.

Cultivation When the seedlings are about 2.5cm (1in) high, thin them to 7–10cm (3–4in) apart for large beets, and 4–5cm (1½–2in) to produce small, round beets for pickling.

Harvesting Harvesting usually runs from early summer to mid-autumn, although beetroot can be harvested at any stage of growth depending on the size of beets required. The plants are not fully hardy, however, and should all be lifted for storage by late autumn. Dig up the beets with a garden fork and twist off the leaves, then use immediately or store the roots in a box of moist sand in a cool, dry, frost-free place.

B.v. 'Boltardy'

Covering seeds
After sowing, draw soil over the seed drill with the back of a rake.

Removing leaves
After digging up beetroot, twist off leaves before storing the roots.

Freezing produce
In addition to storing root vegetables in sand (see opposite), you can also freeze many vegetables. Not all lend themselves to this method of storage, as those with a large amount of water in their structure will freeze less well than those without.

The vegetables listed here will keep their flavour and structure if frozen in the manner suggested. To blanch vegetables, simply plunge them in boiling water for one minute. Drain and cool.

Blanched Asparagus, aubergines, beetroot, broad beans, broccoli, Brussels sprouts, calabrese, carrots, cauliflowers, cabbages, courgettes, French beans, kale, kohl rabi, marrows, parsnips, peas, potatoes, runner beans, spinach, spring onions, swedes, sweetcorn, tomatoes, turnips.

Shredded, pureed, diced or sliced Aubergines, cauliflowers, cabbages, celery, kohl rabi, marrows, swede, turnips.

Frozen when young Beetroot, carrots, parsnips, turnips.

Salsify
Tragopogon porrifolius

T.p. 'Sandwich Island'

A hardy biennial plant, salsify is usually grown for its creamy white, fleshy roots, although its shoots are also edible. Because of its delicious flavour, it is often called the 'vegetable oyster'.

In order to achieve maximum growth, salsify requires a deep, well-drained, fertile soil.

Sowing Sow seed in drills 1cm (½in) deep and 15cm (6in) apart, in spring. Fresh seed gives the best results, as salsify seed loses viability very quickly.

Cultivation Thin the seedlings to 10cm (4in) apart soon after germination. To encourage rapid growth, keep the plants weed-free and well watered.

Harvesting The roots will be ready to harvest from late autumn onwards. In mild areas, the roots can be lifted and used as required, but in colder areas the roots should be lifted and stored in boxes of sand (see opposite) before winter frosts set in.

Radishes
Raphanus sativus

R.s. 'French Breakfast'

Although usually grown for their swollen roots, which have a 'hot' flavour, radish leaves and their crisp young seed pods also make a useful addition to salads. The swollen roots come in a range of colours, shapes and sizes, and if several types are grown it is possible to have radishes all year round.

Most radishes are ready for harvesting 14–21 days after sowing and are therefore good for growing as a catch crop or for intercropping between vegetables such as Brussels sprouts and leeks, which mature much more slowly. Their rapid germination and growth is ideal for covering the ground quickly, especially when sown broadcast, which makes radishes an ideal 'mulch crop' to smother out annual weeds. They prefer a light, well-drained, fertile soil.

Sowing Sow seed thinly in drills 13mm (½in) deep and about 15cm (6in) apart. For a continuous supply, sow seed in small batches at 10 day intervals from early spring to early autumn. The seed will keep for up to 10 years if kept cool and stored in an airtight container.

Cultivation Radishes produce poor plants if overcrowded, and ideally they should be about 3cm (1in) apart. Watering is essential: drought will make the roots woody or encourage the plants to bolt.

Harvesting Radishes are ready to harvest when the roots are about 3cm (1in) across at their widest point. Grip the plant firmly by its leaves and pull gently. If the soil is dry, water the plants the day before harvesting so that they will pull out of the ground easily.

Thinning
Radish seedlings should be thinned as they grow to keep them strong and healthy.

Scorzonera
Scorzonera hispanica

S.h. 'Russian Giant'

This hardy, perennial plant is usually grown as an annual, similar to carrots, for its thick, fleshy roots. These are about 20cm (8in) with a shiny, black skin, and have a distinctive flavour when cooked. The young shoots (chards) and flower buds are also edible. Scorzonera is a good source of iron and fairly easy to grow. It needs to have a deep, fertile soil in order to do well and produce a good crop.

Sowing Sow seed thinly in drills 1cm (½in) deep and 20cm (8in) apart, in spring.

Cultivation Thin the seedlings to 10cm (4in) apart soon after germination. In order to achieve maximum growth, keep the plants weed-free and make sure they are well watered.

Harvesting The roots will be ready to harvest from late autumn onwards. In mild areas, the roots can be lifted and used immediately, but in colder areas they should be lifted and stored in boxes of sand before the winter weather sets in.

The roots can be over-wintered in the ground and covered with straw in the early spring. The young shoots will emerge through the straw, and these (and the flower buds) can be harvested when they are about 10cm (4in) high.

Storing root vegetables

A traditional way to store root vegetables, such as turnips, carrots and beetroot, is in a wooden box, laid in a bed of loose straw or sand and then covered with straw or sand.

Place in a cool, dry, frost-free area, such as a garage. The length of time that vegetables may be stored will depend not only on the vegetable type and cultivar but also the conditions within the store. Generally, they will survive for a few months in reasonable shape.

Onions

Allium cepa

The strong-flavoured bulbs of onions are invaluable in the kitchen for a wide range of dishes. They are grown as annual plants, with the brown- or yellow-skinned cultivars being the most popular with gardeners.

Onions are tolerant of cool temperatures and even frost, especially in the early stages of development, with low temperatures often producing a better-quality crop. They have a long growing season, and for good skin quality and colour the bulbs need plenty of bright sunshine in the period just before harvesting. Onions prefer a well-drained, fertile soil, which has been well dug to encourage the plants to root deeply and enable them to grow well in dry conditions. Onions will be ready to harvest 14 weeks after spring sowing or 36 weeks after autumn sowing.

Sowing In early autumn or early spring, sow seed in drills 1.5cm (½in) deep and about 30cm (12in) apart, with 2.5cm (1in) between the seeds. These spacings should produce bulbs 7.5–10cm (3–4in) across at harvest time.

A. cepa

Cultivation Onions suffer from weed competition, and keeping the plants weed-free by hoeing between rows until they establish (this takes about 6 weeks) is critical. Remove any flower heads on the onions as soon as they are seen, or dig up the plant, to ensure the plant's efforts are concentrated on the bulb.

Harvesting Onions are ready for harvesting when the leaves turn yellow and the tops keel over. The process can be speeded up by bending over the tops by hand, but this must be done carefully or the bulb may be bruised and will start to rot when in store.

Lift the bulbs gently with a garden fork and allow them to dry naturally (see right) before storing in a cool, dry, frost-free place. Onions rarely store well beyond mid-spring, and will start to produce new top growth after this time.

Harvesting and storage

Once the onions have swelled to an appropriate size and the leaves have turned yellow, they can be harvested. Lift the bulbs carefully, to avoid damaging or bruising them, and spread them out to dry.

A raised, open-slatted rack covered with a plastic sheet supported on a cloche frame, will ensure the onions do not turn mouldy before they dry, as plenty of air must circulate around the bulbs. Spread the onions out to improve air circulation. Once dry, you can hang the onions on string indoors (see opposite).

Drying out
Onions left to dry in the sun may need protection from rain.

Bolted plants
Onions that have started to produce seed should be dug up and discarded.

Overwintering
Autumn-sown onions may need to be protected if the weather is very severe.

Bending leaves
Gently pushing over onion leaves when the tips start to turn yellow helps the tops die quickly.

Shallots
Allium cepa Aggregatum Group

A.c. 'Dutch Yellow'

These onion-like, yellow- or orange-skinned bulbs, which develop into a clump of up to 12, have a distinct flavour and are eaten raw or cooked.

Shallots like a fertile, well-drained, soil which has been well dug, as this encourages the plants to root deeply and grow well in dry conditions. For best results, the bulbs need lots of sunshine just before harvesting.

Sowing From late winter to early spring, shallowly plant virus-free sets 15cm (6in) apart, with 25cm (10in) between rows, into a soil with a seedbed-like tilth that has then been firmed down to discourage birds from disturbing the soil.

Cultivation Follow the same guidelines as for onions (see left).

Harvesting The bulbs are ready to harvest when the leaves have died down. Lift them with a garden fork.

Firming soil
Press on the soil to firm it down before planting the shallots.

Garlic
Allium sativum

This hardy vegetable, with its characteristic strong flavour that makes such a valuable contribution to both cooked dishes and salads, is far easier to grow than many gardeners realize. There are two distinct forms, one with white skin and the other with purple.

Garlic has a long growing period, but will survive outdoors throughout the winter if grown in a light, dry, well-drained soil. On wetter soils, the plants should be grown on ridges to improve drainage.

The best crops come from autumn plantings, because most garlic requires about 6 weeks of cool weather (at 0–10°C/32–50°F) to promote good growth the following season.

Sowing Dig over the soil deeply before planting in autumn. Split the bulbs into

Planting
Garlic cloves should be pushed into the soil, base first.

Drying
Hang up garlic in a cool, frost-free place to dry out naturally.

A. sativum

individual 'cloves' and push these into the soil, so that the top (pointed end) of the clove is approximately 2.5cm (1in) below the soil surface. For maximum yields and even bulb development, plant the cloves in a square arrangement at a spacing of 18cm (7in).

Cultivation As they develop, the bulbs will gradually work their way up to the surface of the soil.

Harvesting The bulbs will be ready to harvest as soon as the leaves begin to turn from green to yellow. A delay in harvesting will result in shrivelled bulbs – these will be usable in the kitchen, but will deteriorate in storage. Lift the bulbs gently with a garden fork and allow them to dry naturally before storing in a cool, dry, frost-free place. In these conditions, they will keep for up to 10 months.

Stringing onions and garlic
After harvesting, hang up onions and garlic to dry in a cool frost-free place.

To keep them tidy, you can hang the bulbs on a length of string. Simply knot a length of string or raffia and hang it from a hook so that it forms a loop. Weave the dried stem of the first onion (or garlic) through the base of the loop and then add each bulb in turn in the same way.

Finally, hang the string of bulbs from the wall or ceiling in a place that is cool and dry.

Securing the bulbs
Weave each bulb on to the string loop, as shown, pulling the stem taut to secure.

Fruiting vegetables

Many of these vegetables, such as peppers, aubergines, peppers and melons, originate from tropical and sub-tropical regions and need very warm or in some cases subtropical (21–30°C/70–86°F) temperatures to ripen. Despite this, they can be grown successfully outdoors in southern temperate regions, and inside or in a green-house in cooler northern areas. Other fruiting vegetables, such as globe artichokes, marrows, courgettes, pumpkins and sweetcorn can be germinated indoors but will ripen outdoors. With some plants (such as melons, marrows and pumpkins), fertilization can be a problem, and it is often best to pollinate by hand.

Tomatoes
Lycospersicon esculentum

This popular fruiting vegetable is grown as an annual and requires long, warm summers to really perform well. Given the right conditions, some cultivars can reach 2.5m (8ft) high. Bush tomatoes have no obvious main stem but produce several fruit-bearing branches of about the same size. Cordon tomatoes have a dominant main stem which carries fruit trusses along its length.

Tomatoes prefer a fertile, well-cultivated soil. They will also grow successfully in pots, troughs and growbags, but regular watering is essential to produce a good yield of larger fruit. Cropping usually starts within 12–14 weeks of transplanting.

Sowing For outdoor culti-vation, sow seed in late spring. Place individual seeds in 10cm (4in) pots and ger-minate at 15°C (60°F), hard-

L.e. **'Phyra'**

ening off in a cold frame for 10 days before planting out.

Cultivation The best growth is achieved at tem-peratures of 20–25°C (68–78°F), and the plants and their fruits can be dam-aged when temperatures fall below 10°C (50°F), so in colder climates tomatoes are usually grown under glass or in plastic tunnels. Plant out the young plants as the first flowers open.

Plant out bush types first, as they are the hardiest group. Space the plants about 90cm (3ft) apart: closer spacings will produce earlier crops, wider spacings a later but heavier yield. The plants can spread along the ground, per-haps on a mulch of straw or plastic. Plant cordon types at a spacing of 75cm (30in) and train them up canes. Remove any side shoots as they develop, so the plants' ener-gy goes into fruit produc-tion. As the fruits develop, apply a high-potash feed every two weeks to help them swell. When five fruit trusses have formed, remove the main stem at two leaves above this point, to encour-age even growth. Then remove the canes and lay the plants on straw to encourage quicker ripening. To extend the growing season, cloches or polythene tunnels can be used for protection.

Harvesting Pick the fruits as they ripen and remove any leaves covering the fruit to encourage more to do so. If frost threatens in autumn, uproot the plants and hang up in a dry, frost-free place to allow the remaining fruits to ripen.

Pinching out side shoots
Snap out any side shoots to channel the plant's energies into producing fruit.

Removing main shoot
Break off the main shoot two leaves above the fifth truss to encourage the fruits to develop.

Tomato types
Tomatoes come in many shapes and sizes, from the large, thick-skinned 'beef-steak' tomatoes, which hail from America, to the more traditional 'Marmande' types and small, multi-trussed 'cherry-' and 'currant-fruit-ed' cultivars. A vast range of fruit colours takes in shades of red, pink, orange and yellow, or even combinations of these, which show as striped flecks on the skin and flesh of the fruit.

Tomato sizes
'Beefsteak' varieties are the largest, Cherry types smallest and 'Marmande' medium-sized.

'Beefsteak'
'Marmande'
Cherry

Sweet peppers
Capsicum annuum Grassum Group

C.a. 'Mavras'

These annual plants are grown for their characteristic bell-shaped fruits. When ripe, the fruits can be red, yellow, orange and even bluish black, depending on which cultivars are grown.

Sweet peppers prefer a deeply cultivated soil, but also do well in growbags, pots and troughs; make sure the soil or compost is slightly acidic. They require an average temperature of around 21°C (70°F) and fairly high humidity.

Easy-to-grow cultivars such as 'Bell Boy' and 'Yellow Bell' will be ready to harvest as green fruits 14 weeks after planting out, and 3 weeks later for coloured fruits.

Sowing Sow seeds individually in peat pots in mid-spring and germinate at 18°C (64°F). Young plants will be ready to plant out 10 weeks later.

Cultivation Plant out 75cm (30in) apart. When the plants reach 75cm (30in) high, stake them individually and pinch out the growing point to encourage bushy growth. Spray them with water regularly to keep the humidity high. Once the fruits have started to develop, apply a high-potash feed every two weeks to encourage them to swell.

Harvesting Pick the ripe peppers by cutting through the stalk about 2cm (³⁄₄in) from the top of the fruit.

Chilli peppers
Capsicum frutescens

C.f. 'Apache'

These plants are grown for their small, thin tapering fruits which are green or red when mature, depending on the cultivars grown. The flavour is often very hot, with even the mildest increasing in strength as the fruits mature. The plants can grow up to 60cm (24in) high and 45cm (18in) across, while dwarf cultivars suit pots or growbags.

Chilli and cayenne peppers require an average temperature of around 21°C (70°F) and fairly high humidity, so are often grown under protection.

The easy-to-grow cultivars such as 'Apache' and 'Red Chilli' are ready to harvest about 17 weeks after planting out, but the riper the fruit, the hotter the flavour – the seeds being the hottest part.

Sowing Sow seeds individually in peat pots in mid-spring and germinate at 18°C (64°F).

Cultivation Plant out 45cm (18in) apart, and when the plants reach 45cm (18in) high pinch out the growing point to encourage bushy growth. Spray the plants with water regularly to keep the humidity high.

Harvesting When frost is imminent, pull up the plants and hang them upside down in a frost-free place, where they will continue to ripen and can be used as needed.

Aubergines
Solanum melongena

S.m. 'Slice Rite'

The 'eggplant' is grown for its egg-shaped fruits, which are usually a blackish purple but may be white flushed or completely white in cultivars such as 'Easter Egg'.

The plants can reach 75cm (30in) high and 60cm (2ft) across and have a deep root system. They therefore prefer a deep, fertile soil, but will also grow well in containers if fertilized and watered generously. Grow in a warm, sheltered spot, as aubergines are susceptible to wind damage. The fruits will be ready to harvest 16 weeks after planting out.

Sowing Sow seed in small pots in mid-spring, and

Harvesting aubergines
Cut through the stalk 2cm (³⁄₄in) from the fruit.

germinate at 25°C (78°F). After germination, you will need to lower the temperature to about 17°C (62°F) – if higher than this, the plants will become spindly and prone to falling over.

Cultivation Plant out as the first flowers start to open, but after all risk of frost has passed. Space the plants 75cm (30in) apart, and stake them individually to provide extra support. When the main stem reaches 45cm (18in) high, pinch out the growing point to encourage bushy growth. Once the fruits have started to develop, apply a high-potash feed every two weeks to help them swell. To grow large aubergines, allow about five fruits to develop on each plant, removing all other flowers.

Harvesting Pick the fruits when they are fully swollen, shiny and firm with a smooth skin, cutting the stalk about 2cm (³⁄₄in) from the top of the fruit. If left too long before picking, the flesh will become bitter.

Cucumbers
Cucumis sativa

C.s. 'Femdan'

These tender plants are grown for their characteristic fruits with a high water content. Some cultivars have a bushy, compact habit while others can trail over several metres. The latter can be trained vertically to save space in small gardens.

Outdoor cucumbers tend to be much easier to grow than indoor types as they are less susceptible to disease and do not have the same requirements for high temperatures and humidity.

Cucumbers will not tolerate temperatures below 10°C (50°F), so a frost-free environment is essential. The plants will do well in loam-less compost in growbags and, as they need lots of water, will also thrive using 'ring culture'. In this, the plants are grown in compost-filled, open-bottomed pots on a gravel bed where they develop two sets of roots, one within the compost for nourishment, the other growing into the gravel for water. The fruits will be ready to harvest about 16 weeks after sowing.

Sowing In mid-spring, sow seeds, individually in 7.5cm (3in) pots, at a temperature of 18–30°C (64–86°F).

Cultivation Once the risk of frost has passed and the seedlings are 30cm (12in) high, gradually harden off those to be grown outside. Plant at least 40–45cm (16–18in) apart, with 90cm (36in) between rows, to allow lots of light to reach the plants. Train trailing types vertically as cordons up nets or strings at least 2m (6ft) high. Twist support strings around the plants to hold them upright. As the main stem grows upwards, trim back the side shoots to two or three leaves.

Harvesting The fruits will be ready to harvest by late summer. Cut them from the plant, leaving a stalk of about 2.5cm (1in) on each fruit.

Planting seeds
To avoid root disturbance, cucumber seeds are sown into pots.

Courgettes and marrows
Curcubita pepo

C. pepo

Grown for their long, cylindrical fruits, marrows come in a range of colours from white, through yellow, to deep green; some cultivars, such as 'Tiger Cross', are a mixture of green and creamy white stripes. Marrow fruits will be ready to harvest about 16 weeks after sowing.

Courgettes are cultivars of marrows, but their fruits are harvested while they are still immature – about 6–8 weeks after sowing – and the skin is smooth and shiny. Numerous new courgette cultivars have been introduced, with fruit colours ranging from the dark green of 'Ambassador', through lighter shades, to the yellow of 'Taxi'.

Sowing In spring, soak the seeds overnight and then sow individually in 7.5cm (3in) peat pots at a temperature of 15°C (59°F).

Cultivation Harden off the young plants before planting out. Plant bush types 90cm (36in) apart; trailing cultivars will need at least 2m (6ft) all round unless trained vertically, when they can be planted at the same spacing as bush types. Immediately after planting out, make sure that the plants are protected from overnight frost.

Each plant needs a minimum of 13.5 litres (3 gallons) of water per week. Mulch with a layer of organic matter at least 10cm (4in) deep, to retain soil moisture. Cut away any leaves shading the fruits. As the fruits start to swell, remove any male flowers close by to prevent the fruits developing a bitter taste.

Harvesting Although they can grow much larger, marrows are usually harvested when the fruits are about 45cm (18in) long and 15cm (6in) in diameter. Such mature fruits, with their seeds formed, can be stored for several months in an airy, frost-free environment. Pick courgettes when they are 10–15cm (4–6in) long. Regular picking encourages the production of further flowers and fruits.

Removing growing tip
Cut out shoot tips later in the season to help fruit develop fully.

Storing marrows
Suspend produce from beams in loosely woven mesh sacks.

Squashes and pumpkins

Cucurbita pepo, C. maxima, C. moschata

C.p. 'Tivoli'

These tender plants are grown for their unusual fruits, which vary tremendously in shape and size – from the large, orange fruits of the traditional Hallowe'en pumpkin to the distinctive 'Turk's Turban' squash. They can weigh up to 227kg (500lb) each and come in a range of colours from yellow to grey-green.

Squashes and pumpkins grow best in a warm, sheltered position and are generally ready to harvest about 16–20 weeks after sowing. 'Gold Nugget' is a useful cultivar, producing fruits which can weigh as much as 1kg (2¼lb), even though this very compact plant is one of the earliest to mature.

Sowing In mid- to late spring, soak the seeds overnight in cold water and then sow individually in 7.5cm (3in) pots. Raise at 12–14°C (54–57°F).

Cultivation Harden off the young plants for 2–3 weeks before planting out once the danger of frost is minimal. However, if frost is forecast, make sure that the plants are protected with fleece. Plant bush types 90cm (36in) apart; trailing cultivars need at least 2m (6ft) all round.

Each plant requires a minimum of 13.5 litres (3 gallons) of water per week. Mulch with a layer of organic matter at least 10cm (4in) deep, to retain soil moisture. Cut away any leaves that shade the fruits. As the fruits start to swell, remove any male flowers that are close by to prevent the fruits developing a bitter taste.

Harvesting Although they can grow much larger, the fruits are usually harvested when about 20–25cm (8–10in) across, or when the foliage starts to turn yellow and the fruit stems start to crack. This is often just before the first hard frosts occur. After severing the fruit from the parent plant, dry it for about 10 days outdoors, using the warmth of the sun to improve storage quality. Place the fruit in a string or netting bag, and hang in an airy, frost-free place at a temperature of 10°C (50°F) for up to six months.

Protecting seedlings
Inverted jam jars can be used to protect young plants.

Ripening pumpkins
Lay black plastic sheeting underneath ripening pumpkins and squashes to keep them off the ground.

Melons

Cucurbita melo

C. melo

These tender tropical plants are grown as annuals and prefer temperatures of 25°C (77°F) or above. They need full sun to do well and are damaged by low temperatures (10°C/50°F), so must be in a sheltered position. They can be grown as horizontal bush plants or as cordons up canes.

There are three main types of sweet melon: cantaloupes have thick, rough, grey-green coloured skins, casabas have smooth green or yellow skins, and musk types produce the smallest fruit and have yellow or orange skins. The musk, or honeydew, melons are the easiest to grow.

Sowing Sow seeds two to a 7.5cm (3in) pot in a temperature of 18°C (64°F) in early spring. If both seedlings germinate, the weaker one should be removed after they have been transplanted, usually six weeks after germination.

Cultivation Space the young plants 1m (3ft) apart with 1.5m (5ft) between the rows on a slight mound about 10cm (4in) above the surrounding soil.

Harvesting Usually 12–15 weeks after transplanting, remove the fruits by cutting through the stalk.

Sweetcorn
Zea mays

Z.m. 'Sweet Nugget'

Grown for its sweet-tasting yellow 'cobs', this tender annual crop must have as long a growing season as possible. This often means starting plants early under protection, before planting out from late spring onwards. The extra trouble is well worthwhile, because freshly picked cobs are the most nutritious and have by far the best flavour.

Sowing Sow seed under protection, with three seeds to a 7.5cm (3in) pot. Outdoors, sow seed from mid-spring onwards in a seedbed in a warm, sheltered spot.

Cultivation Sweetcorn relies on the wind to pollinate the plants later on. To facilitate this, plant in square or rectangular, 6-row blocks, with the plants spaced 35cm (14in) apart all round. Before transplanting seedlings grown in pots, cover the planting area with black plastic to warm the soil. When the seedlings are 15–20cm (6–8in) high, insert the young plants into the soil through the plastic and shelter them from wind for the first week after planting. Most of the plants will produce four or five cobs – to get large cobs, water the plants well as the cobs are developing.

Harvesting The cobs will be ready to harvest from late summer to mid-autumn. When the tassel ('silk') at the top of the cob starts to turn brown, snap the cob from the main stem.

Planting
Sweetcorn should be planted in a block in order to aid wind pollination.

Globe artichokes
Cynara cardunculus Scolymus Group

C.c. 'Green Globe'

These large, bushy perennials are grown for their greenish-purple flower bracts and have a cropping life of three years.

Sowing Sow seed 2.5cm (1in) deep in a seedbed in early spring in rows 30cm (12in) apart with 10cm (4in) between the seeds. Transplant the young plants into their cropping site in early summer. These plants will be variable, however, so division of named varieties is preferable. Remove well-rooted suckers from established plants in early spring and replant, leaving at least three shoots on the parent plant to produce new flower heads.

Cultivation Before planting, spread a 10cm (4in) layer of well-rotted manure and dig the ground to one spade's depth. Plant out young plants about 5cm (2in) deep and 90cm (36in) apart all round, and trim back the shoots by half their length to prevent wilting. After planting, spread a 10cm (4in) layer of manure around the plants to reduce weeds and moisture loss. Protect over winter with a layer of straw, until early spring, when each plant will produce two or three shoots to bear the flower heads.

Harvesting From early summer to early autumn, depending on the age of the plants, each stem will carry one primary flower head and several secondary ones. These should be cut when they are about 10cm (4in) across, removing each one with a 10cm (4in) section of stem.

Dividing artichokes
Dig around the plant's base to remove well-rooted side shoots.

Trimming tops
This will stop the leaves wilting and help plants establish quickly.

Stems

Stem vegetables such as celery, celeriac, kohl rabi, Florence fennel, leeks and rhubarb are cultivated for their edible, swollen stems. To grow successfully, almost all of them require cool temperatures (below 24°C/75°F) and a long growing season. Florence fennel, however, will tolerate temperatures up to 18–30°C (64-86°F) and has a short growing season, and kohl rabi also matures quickly.

Celery
Apium graveolens

Celery is grown for its crisp, blanched leaf stalks, which can be white, pink or red. Newer, self-blanching forms are easier to grow as they do not need to be artificially blanched. Celery needs a sunny, open site with deep, stone-free, well-drained, fertile soil that has had plenty of organic matter incorporated. To prevent plants from 'bolting' or producing stringy leaf stalks, it is important to keep them growing steadily.

Celery will be ready to harvest 7–8 months from sowing, by which time each plant will be about 45–60cm (1½–2ft) high.

Sowing Sow seed in trays or peat pots under protection from early to late spring to establish successional crops. Place seed on the surface of the compost, as it needs light to germinate. Self-blanching celery needs warmth to germinate – the temperature should be above 10°C (50°F).

Harvesting celery
The tops and roots of celery plants should be removed as soon as they have been dug up.

A. graveolens

Cultivation About eight weeks after sowing, harden off the seedlings in a cold frame. From late spring on, when the plants have developed five to six 'true' leaves, plant them out. Celery needs plenty of water to grow quickly and remain crisp. Celery that needs blanching should be planted 45cm (18in) apart, into trenches 30cm (12in) deep and 45cm (18in) wide. For self-blanching celery, plant closely, 25cm (10in) apart, with 25cm (10in) between rows. There is no need to trench. For trench celery, wrap a 25cm (10in) paper collar loosely around each plant when they reach 30–45cm (12–18in) high. Tie in position and half-fill the trench with soil to blanch the celery stalks. Three weeks later, fill the trench until the soil is level with the surrounding ground. Four weeks later, add another paper collar to each plant and 'earth up' with a further 15cm (6in) of soil.

Harvesting Harvesting for trench celery can begin in late autumn, when the leaf stalks are crunchy to eat; the pink and red forms are the hardiest and will be harvested last. Dig out the soil around each plant, lift the celery and remove the paper collars, then cut off the head and roots. Self-blanching celery can be harvested from late summer onwards. Celery can be left in the ground over winter.

Celeriac
Apium graveolens Rapaceum Group

A. g. Rapaceum Group

This vegetable is grown for its celery-flavoured, swollen stem, which takes six months to mature after sowing. It can be cooked or used raw.

Grow celeriac in a sunny, open site in free-draining soil. It may eventually reach 75cm (30in) high.

Sowing Sow seed in trays or modules under protection, at a temperature of 16°C (61°F) from early spring onwards for a continuous supply.

Cultivation About six weeks after sowing, harden off the seedlings in a cold frame. Plant them out in rows 30cm (12in) apart, with 40cm (16in) between the plants, with the stems just visible on the soil surface. In late autumn, remove the outer leaves to encourage the stems to swell, and mulch with straw to protect from severe frost.

Harvesting Harvest celeriac from early autumn until the following spring, digging up the plants with a garden fork. However, plants will survive in the ground in most sites.

Florence fennel
Foeniculum vulgare Azoricum Group

F.v. **'Zefa Fino'**

Florence fennel is grown for its succulent bulb, which has a distinctive aniseed flavour, the edible part being the swollen bases of its decorative, feathery leaves.

It prefers well-drained but moisture-retentive, fertile soil which has had plenty of organic matter incorporated six to eight weeks before planting. The bulbs are ready to harvest about 15 weeks after sowing.

Sowing Sow seed in modules under protection from early spring onwards. Set in a temperature of 16°C (61°F) if growing in a greenhouse; seeds germinated in a polytunnel require 12–14°C (54–57°F), while those in a cold frame need 10°C (50°F).

Cultivation About six weeks after sowing, harden off the seedlings in a cold frame. Plant them out from early summer onwards, after two 'true' leaves have developed, in rows 30cm (12in) apart and with 40cm (16in) between plants. When the bulbs begin to swell, cover the lower half with soil to blanch them.

Harvesting The bulbs will be ready to harvest from late summer onwards, when they are about 10cm (4in) across. Cut them off at soil level and trim away the leaves. Fennel can withstand light frosts only, and does not store well.

Asparagus
Asparagus officinalis

A.o. **'Franklim'**

This herbaceous perennial can produce crops of its delicious shoots ('spears') for up to 25 years, so requires a permanent site. If possible, plant only male cultivars such as 'Franklin' or 'Sorbonne', which produce much higher yields than female ones. The plants must be at least three years old before harvesting can begin.

Asparagus prefers deep, fertile, well-drained soil which has had plenty of organic matter incorporated into it 2–3 months before planting. In spring, before the spears emerge, the soil is often topdressed with salt, which controls weeds but does not harm the crop.

Cultivation Asparagus plants grown from seed give a variable crop, so it is best to purchase one-year-old asparagus crowns ready for planting. Plant crowns in early spring, 10–15cm (4–6in) deep and 45cm (18in) apart, in ridge-bottomed trenches 30cm (12in) apart. Cut down and remove all top-growth in late autumn as it turns yellow.

Harvesting Harvesting usually begins in mid-spring and lasts for eight weeks. When the spears are 15cm (6in) high, cut them off with a sharp knife, slicing through the stem 2–3cm (1–1½in) below soil level. Keep the cut spears covered to prevent them drying out.

Harvesting asparagus
Cut the young stems just below soil level with a sharp knife.

Maintaining the plants
Chop old stems down to ground level in autumn.

Kohl rabi
Brassica oleracea Gongylodes Group

B.o. **'Trero'**

Kohl rabi is grown for its nutritious, globe-like, swollen stem. There are both green- and purple-skinned forms, both of which grow to a height of 60cm (24in). Kohl rabi thrives in hot, dry conditions, and at the height of summer, the stems will be ready to harvest eight weeks from sowing.

Sowing Sow seed thinly in drills 2cm (¾in) deep and 30cm (12in) apart, in a well-prepared, finely sieved seedbed. Sow the quicker-maturing, green-skinned types from mid-spring to midsummer, and the hardier, purple-skinned types from mid- to late summer.

Cultivation As the first 'true' leaf develops, thin seedlings to 20cm (8in) apart.

Harvesting The swollen stems are ready when they are about 8–10cm (3–4in) across. The newer cultivars can grow much larger, as they remain tender.

Harvesting kohl rabi
Cut through the tap-root just below the swollen stem.

Leeks

Allium porrum

A. porrum

Rhubarb

Rheum x *hybridum*, syn. *R.* x *cultorum*

R. x h. 'Timperley Early'

One of the hardiest of winter vegetables, leeks have a long cropping season, from early autumn, through winter, and into late spring of the following year.

They are grown for their white, fleshy leaf bases, which form a stem-like shank or 'leg'. Early types take 28 weeks from sowing to harvest; late-season ones need up to 40 weeks to mature.

Leeks prefer light, loamy soil, and their fibrous root system also helps to improve soil structure.

Sowing In late spring sow seed thinly, 3cm (1in) apart, in drills 3cm (1in) deep and 30cm (12in) apart.

Cultivation Transplant seedlings when they are about 20cm (8in) high, the main planting season being midsummer. Incorporate a dressing of high-nitrogen fertilizer into the soil surface before planting. The best yields come from planting at a spacing of 15cm (6in), with 30cm (12in) between the rows. Quality is determined by the depth of planting, which blanches the shank: the aim is to obtain 15–20cm (6–8in) of white shank. Push a dibber into the ground to a depth of 15cm (6in), drop the plant into the hole and fill the hole with water so the soil will fall back into it.

Harvesting Harvest leeks when their leaves start to hang down, from early autumn onwards, by lifting them with a garden fork. Mid- and late-season cultivars will tolerate winter climes without protection.

Often regarded as a fruit, but technically a vegetable, this herbaceous perennial is grown for its edible leaf stalks, which can be used for desserts and jam making from mid-spring onwards.

Rhubarb, which matures to a height of 30cm (12in), can be grown in the same plot for many years, but the well-drained, fertile soil must be dug deeply and plenty of organic matter incorporated prior to planting.

Planting In late autumn or early winter plant one-year-old crowns about 1m (3ft) apart, with the young shoots ('eyes') just above soil level. If they are planted too deeply, the eyes will rot away.

Cultivation Mulch the crowns well, keep the soil moist, and provide a generous feed of balanced fertilizer after harvesting. Cut off any flowering spikes as they emerge in the spring and summer, and remove any spindly, unwanted leaves as they occur.

The crop can be advanced by as much as three weeks if covered with loose straw to protect the developing leaves and stalks from frost damage. Alternatively, cover with an upturned pot or bucket.

Harvesting Pick the rhubarb when the stalks are about 30cm (12in) long and deep pink in colour. Grip each stalk as close to its base as possible and and pull it gently from the crown with a twisting action. Cut off the leaves and discard, as these are not edible.

Transplanting leeks
If the soil is very dry, water each hole before planting seedlings.

Harvesting leeks
Use a garden fork to gently lift leeks from the soil.

Forcing rhubarb
Place an upturned pot over the crown to force young rhubarb.

Cutting flowering spikes
Remove any rhubarb flowers as soon as they appear.

Growing fruit

It is always possible to grow fruit, even in the smallest of gardens. For most people, 'fruit' conjures up trees in blossom, apple pies and strawberries and cream, which is not surprising, as one of the most satisfying aspects of gardening is picking ripe fruit straight from the plant and eating it at the peak of freshness. There is also a decorative value to fruit: not only is the blossom colourful but there are also the changing hues of the ripening fruit through summer and autumn.

For cultivation purposes, most fruits fall into two main categories: soft fruit (such as currants, raspberries and gooseberries) which grows on bushes or canes or as groundcover, and top fruit (such as apples, peaches, plums and cherries) which grows on trees. Some fruits fall into neither category: grapes and kiwi fruits, for example, are produced on long, trailing vines.

To cultivate fruit, you must first establish which varieties will grow successfully in your climate, although the range and growing season of fruiting plants can be extended by growing them in a greenhouse or conservatory. You should then decide on a suitable site in the garden. Most fruits will thrive if grown in a sunny but sheltered position, the sun being important for ripening and encouraging good fruit colour and flavour. Shelter is needed to keep plants warm and to reduce the risk of wind damage. On a windy site, insect activity is reduced, and this results in

Training fruit trees
Fruit trees can be trained against walls and fences, or along wires, giving good yields from relatively small spaces, like this espalier pear.

restricted pollination at flowering time, and a correspondingly poor crop. Any windbreak, however, must be carefully positioned to avoid cold air being trapped on the site and thus creating a frost pocket – the biggest enemy of most fruit-growing plants being the occurrence of late spring frosts, especially on a sunny slope.

Choosing fruit bushes and trees

Always buy healthy, sturdy bushes and trees that are certified free from virus, in order to minimize attacks from pests and diseases. The shape and cultivar of plant you select, however, will depend on the available space in your garden. Free-standing forms, such as spindle bushes or dwarf pyramids, generally take up far less room than branch-headed bushes, standards and half-standards. To save space, many fruits can also be trained as cordons, espaliers and fans against a wall or fence.

Most fruit trees tend to grow badly on their own roots, so when you buy a fruit tree it usually comprises

two plants that have been grafted together. The top part, or scion, is the cultivar, which is grown for its fruit flavour and colour, while the bottom part, or rootstock, provides a ready-made root system that influences the size and vigour of the tree and the amount of fruit it will yield. Rootstocks are classified according to their vigour and are available from the extremely vigorous through to very dwarfing.

The main advantages of dwarf rootstocks are that fruit is much easier to pick, prune and spray than on larger rootstocks, and the trees fit easily even into the smallest gardens.

Fruit tree formations
The formations below are those most commonly found in gardens.

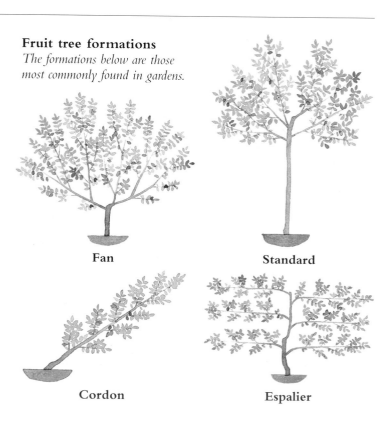

Fan

Standard

Cordon

Espalier

Planting

Most fruit bushes and trees are best planted in late autumn or early winter. If they are container-grown, they can be transplanted at any time, except in very cold, very wet or very dry weather.

Thorough preparation of the planting site is important, so dig the soil well, adding plenty of well-rotted garden compost or manure. The planting hole should be at least as wide as the root system and the plant should be inserted at the same depth as previously, so check for a soil mark on the stem.

All trees should be supported with a stake or, if trained against a wall or fence, they need to be tied to wires. For a tree with bare roots, drive a vertical stake into the planting hole before inserting the plant. For container-grown plants, add an angled stake after planting and then tie the plant to the stake or wires.

Planting a bareroot bush
Spread out the roots and plant so that the uppermost root is 5–7cm (2–3in) below soil level.

Planting a tree
Plant a container-grown tree so that the surface of the compost is 3–5cm (1–2in) below soil level.

Feeding

Most fruits need the essential nutrients of nitrogen, phosphate and potassium on a regular basis. However, nutrients incorporated during planting will only last for the first few years.

After this, topdressings should be applied around the base of trees or bushes during spring or summer. Before applying fertilizer, mark out the area where it should be applied. Using string and a peg, tie one end of the string around the trunk of the tree or bush. Pull the line taut to just beyond the spread of the branches and use the peg to mark a circle. Fertilizer scattered over this area will cover the entire span of the tree's root system.

Nitrogen-based fertilizers are usually given in spring to encourage shoot growth, while phosphate and potash are often needed in summer to encourage fruit development and flower formation for the next year.

Fruit pollination

The transfer of pollen grains from the male to the female parts of a flower is essential for fertilization, so that seeds and fruit can develop. If this occurs in the same flower on the same plant, it is called self-pollination. The transfer of pollen from the male parts of one flower to the female parts of the flower on a different but closely related plant is cross-pollination. Most tree fruits need cross-pollinating. This transfer of pollen is usually carried out by bees or other insects, but fruiting plants such as peaches – which flower in early spring before insects are very active – may need pollinating by hand.

It is possible to grow a single tree with more than one variety on it. These 'family' trees consist of three selected varieties of the same type of fruit, which flower at the same time. This enables them to pollinate one other and produce fruit.

Protecting your crop

At one time or another most fruit bushes and trees need to be protected against birds, other pests, diseases and frost.

Some birds can be a particular nuisance by eating flower buds and the fruit itself. A piece of netting draped over the plant at critical times may be all that is needed in the way of protection, although if the problem is bad or you have several plants, it may be worth investing in a fruit cage. This comprises metal supports covered in wire or plastic netting. However, the netting must be removed in winter, as it will be damaged by the weight of snow.

Unfortunately all fruit crops are prone to attacks from certain pests and diseases but chemical sprays can achieve a dramatic improvement in fruit quality, although they should be used sparingly. Where possible, avoid spraying fungicides and insecticides when the plants are in blossom, as some sprays may also kill or deter pollinating insects.

Flowers and fruits are also vulnerable to late-spring frosts, so early-flowering bushes such as gooseberries should be protected with fleece or heavy netting at night. Always remove netting during the day so that insects can pollinate the flowers.

Boughs bearing heavy crops may need supporting with a forked stick and sacking, especially if the site is particularly windy.

Beating the frost
During prolonged cold weather, strawberries, fruit bushes and fruit trees should be protected at night with fleece or similar material. Always remove again once the temperature has risen above 0°C (32°F).

Keeping birds at bay
Netting can be used to protect ripening fruit from marauders.

Sheltered site
A fan-trained tree grown against a fence for wind protection.

Pruning soft fruit

The aim of pruning soft fruit is to develop a healthy plant in optimum shape to produce a large quantity of fruit. Shoots that have already fruited should be removed, as should any diseased, damaged, dying or dead stems. Specific pruning techniques, however, depend on the growth habit of the plant, and soft fruits grow in three main ways: as canes, bushes and ground cover. Canes are very slender shrubs and their stems develop at ground level or slightly below. Bushes have a basic woody framework that starts at ground level, or just above, and they are generally as high as they are wide. The most popular ground-cover soft fruit is the strawberry, which is a low-growing bedding plant.

Making an impression
Soft fruit bushes can be of ornamental as well as practical value, as this standard gooseberry bush demonstrates.

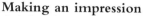

Pruning cane fruit

Cane fruits produce fruit only once on each cane, and should have all the old canes cut down to ground level in summer or autumn, after the fruit has been harvested.

Young cane fruit

To encourage new plants to establish quickly, and strong shoots to merge from soil level around their base, young plants should be pruned immediately after planting, in late autumn to early spring. The plants should be spaced at 30cm (12in) intervals in rows 30cm (12in) apart.

Cut the new canes back to 23cm (9in) above ground level. Tie young canes to their support wires as they develop and remove all flowers in the first season. If plants are to become well established, a fair amount of patience is required. It will be 18 months before a crop can be picked.

In late summer, cut out all canes that were shortened at the time of planting.

Securing new growth
Tie in young canes as they begin to develop.

Removing suckers
Pull up suckers along with any surplus new plants.

Mature cane fruit

Immediately after cropping, remove canes that have fruited, as well as damaged and weak ones. The old canes should be grey or dark brown, while new shoots are usually a light brown colour. Prompt clearance enables the remaining canes to grow unhindered. Also remove suckers and unwanted young plants as they develop and dead, damaged and diseased wood as soon as it is noticed.

To protect canes from wind damage, regularly tie new canes to their support wires, giving each cane equal room – usually one cane every 10cm (4in). The tops of vigorous canes can be further supported in autumn by looping them over the top wire and tying firmly with string.

Each spring, you will need to shorten the canes back to 15cm (6in) above the top support wire, and cut back canes that have frost-damaged tips. Remove some canes from overcrowded sections on the row, so that there is one every 10cm (4in).

Fruited canes
Remove old canes as soon as they have fruited, cutting them at ground level.

Tip pruning
Shorten all canes back to within 15cm (6in) of the top wire in spring.

Pruning bush fruit

Bush fruits, such as gooseberries and red and white currants, which develop branches above ground level, on a short leg, are most commonly grown as bushes with an open centre. They can also be trained as standards or cordons (see pp.106–107). Bush fruits, such as blackcurrants and blueberries, are pruned in a slightly different way because they produce shoots from ground level and fruit on one-year-old shoots. Red and white currants and gooseberries fruit on shoots that are one year old or more and these should be pruned to produce plenty of new wood. All these bush fruits are pruned in winter and early spring.

One-year-old currant bush
Cut back stems by one-half in late winter.

Young bush fruit

In autumn or winter, at the time of planting gooseberries and red and white currants, remove any shoots that are less than 30cm (12in) above ground level to produce a short leg, which will prevent any branches or fruit trailing on the ground. Shorten the remaining shoots by one-half in late winter. The following winter, cut back all new growth by one-half to form the framework of main branches. Prune back any side shoots growing into the centre of the bush or in a downward direction to a single bud. These form the basis of fruiting spurs later.

Two-year-old gooseberry bush
Cut back leaders by one-half and other side shoots back to just one bud in winter.

Black currants

With black currants the majority of fruit is produced on shoots formed the previous year, and, in order to promote the production of new shoots, regular hard pruning each winter is essential. Immediately after planting the new bushes, in autumn or winter, prune all stems to one bud above soil level. The following winter cut out any thin, weak or diseased shoots.

For established black currant bushes, renewal pruning in mid-winter is used. This involves cutting out up to one-third of the oldest, dark-coloured shoots, and removing all thin, weak or diseased ones. Using such a pruning system, the entire top growth of the bush is replaced over a three-year period and thus the full fruiting potential of the bush is utilized. Blueberries are pruned in a similar way except that they are not pruned for the first three years after planting.

Mature bush fruit

Established fruit bushes should have an open centre. This encourages good air circulation through the plants, allows the sun to ripen the fruit and helps to reduce the incidence of pests and diseases. Therefore any low-growing, overcrowded and crossing shoots should be removed in winter or early spring. Picking is easier when the fruit is produced on short spurs, so also shorten side shoots to one bud. Cut out any old, unproductive shoots and encourage strong, young shoots to grow into the available space. Completely remove any shoots on the stem, or leg, below the main framework of branches.

Old, neglected bushes that have not been regularly pruned need more drastic treatment. In late winter or early spring remove some or all of the old wood and retain only healthy, new shoots. This process may need to be repeated the following winter until new stems have replaced all the older ones. To reduce competition, thin out some of the new shoots, retaining only the strongest.

Removing suckers
Removing competing suckers from the trunk of a gooseberry bush.

Renovating gooseberry
Thin out competing stems on neglected or overcrowded bushes.

Pruning strawberries

Strawberries are pruned in late summer or autumn, after the crop has been picked. Cut off the old leaves with secateurs or shears, leaving plenty of room for young, new leaves to emerge. Discarding these old leaves also removes any pests and diseases that might be resident on them.

At the same time cut away any runners, which will weaken the development of the plants (these runners can later be used to form the basis of a new crop). After three years, strawberry plants should be discarded as their fruiting capacity will be much reduced.

Pruning tree fruit

Apple, pear and sweet cherry trees mostly bear fruit on shoots that are two years old or more, and the aim of pruning these trees is to maintain a balance between the number of old, fruit-bearing shoots and the development of new growth, which will eventually produce fruit. Damson and plum trees, on the other hand, produce fruit on shoots that are one year old or more, and these should be pruned to produce plenty of new shoots. Fig and peach trees carry most of their fruit on one-year-old shoots, and these are pruned by removing the shoots that have just fruited.

Most pruning of tree, or top, fruit is done in winter and early spring, when the plants are dormant, although summer pruning can be used to encourage more fruit-bearing spurs to develop, especially with trained trees, such as cordons, espaliers and fans. However, all stone tree fruits, such as plums, peaches, nectarines and cherries, should be pruned in summer whenever possible, to reduce the risk of infection from the silver leaf fungus *Chondrostereum purpureum*, which usually enters a tree through pruning wounds made in winter.

Before any pruning is done, it is important to establish whether the tree is a tip bearer (if it carries its fruit at, or near, the tips of young shoots) or a spur bearer (if it develops fruit along the full length of the young shoot). Tip bearers do not need much pruning and are best grown as bush fruits, standards and half-standards. Spur bearers respond well to pruning and are excellent for intensive forms of tree-fruit growing such as espaliers and cordons.

Encouraging better crops

Ideal weather at blossom time can lead to a larger than average number of flowers being fertilized.

If all of these juvenile fruits are allowed to develop, the tree may produce quantities of undersized and deformed fruits.

The sheer weight of the crop may also cause structural damage to some branches, and retard fruit-bud development for the following year.

To prevent these problems, you should thin out up to 40 per cent of juvenile fruit, if the tree does not naturally shed some itself, in the 'June drop'. This will allow the remaining fruit to develop normally, to full size. Juvenile fruits should be removed by pulling off only the fruits, leaving the stalks behind on the tree.

To promote flower-bud and fruit-spur formation, and thus increase yields, tree fruits such as cordons, which have been trained for intensive fruit growing in a restricted space, can be pruned in midsummer, just before next year's flower buds are formed.

Woody-based side shoots are cut back to one leaf, while side shoots of the current season's growth are reduced to three leaves.

Spur thinning

The continual pruning to encourage the formation of fruiting spurs causes the spurs eventually to become entangled and carry small, poorly coloured and sized fruit. When this occurs, the overcrowded spurs should be thinned in winter.

Remove the older wood, sawing off complete clusters of spur systems if necessary to allow more space for new spurs to develop.

Overcrowded spurs
Dense spur systems will produce large numbers of small fruits.

Spurs after thinning
Older, tangled growth and any thin, weak spurs are cut out.

Pruning standards

Standards, half-standards and bush fruit trees are the most commonly grown free-standing fruit trees. A standard has a clear stem of some 1.8m (6ft) before its branches radiate. A half-standard has about 1.35m (4½ft) of clear stem and bush fruit trees 75cm (2½ft) of clear stem. All are pruned in winter; the aim to maintain an open framework to aid ripening and picking.

Young standards
Remove dead, dying or diseased shoots and thin out congested ones to make the framework even. Shorten leaders by up to two-thirds, and well-spaced shoots arising from the branch framework by one-half, to an outward-facing bud. Tip bearers need no further pruning but spur bearers should have shoots that are not needed for the basic framework shortened to four or five buds to encourage fruiting spurs to form.

Mature standards
Continue to prune as for young standards, stimulating some new growth and maintaining an open structure so that the tree crops well on a regular basis and the fruit is of good quality. The exact pruning needed will vary each year depending on the type, the growth, and the general habit of the tree.

Controlling vigour
Cut vigorous leading shoots by half to help lateral shoots develop.

How to prune cordons

Cordons are specially trained, angled trees that have been intensively pruned so that they have generally only one main stem. Because they are compact, having no major branches, they take up little space in the garden and they are convenient to manage. Pears, apples and some bush fruits (see p.105) are best suited to training as cordons.

Each cordon is grown at a 45° angle against wires, 60cm (2ft) apart, secured to a fence, wall or set of posts, 10cm (4in) by 10cm (4in) square and 2.1m (7ft) high. A bamboo cane, set at 45°, is tied to the wires and the cordon trained along it.

Young cordons

Training of young cordons starts immediately after planting, in winter, when each tree is positioned with the graft union uppermost on the stem, to reduce the risk of breakage. Immediately after planting, secure the main stem to the bamboo cane, in several places, and cut all side shoots back to 10cm (4in). To allow the tree to become fully established before it produces fruit, remove any flowers the first spring after planting.

Mature cordons

To ensure that cordon trees keep on producing a constant supply of fruit buds, and to suppress vigorous shoot growth, most pruning is carried out in summer, with shoots being pruned in succession as they mature.

Once young shoots have become woody at the base, all side shoots of the current season's growth on the main stem or branches are cut back to three leaves above the basal cluster of leaves. At the same time any new shoots growing from older side shoots and from spurs are shortened to just one leaf above the basal cluster.

Some spur thinning may be required in winter to prevent congestion.

Winter pruning
Cut all side shoots back to 10cm (4in) in the first winter.

Disbudding
Remove flowers in the first spring, so the tree can establish itself.

Summer pruning
Cut back side shoots to within three leaves above the base cluster.

How to prune espaliers

The fruitfulness of a tree can be increased by training its branches horizontally, into an espalier, for example. This tree form has pairs of shoots – trained in two or three tiers – growing at right angles to the main stem. The tiers are trained along horizontal wires set about 40cm (16in) apart and secured to a wall, fence or set of posts, 10cm (4in) by 10cm (4in) square and 2.1m (7ft) high. This type of training is best suited to apple and pear trees.

Young espaliers

After planting a young espalier, in winter, cut back the main stem just above the bottom wire, ensuring there are two healthy buds below it. As it develops, tie the new leader to a vertical bamboo cane; also secure two vigorous side shoots to canes set at 45° to the wires. Shorten to two or three leaves or remove any other side shoots. In winter cut back the leader just above the second wire, ensuring there are two healthy buds below it.

In subsequent summers, repeat this process, treating the three new shoots arising from the vertical stem in the same way as those in the first year, until the required number of tiers has been achieved. Gradually lower each tier of side shoots until they are lying along the wires. Do not tie them into a horizontal position too early or extension growth will be checked.

Mature espaliers

Once established, espaliers are pruned in the same way as mature cordons (see above), except that any terminal growths on vertical and horizontal tiers of the espalier should also be kept pruned back. The whole idea of an espalier tree is to produce horizontal, spur-bearing platforms to carry the fruit – but on older trees, these spur formations may become complicated and overcrowded.

During the winter, when the fruit buds on the spurs are easy to see, relieve this overcrowding by cutting out any thin, weak or damaged spurs, as well as removing any spurs that are developing on the underside of the horizontal branches.

Young espalier
Removing side shoots on a two-year-old espalier.

Pruning fans

Growing a fruit tree, such as a cherry, in a fan shape can be very attractive but is not suitable for a small garden, as a fan occupies more space than a cordon or espalier. A fan has a series of lateral shoots (ribs) and sub-laterals radiating out in an arc from a short stem, or leg, and is usually grown against a wall or fence.

The aim of pruning a fan is to provide a constant supply of young shoots to replace the old cropping wood. This is usually done after harvesting, when the fruiting shoot is removed and a young shoot from just below the point where the cut was made is tied in its position instead. Tie in the shoot from the end bud of each rib and encourage suitably spaced shoots to grow on the upper side of each rib and one on the underside. Remove any shoots that grow towards or away from the supporting wall or fence.

Fruit

Fruit is a popular crop, with birds and insects as much as with gardeners, so one of the first priorities is to find ways to protect the crop once it is nearly ripe. Netting soft fruit is imperative if you wish to have decent yields, as is correct pruning. These days, modern plant breeding has done much to ensure that good results are obtained with relatively little effort. It is important to remember that some fruits (citrus, apricots and nectarines in particular) are not frost-hardy and will require protection in cold climates.

Currants
Ribes nigrum, R. rubrum

R.n. 'Baldwin'

R. r. 'Versailles' Blanche'

Currants are grown for their juicy red, white or black fruits, which are used in pies and other desserts and for making jams and jellies. Redcurrants are high in pectin and can be added to other fruits when making jam to aid setting. A variety of the redcurrant is the white currant, which has similar cultivation needs.

All red- and white-currants have a similar, upright habit and are quite vigorous; they can easily reach 1.5m (5ft) high and across. In good conditions, blackcurrants will grow even larger: up to 1.5m (5ft) high and 2.1m (7ft) across. However they have a greater variety of habit and vigour, 'Ben Sarek' being the most compact blackcurrant variety you can buy.

Currants prefer an open, sunny position but struggle on exposed, windy sites. Almost any soil will do for red- and whitecurrants, provided it is well-drained but moisture retentive, while blackcurrants require a very fertile soil to do well, although they will produce some fruit even if they are badly neglected. All currants will be ready to crop 12–18 months after planting.

Planting Add plenty of bulky organic matter to the soil before planting. Plant when the bushes are dormant, in autumn and winter. Space bushes 1.5m (5ft) apart.

Cultivation In early spring, mulch the plants with well-rotted compost or manure to a depth of 10cm (4in) to help control weeds and retain moisture. Water the bushes thoroughly in dry periods, especially when the fruit is swelling, as the roots are shallow and can easily suffer from drought.

R. r. 'Jonkheer van Tets'

You will need to net the fruit once the currants start to change colour in order to protect them from birds.

Training and pruning red- and whitecurrants
In late winter or early spring, cut back the main leaders and strongest side shoots of red- and white-currants by one-quarter, and the weaker ones to just one outward-facing bud. This will encourage the formation

Soaking roots
Leave the roots of any bare-rooted bush in water before planting.

Trimming roots
Remove any damaged roots before planting.

of fruiting spurs. You should aim to develop an open-centred bush, which will promote good air flow and help to reduce the chance of pests and disease colonizing the plant.

It is also important to maintain a clear stem, or 'leg', of at least 15–20cm (6–8in) between the lowest branch and ground level, as the fruits hang in long trusses which will tend to trail on the soil if the branches are too low.

Training and pruning blackcurrants

Prune black currants in autumn, immediately after leaf-fall. Remove up to one-quarter of the stems, choosing those that are darkest in colour, to make room for new ones. Black currants produce most of their fruit on shoots made in the previous season, and on regularly pruned bushes no stems should be more than four years old.

Harvesting Never pick currants until they are fully ripe. The uppermost berries on the truss ('strig') will ripen first and the lowest several days later, so wait until all of them are ripe before removing the entire strig from the branch.

Blackcurrants will be ready to harvest in midsummer and red and whitecurrants in mid- to late summer. Cropping can continue for 10–14 days.

Pruning for shape
Aim to create an open, balanced structure so that air can circulate.

Gooseberries
Ribes uva-crispa var. *reclinatum*

R. u-c. 'Invicta' var r.

Gooseberries are grown for their green, yellow, creamy white or occasionally red fruits, which can be used in jams, wines and desserts.

Gooseberries grow well in a sheltered position in full sun or partial shade, and need well-drained but moisture-retentive, fertile soil. Mature bushes usually reach about 1.2m (4ft) high. Fruits will be ready to crop 12–18 months after planting.

The plants flower in early spring, so beware of potential frost pockets when planting, and heavy netting or fleece may be needed to protect the flowers and early fruits. Remove netting during the day, however, to allow insects access for pollination.

Planting Before planting add plenty of bulky manure

Gooseberry sawfly
Sawfly larvae will strip the leaves off a gooseberry bush, as here.

to soil that is not particularly fertile. In late autumn or early winter, plant goose-berries 1.2m (4ft) apart, with 1.5m (5ft) between rows.

Cultivation Apply a mulch, 10cm (4in) thick, of well-rotted manure or compost in spring, after plants have been pruned, to help control weeds and prevent the soil drying out. The bushes should then need watering only during very dry periods. In summer, the bushes may need to be covered with netting to protect the fruits from birds.

Training and pruning
Prune gooseberry bushes in late winter or early spring and aim to develop an open-centred bush to promote air flow and protect against pests and disease.

Birds, such as finches, often feed on the buds in winter, and any damaged wood should be removed. Cut back the main leaders by one-half and reduce the strongest side shoots to about 7.5cm (3in). The weaker shoots should be cut back to 2–3cm (1–1½in) to encourage the formation of fruiting spurs.

Harvesting The fruits can be picked while still green for cooking, from early to midsummer, when they are about the size of marbles. They will ripen from midsummer onwards, and will gradually become softer and sweeter, developing their final, red colour.

Frost protection
Cover bushes with fleece or heavy netting in cold weather.

Blueberries
Vaccinum corymbosum, V. australe

V. c. 'Bluecrop'

Grown for their delicious white-bloomed, dark blue fruits, blueberries require cool, moist, acid soil. The bushes will do best in an open, sunny position but will also tolerate partial shade, although they must be protected from cold winds. A mature blueberry bush will grow 1.2–1.5m (4–5ft) high. Bushes can be cropped for the first time two years after planting.

Planting Plant the bushes at any time from late autumn to early spring, into soil that has had 10cm (1in) of peat added. Space plants 1.2–1.5m (4–5ft) apart.

Cultivation Mulch in early summer with a 10cm (4in) layer of well rotted manure to keep roots moist and control weeds. In dry periods, water with collected rainwater if your tap water is alkaline.

Training and pruning
Blueberries do not require pruning until three years after planting, when the four oldest shoots should be cut back to soil level each winter.

Harvesting Harvesting begins in late summer and lasts several weeks. Pick only the ripest fruits: those which are dark blue, with a white bloom, and slightly soft. Pull them gently from their stalks with a finger and thumb.

Blackberries
Rubus fruticosus

R.f. **'Thornfree'**

Most blackberry cultivars produce heavy crops of large, well-flavoured, glossy black fruits. Although the plants are notoriously prickly, there are several thornless cultivars such as 'Oregon Thornless'.

Blackberries need well-drained, fertile soil and prefer a sheltered, sunny position, although they will also tolerate partial shade. They can be cropped for the first time two years after planting.

Planting Plant the canes, 15cm (6in) deep and 3–5m (10–15ft) apart, in well-prepared soil at any time from late autumn to early spring. To make cropping easier, set them in rows spaced 3–5m (10–15ft) apart. After planting, cut back the stems to 25cm (10in) above soil level.

Cultivation Mulch the bushes with a layer of organic matter 10cm (4in) deep and water the plants well during dry periods.

Training and pruning Blackberries are very vigorous, often growing 4m (12ft) in a year, and must have a strong support system to keep them manageable.

Select posts, 10 x 10cm (4 x 4in) square and 3m (10ft) long, and insert these 90cm (36in) into the ground. Fix six horizontal wires, 30cm (12in) apart, to the posts, starting 30cm (12in) above ground level. Then, as they develop, train the canes into a 'fan' arrangement along the wires and tie in position.

Harvesting Cropping can start in mid- or late summer and should last three weeks. When completely black, the ripe berries can be picked by pulling the berry together with its core, or 'plug', from the plant. Pick carefully, as they are easily damaged.

Severing rooted runner
Once it has been rooted, cut the young plant from its parent.

Raspberries
Rubus idaeus

R.i. **'Autumn Bliss'**

Raspberries are grown for their good crop of delicious fruit which may vary in colour from a blackish red to golden yellow, depending on the cultivar. Raspberries prefer cool seasons, lots of moisture and a well-drained, fertile soil rich in organic matter. They enjoy a sheltered, sunny position but will also grow in partial shade, especially on dry, exposed sites with light, sandy soil.

There are two types of raspberry: summer-fruiting and autumn-fruiting. Both grow 1.4–2.1m (4½–7ft) high. Harvesting begins from the second year after planting.

Planting Canes can be planted at any time from late autumn to early spring. Add wood ash or another potash fertilizer to the soil before planting. Plant the canes 45cm (18in) apart, in rows 1.8m (6ft) apart. Then cut the newly planted canes back to 23cm (9in) above soil level. Once established, they will sucker profusely; if this is a problem, line the sides of the planting trenches with plastic to contain their spreading habit.

Cultivation Raspberries prefer a cool root run and benefit greatly from mulching with a layer of organic matter 10cm (4in) deep, to help control weeds and retain moisture. Remove the flowers in the first year.

Training and pruning Some cultivars are very vigorous and will produce new canes well over 2m (6½ft) high in a single season. To keep them manageable, use stout posts, 2.4m (8ft) long, and insert them 90cm (36in) into the ground. Fix three wires to the posts 75cm (30in), 1.2m (4ft) and 1.5m (5ft) above ground level. Tie

Planting raspberries
Shorten canes back to 23cm (9in) immediately after planting.

young canes to these wires immediately after the canes that have fruited have been cut down. In autumn, loop over the tops of tall canes and tie them to the top wire. Cut these loops back to 15cm (6in) above the top wire in late winter or early spring, if required.

Prune summer-fruiting raspberries immediately after the crop has been picked, cutting down all canes that have fruited to ground level and removing them, so that only the young canes remain. Prune autumn-fruiting types in late winter, before new growth appears, cutting back the fruited canes to ground level to stimulate the production of new canes.

Harvesting Raspberries are fully ripe when they can be picked cleanly from the fruit stalk, leaving the core, or 'plug', behind. Pick carefully, gripping the fruit gently between finger and thumb.

Training raspberries
Wires stretched between stout posts provide support for canes.

Fruiting raspberries
After the harvest, cut all fruiting canes down to ground level.

Strawberries

Fragaria x *ananassa*

These low-growing, herbaceous plants are grown for their delicious red, occasionally yellow, fruits.

Strawberries, which grow to 45cm (18in) high and 60cm (24in) across, will tolerate most soils that are well-drained. They are relatively short-lived with a cropping life of about three years, so new plants should be planted on a regular basis. The second year is the most productive.

Planting Plant in early autumn at a distance of 45cm (18in) apart and 75cm (30in) between the rows. Plant on a very slight mound with crowns at ground level. The plants must be firmed well and watered.

Cultivation Newly planted strawberries have a shallow root system and must be kept watered until well established. As the fruits develop, they will hang down onto the soil, so a mulch of straw will prevent them from marking and rotting; black plastic can be used as an alternative, but fruits actually touching it may become scorched in hot weather.

Pruning Cut off any runners (modified side shoots) bearing new young plants in summer. Cut down the foliage to approximately

Planting
Young strawberry plants are planted in well-prepared soil.

F. x *a.* 'Calypso'

10cm (4in) above soil level in the autumn, after picking has finished.

Harvesting Harvesting begins in early summer for early-fruiting cultivars, and continues through to autumn for perpetual-fruiting types (see panel). Pick the berries complete with their stalks, when they are red over about three-quarters of their surface and handle them as little as possible, as they are easily bruised. Pick fruits every other day, as they deteriorate fast. Fruits intended for freezing and preserving can be picked slightly earlier than those destined for dessert.

Tidying up
Cut out old leaves and runners once harvesting is over.

Strawberry types

Three kinds of berry
Summer (top), Alpine (right) and Perpetual (bottom).

Strawberries are divided into three distinct groups:
• **Alpine strawberries** produce a light crop of small, delicately flavoured fruits. Reliable cultivars include 'Alpine Yellow'.
• **Perpetual strawberries** flower and fruit in midsummer and again in mid-autumn. Reliable cultivars include 'Gento'.
• **Summer-fruiting strawberries** produce a heavy crop over a three- or four-week period in summer. The season can be extended by selecting cultivars carefully: 'Elvira' fruits early, 'Cambridge Favourite' in mid-season and 'Domanil' late.

Apples

Malus domestica

M. d. 'Discovery'

Apples are one of the most popular fruits, with a wide variety of flavours and uses, as well as a cropping and storing season that runs from late summer to mid-spring. They grow well in most soils, but prefer deep, well-drained soil that does not dry out too quickly in summer.

Most apple cultivars must be cross-pollinated with another cultivar to produce fruit, so it is important to grow cultivars with flowering periods that overlap.

Planting Plant in late autumn or early winter into a well-cultivated soil with plenty of organic matter added. Planting distances vary according to the rootstock used, but an average would be 3 x 4m (9 x 12ft) apart.

Cultivation In early spring apply an organic mulch to a depth of 10cm (4in) to help retain moisture and control weeds. Water the trees in dry summer periods or the fruits may drop prematurely.

Pruning Most tree and bush forms of apple require moderate pruning in winter to stimulate growth for the next season's fruit, so that they will crop well on a regular basis and maintain an open, well-balanced structure The pruning required will vary from year to year, depending on the season and growth of the tree, but strong shoots and leaders should generally be reduced by one-third of the current season's growth, and laterals cut back to four or five buds. The

fruiting habit of the tree must be considered. Spur-bearing trees such as 'Jester' and 'Cox's Orange Pippin' require spur thinning and pruning (see panel, p.187). Tip-bearing cultivars such as 'Discovery' and 'Worcester Pearmain', which produce the majority of their fruit on the tips of the branches, will need 'renewal' pruning, or cutting back in winter to a growth bud to remove bare, unproductive wood.

Harvesting To test whether apples are ripe, lift one in the palm of your hand and twist it slightly. If the apple and stalk come away from the spur easily, then it is ready. Handle apples with care, as they will deteriorate rapidly if bruised. To store, wrap each fruit individually in greaseproof paper and place in a well-ventilated container in a cool place. Early-season apples will be ready to harvest between late summer and early autumn and should be eaten within a few days of picking. Mid-season cultivars should be picked from early to mid-autumn, and late-season apples should be picked from mid- to late autumn, both before they are fully ripe. They will continue to ripen in store, ready for use from midwinter into late spring.

Winter pruning
Removing the end quarter of the current season's growth from leader shoots.

Apple and pear varieties
Not all apple and pear trees are self-fertile and those that are not will need to have a suitable tree nearby with which they can cross-pollinate. Check which pollination group the tree belongs to when you buy it, and perhaps purchase a suitable companion that will cross-pollinate with it. Without pollination, there will be no fruit. Ideally plant two or more from compatible groups that flower at the same period.
Apple varieties Mid-season apples (compatible pollinators) 'Bramley's Seedling' (cooking), 'Blenheim Orange' (cooking), 'Cox's Orange Pippin' (dessert) 'Worcester Pearmain' (dessert) **Late season apples (compatible pollinators)** 'Gala' (dessert), 'Orleans Reinette' (dessert), 'Encore' (cooking)
Pear varieties (Self-fertile or compatible pollinators) 'Conference', 'Beurré Superfin', 'Fondante d'Automne', 'Marie-Louise

Harvesting
When the apple and stalk separate easily from the branch, the fruit is ready for picking.

Pears

Pyrus communis

***P. c.* 'Conference'**

This very popular fruit can be used fresh in desserts or for cooking and preserving.

Pears are almost as easy to grow as apples, but prefer a warmer climate and flower earlier, so are more susceptible to spring frost damage. They need deep, fertile soil that is moisture-retentive, as they are sensitive to drought. Ideally, at least three different cultivars of pear should be grown in close proximity to allow cross-pollination to occur.

Planting Plant in late autumn or early winter at a spacing of 3 x 3m (10 x 10ft) apart, into a deeply cultivated soil containing plenty of well-rotted organic matter.

Stimulating growth

When a pear tree has ceased to produce new growth, cut back to two- or three-year-old wood. This can be recognised by the annual growth rings on a stem.

Cultivation In early spring, apply an organic mulch 10cm (4in) deep to control weeds and, more importantly, to retain moisture, as dry summer soil can cause the crop to abort.

Pruning Pear trees produce fruiting spurs easily, usually on two- and three-year-old shoots, and will need quite a lot of spur thinning (see p.180) and renewal pruning – cutting back in winter to a growth bud to remove areas of bare, unproductive wood. Most forms of pear require moderate pruning in winter to stimulate the following season's growth and fruit, and to maintain an open structure. The pruning needed will vary from year to year, but strong shoots and leaders should generally be reduced by one-third of the current season's growth and laterals cut back to four or five buds.

Harvesting Timing is critical: pears must be picked before they ripen or they will rot almost immediately in store. To keep pears, place them in a cool, dark position at 0–1°C (32–34°F).

Early-season pears will be ready to harvest between late summer and early autumn, and should be cut from the tree with secateurs.

Mid-season cultivars should be harvested from early to mid-autumn and late-season pears from early winter. They will continue to ripen in store. Always use the smallest fruits first.

Spur systems

With spur-bearing cultivars, apples and pears are produced on shoots that are two years old or more, and the fruits are usually borne in clusters on short, twiggy growths called 'spurs'.

The branches will carry two types of bud: large, swollen buds, which produce flower clusters and then fruit buds (spurs), and other much smaller, pointed growth buds, which develop into shoots for the following year or into laterals (side shoots). These spur systems may become overcrowded over a number of years, and can be thinned out or in some cases removed entirely.

Creating spurs

Lateral shoots should be pruned back to five buds in the winter, to encourage fruiting spurs.

Recognizing bud types

The shoots that are two years or older on this spur system generally contain both pointed growth buds and swollen flower buds.

Plums
Prunus domestica

P. d. 'Giant Prune'

This fruit can be eaten fresh or used for cooking, bottling and jams, but as the trees flower in early spring there is a risk of frost damage.

Plums prefer deep, well-drained soil and a warm, sheltered site. Different cultivars should be grown close together to ensure adequate pollen is available, even for the so-called self-fertile cultivars.

Planting Plant in late autumn or early winter into a deep, well-prepared soil with plenty of well-rotted organic matter. Plants should be spaced 3–4m (9–12ft) apart.

Cultivation In spring, apply an organic mulch, 10cm (4in) deep, to help retain moisture and control weeds. Water the trees in dry periods, or the fruits may drop prematurely. Some thinning of the crop may be necessary in midsummer to avoid major branches breaking under the weight of the fruit. Reduce each cluster to a maximum of five fruits.

Pruning Plum trees should be about 3m (10ft) high, so that most of the fruits can be reached from the ground. If the tree is cropping regularly, do as little pruning as possible. All pruning should be done in late summer to reduce the risk of attack from silver-leaf fungus. Thin out overcrowded branches by removing some completely, and try to keep the rest to about 1.5m (5ft) in length.

Harvesting The ripe fruits will be ready to harvest from midsummer to mid-autumn. Plums for cooking should be picked while still firm; those for dessert when they are slightly soft. Plums do not store well and should be eaten within a few days of picking.

Thinning dense clusters
Remove some fruit, leaving all the stalks on the tree.

Damsons
Prunus insititia

P. i. 'Bradley's King Damson'

These dark purple fruits are noted for their sour taste, which makes them more suitable for cooking and preserving than for eating fresh.

Most cultivars are self-fertile. The trees, which flower in mid-spring, often grow too large for the average garden unless grafted onto a dwarfing rootstock, in which case they can grow to 4m (12ft) high.

Damsons tolerate more rain and will do well with less sunshine than plums. They enjoy a deep, well-drained soil.

Planting Plant in late autumn or early winter into a well-prepared planting hole with plenty of well-rotted manure added. The plants need to be at least 4 x 4m (12 x 12ft) apart.

Cultivation Follow the same guidelines as for plums (see left).

Pruning As with plums, the fruits are carried on the previous season's growth and on spurs carried on older wood. Very little pruning is needed if the tree is cropping regularly. If any pruning is necessary, due to overcrowded or broken branches,

Heavily laden branch
Use a padded, forked stick to support and protect a heavily laden stem.

it should be carried out in summer, to reduce the risk of attack from silver-leaf fungus, to which damsons are prone.

Harvesting Allow the fruits to ripen on the tree. They will be ready to harvest from early to mid-autumn. Damsons for cooking should be picked while still firm; those for dessert when they are slightly soft to the touch.

Greengages
Prunus domestica

P. d. 'Reine Claude de Brahy'

Greengages, which are in fact coloured yellow or green, are ideal for eating fresh or bottling. The trees however tend to produce only about two-thirds of the yield of dessert plums.

Like plums, greengages prefer a deep, well-drained soil and a warm, sheltered site to encourage pollinating insects. They need more sunshine than plums, and most cultivars are self-fertile.

Planting Plant in late autumn into a well-prepared planting hole with plenty of well-rotted manure. Plants should be spaced 3-4m (9-12ft) apart.

Cultivation In spring, apply an organic mulch, 10cm (4in) deep, to help retain moisture and control weeds. Water the trees in dry summer periods, or the fruits may drop prematurely. Some thinning of the crop may be necessary in midsummer, otherwise major branches may break under the weight of the fruit. Reduce each cluster to a maximum of five fruits. Ripening greengages are prone to splitting and rotting in wet weather, and attack from birds and wasps in hot weather, so may need protecting with netting.

Pruning Ideally, greengage trees should be about 3m (10ft) high, so that most of the fruits can be reached from the ground. The fruits are carried on the previous season's growth and on spurs carried on older wood. If the tree is cropping regularly, do as little pruning as possible. All pruning should be carried out in summer, after fruiting, to reduce the risk of attack from silver-leaf fungus. Thin out overcrowded branches by removing some completely, and try to keep all branches to about 1.5m (5ft) in length.

Harvesting Allow the fruits to ripen on the tree. They will be ready to harvest from midsummer to mid-autumn. Greengages for cooking should be picked while still firm; those for dessert when they are slightly soft to the touch.

Cherries
Prunus avium

P. a. 'Morello'

Sweet cherries are delicious eaten fresh. The trees are very vigorous and are usually grafted onto a dwarfing rootstock. Because sweet cherries flower very early – in midspring – they need protection from frost. For this reason, they are often trained against a wall or fence. They require a deep, well-drained, moisture-retentive soil.

Planting Plant in late autumn or early winter. into a well-cultivated soil which has had plenty of well-rotted manure added. Space plants 5–7m (15–20ft) apart.

Cultivation In early spring, feed the tree with an organic mulch, 10cm (4in) deep. Water in dry periods and in early summer drape the tree with netting to protect the fruits from birds.

Training and pruning All pruning should be carried out in summer, after fruiting, to promote fruit-bud formation. Each late summer, select two new lateral growths from each branch, tie them into any available space, and remove any other laterals or pinch them back to six leaves.

Harvesting The fruits will be ready to harvest in summer. Pick fruits for freezing when still firm, and those for cooking or dessert when slightly soft.

Shortening laterals
Cut lateral shoots to four or five buds to encourage fruiting spurs.

Tying in new growth
Secure young shoots to the network of supporting wires.

Peaches
Prunus persica

P. p. 'Garden Lady'

Peaches are grown for their downy fruits, eaten fresh or used cooked for desserts and jams. Peach trees will grow in any fertile, moisture-retentive, well-drained soil that is rich in organic matter. They benefit from a sheltered, sunny position, so are often grown against a wall in a fan shape. Flowers in mid-spring are vulnerable to frost. Peaches can be grown as single plants, as almost all cultivars are self-fertile.

Planting Plant in late autumn or early winter at a spacing of 4 x 4m (12 x 12ft) into a deep, well-drained soil. Add plenty of well-rotted manure to the planting hole.

Cultivation Follow the same guidelines as for cherries (p.115). Pollination can be assisted by dabbing each flower with a camel-hair brush. If the crop is heavy, thin out when the fruits are about 2.5cm (1in) across. Aim for one fruit to every 20–25cm (8–10in) of stem.

Training and pruning Peaches produce fruit only on the previous season's growth. Prune in spring to provide a regular supply of new shoots, which will form the ribs/branches of the fan.

Harvesting The fruits will be ready to harvest in mid- to late summer. They are ripe when the flesh yields to gentle pressure if squeezed.

Dwarf peach
Some peaches are ideal for growing in pots, where space is limited.

Peach leaf curl
This fungal disease distorts and causes leaves to fall prematurely.

Nectarines
Prunus persica var. *nectarina*

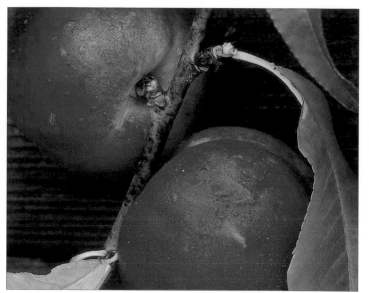

P. p. var. n. 'Harko'

Nectarines are similar to peaches but are smooth-skinned rather than downy, and are less hardy than their close relatives.

Nectarines, like peaches, will grow in any fertile, moisture-retentive, well-drained soil that is rich in organic matter. They also like shelter and full sun and, as they flower in mid-spring, can be vulnerable to frost.

Nectarines can be grown as single plants, as almost all cultivars are self-fertile.

Planting Plant in late autumn or early winter into a deep, well-drained soil with plenty of well-composted organic matter incorporated into the planting hole. Plant trees 4 x 4m (12 x 12ft) apart.

Cultivation In spring, feed the trees with an organic mulch, 10cm (4in) deep. Pollination can be assisted by dabbing flowers with a camel-hair brush. Water in dry summer periods, or the fruits may drop prematurely. In early summer, drape the tree with netting to protect fruits from birds. If the crop is heavy, thin when the fruits are about 2.5cm (1in) across, aiming for one fruit to every 20–25cm (8–10in) of stem.

Training and pruning Nectarines produce fruit only on the previous season's growth. Prune in spring to encourage new shoots and tie them into any available space. These will replace fruiting branches, which should be removed immediately after cropping.

Harvesting The fruits will be ready to harvest in summer. Pick when the flesh yields slightly to pressure when squeezed between finger and thumb. Nectarines will store for up to one month if kept in a cool place, but handle them with care as they bruise easily.

Protecting nectarines
Cover the tree with netting to protect the fruit from birds.

Apricots
Prunus armeniaca

P. armeniaca

This succulent, yellow-skinned fruit can be eaten fresh or used for jams and preserves. Apricots are more difficult to grow than other 'stone fruits' such as peaches and nectarines, because they suffer from drought-induced bud drop late in the season. A warm, sheltered site is best, as the early (mid-spring) flowers are susceptible to frost.

Planting Plant from early autumn until late spring when the plant is dormant. Apricots prefer a deep, slightly alkaline, well-drained soil with lots of organic matter. Space plants 4–4.5m (12–14ft) apart.

Cultivation In spring, feed the trees with an organic mulch, 10cm (4in) deep. Pollination can be assisted by gently dabbing each flower with a camel-hair brush. Water in dry summer periods and in early summer drape the whole tree with netting to protect the fruits. If the crop is very heavy, thin when the fruits are about 2.5cm (1in) across, aiming for one fruit to every 20–25cm (8–10in) of stem.

Training and pruning As the fruits are carried on one-year-old growth and on

Spring blossom
A warm wall provides vital shelter for delicate, early spring blossom.

spurs on older wood, all pruning should be carried out in summer to reduce vegetative growth and promote fruit-bud formation. Each early summer, select two new lateral growths from each branch, tie them into any available space, and either remove surplus branches or pinch them back to six leaves.

Harvesting Allow the fruits to ripen on the tree; they will be ready to harvest in late summer. Pick them when they come away from the stalk easily and use immediately, as apricots do not store well.

Figs
Ficus carica

F. c. 'Rouge de Bordeaux'

Figs, which are among the oldest fruits in cultivation, vary in colour from green to reddish-brown. They are used for making desserts and preserves and are also eaten raw.

These evergreen trees like fertile, deep soil that is slightly alkaline, and a warm, dry climate. They can be planted in a brick- or concrete-lined plot to restrict their overall size and to increase their fruiting potential. As a guide, a pit 60 x 60 x 60cm (2 x 2 x 2ft) will confine a fig tree to a mature size of 2.4m (8ft) high and 5m (15ft) wide. Self-fertile fig flowers are produced internally and develop with the embryo fruit.

Planting Fig trees can be planted at any time of year in a deeply dug soil containing plenty of organic matter. Plants should be spaced 4–5m (12–15ft) apart.

Cultivation In early spring, feed the trees with an organic mulch, 10cm (4in) deep, to help retain moisture and control weeds. Water in dry summer periods, or the fruits may drop prematurely. In early summer, drape the whole tree with netting to protect the fruits from birds.

Protect the young fruits from frost by covering the whole tree with fleece.

Pruning In early spring, cut out the old fruited wood as well as any that is frost damaged. Prune back weak, young shoots to a single bud to encourage new shoots.

Harvesting Allow the fruits to ripen on the tree; this can take up to one year before they are ready to harvest, in summer and autumn. The figs are ripe enough to pick when the flesh yields to pressure if squeezed gently between finger and thumb.

Concrete-lined plot
Figs produce more fruit if the root spread is restricted.

Grapes
Vitis Hybrids

V. vinifera 'Schiava Grossa' syn. *V.v.* Black Hamburgh'

Grapes are one of the oldest of domesticated fruits and can be eaten fresh, processed for juice or used in wine-making. Borne in bunches, the fruits are blackish-purple, greenish-white or yellow in colour. Grape vines may reach up to 20m (70ft) when mature and will grow in any fertile, moisture-retentive, well-drained soil that is rich in organic matter. Their flowers, in mid-spring, are susceptible to frost damage. The vines should start to produce fruit in the fifth or sixth year after planting.

Planting Vines may be planted at any time of year.

Cultivation In spring, apply an organic mulch, 10cm (4in) deep. Water the vines in dry summer periods, especially while the fruits are swelling, or they may shrivel and drop. In early summer, drape the plant with netting to protect the fruits. If the bunches are very heavy, thin the crop when the grapes are about the size of peas.

Training and pruning
There are many training methods for grape vines, but the Guyot system is widely used where space is limited. Vines trained by the Guyot method should have all old, fruited wood cut out in winter, leaving only three replacement shoots. Tie two of these shoots down, one on either side of the third, central shoot, and prune the third shoot back to three strong buds. Six weeks before the fruits are to ripen, remove any overcrowded shoots and leaves that are obscuring them.

Harvesting The fruits will be ready in autumn when they are sweet to taste. Cut ripe bunches with a short section of stalk and place in a container lined with tissue paper. If not bruised, grapes will keep for up to two months in a cool, dry store.

Guyot method
A young Muller-Thurgau vine, trained by the Guyot method.

Removing leaves
Remove any overcrowded shoots or leaves that are obscuring the grapes about six weeks before the fruits are expected to ripen.

Vines for outdoor cultivation
These fall into two main groups; those suitable for dessert and those suitable for wine. Fruit is either black (B), white (W) or golden (G).
Dessert 'Brant' (B)
'New York Muscat' (W)
'Perle de Czaba' (W)
'Muscat Bleu' (B)
'Noir Hatif de Marseille' (B)
'Tereshkova' (B)
Wine 'Huxelrebe' (W)
'Bacchus' (W)
'Pinot Noir' (B)
'Siegerrebe' (G)
'Muller Thurgau' (W)
'Riesling' (W)

Kiwi fruit
Actinida deliciosa, syn.
A. chinensis

A.d. 'Jenny'

This extremely vigorous climbing plant is grown for its hairy-skinned, gooseberry-like fruits, which are about 7.5cm (3in) long and 5cm (2in) across.

Male and female flowers are carried on separate plants, and both must be planted for a crop of fruit to be produced. Generally, one male plant, for example 'Tomuri', should be planted for every 8–9 female plants such as 'Allison'.

Kiwi fruit grow well in a sheltered, sunny position but will also tolerate partial shade. They need a deep, well-drained, fertile soil. The vines flower in early summer and should start to produce fruit in the third or fourth year after planting.

Planting Plant the vines at any time from late autumn until early spring. To make cropping easier, space the plants 4m (12ft) apart, in rows 5m (15ft) apart.

Cultivation In early spring, feed the plants with an organic mulch, 10cm (4in) deep, which will also help to control weeds and retain moisture. Water well during dry periods, to help the fruit to swell and keep the new canes growing vigorously.

Training and pruning
The vines often grow 4m (12ft) in a year, and must have a support system to keep them manageable.

Select posts 10 x 10cm (4 x 4in) square and 3m (10ft) long and insert them 90cm (36in) into the ground. Fix four horizontal wires, 50cm (20in) apart, to the posts, starting 50cm (20in) above ground level. In spring, train the young canes out along the wires and tie them into position as they develop. Cut back the fruit-bearing side shoots to three buds when the plant is dormant. The discarded canes may need to be cut into two or three sections to make removal easier.

Harvesting The fruits will be ready to harvest in late summer or early autumn. They are fully ripe when they begin to feel soft to the touch if squeezed gently between finger and thumb, and can be picked by snipping through the fruit stalk with secateurs. The fruits must be handled carefully as they are easily damaged.

Storing and preserving fruit

The traditional method for storing tree fruit, such as apples and pears, is on slatted benches in a cool, dry loft. Lemons can also be stored in this way. Air must circulate around the fruit to prevent rotting.

Take care when picking and handling fruit for storing, as bruised fruit will quickly cause other fruit to rot if they touch. Soft fruit and some tree fruits can be frozen or preserved, either in syrup or as a conserve. Those with lots of hard pips are better strained and turned into jelly.

Fruits that freeze well

Apples, apricots, blackberries, blueberries, cherries, currants, damsons, plums and greengages, gooseberries, grapes, peaches, nectarines, raspberries.

Citrus fruits
Citrus sinensis, C. limon, C. paradisi

C. sinensis

C. limon

Oranges (*Citrus sinensis*), lemons (*C. limon*) and grapefruit (*C. paradisi*) belong to the citrus family, grown for their refreshing fruits. These are excellent for eating raw or for making desserts, preserves and drinks, and their peel adds zest to cooking.

All citrus are evergreen, sub-tropical trees, which can withstand frost only for short periods. Most citrus are self-fertile and do not require a pollinator, and many are capable of producing fruits with just a few or even no seeds at all. Citrus do not flower and fruit on a seasonal basis but as a response to warm, humid conditions, and there will often be flowers and fruit present on the tree at the same time. Trees should start to produce fruit four or five years after planting.

Citrus trees prefer deep, well-drained, fertile soil, full sun and a warm, dry climate. They can be grown in containers to restrict their overall size, and can be overwintered indoors in cool climates to protect them from frost.

Planting When grown outdoors most citrus will form quite large plants, often needing a 7 x 7m (21 x 21ft) space. They can be planted at any time of year.

Cultivation In late spring, apply an organic mulch, 10cm (4in) deep, to help retain moisture and control weeds. Water the trees in dry summer periods, or the fruits may drop prematurely. In early summer, drape the whole tree with netting to protect the fruits from birds. Protect the young fruits from frost by covering the whole tree with fleece.

Pruning Remove any dead, damaged or diseased branches and prune back long, new growth to encourage bushier plants. Lemon trees can become straggly after a few years and benefit from an occasional hard pruning in early spring, when they should be cut back by two-thirds.

Harvesting Citrus fruit may take up to eight months to ripen. When the flesh yields to gentle pressure, they should be cut from the tree with secateurs.

Watering test
If soil is dry several centimetres into the pot, it needs watering.

Cleaning stems
Remove any shoots below the graft union with the thumb.

Liquid fertilizer
Apply a foliar feed every week, or every two weeks in winter.

The herb garden

Herbs have become increasingly popular for culinary purposes, and even for general medicinal use. They are extremely versatile, producing roots, stems, flowers, seeds and leaves that can have multiple uses, even when they come from the same plant. If you design the herb garden in an attractive, formal way, with the squares or segments divided into different families or species of herbs, it will make using the herbs much simpler. Herb gardens have been popular for centuries, and there is no shortage of information on how to design them, and the best herbs to grow for different purposes. Ideally, however, you should limit your ambitions to a few good, all-round culinary herbs, and some that have medicinal uses. Do not be tempted into practising with home remedies: leave it to the experts, as some herbs are extremely powerful and could endanger your health.

Designing a herb garden

You do not need to come up with an elaborate plan for a herb garden – a small, informal patch close to the kitchen will suffice if you just want to grow a few, well-chosen favourites.

For those looking for a more attractive design, one of the simplest is based on the spokes of a wheel, with each segment being used for a different herb. It pays to put a handsome architectural plant in the hub of the wheel to give the garden structure. A clipped box bush would be good, as would a standard fruit tree, such as a gooseberry, or a standard rose.

The design below will work as well for culinary herbs as for medicinal ones; on the whole, it is best not to mix the two categories.

Much depends on whether your herb garden is ornamental or practical. In either case, if the herb garden is larger than 2m (6ft) in diameter, it will pay to ensure that the paths between the segment are large enough to walk on, so you can tend the garden easily.

If, on the other hand, you have very little space, you can adapt the design to a large-diameter container, simply using fewer herbs in each segment.

The herb garden, left, has six different culinary herbs. A similar design could include medicinal herbs, such as:
a) pot marigold (*Calendula officinalis*)
b) chamomile (*Chaemaemelum nobile*)
c) lavender (*Lavandula angustifolia*)
d) lemon balm (*Melissa officinalis*)
e) mint (*Mentha* spp.)
f) feverfew (*Tanacetum parthenium*)

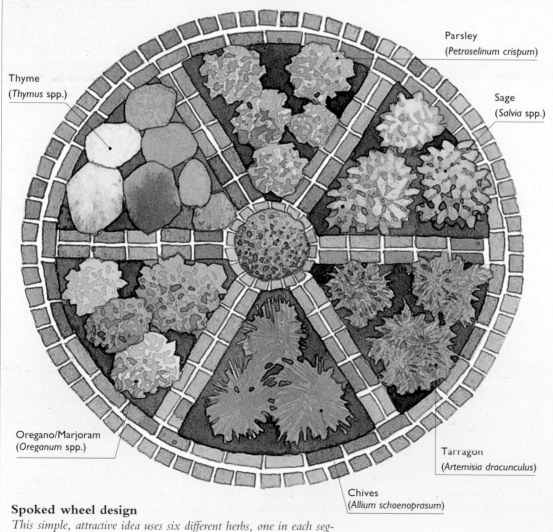

Thyme
(*Thymus* spp.)

Parsley
(*Petroselinum crispum*)

Sage
(*Salvia* spp.)

Oregano/Marjoram
(*Oreganum* spp.)

Tarragon
(*Artemisia dracunculus*)

Chives
(*Allium schoenoprasum*)

Spoked wheel design
This simple, attractive idea uses six different herbs, one in each segment of the wheel. An ornamental plant is the focal point in the hub.

Medicinal herb display
An attractive collection of medicinal plants in a container: wormwood, tansy, feverfew and hyssop.

Choosing herbs

The herbs you choose to grow are very much a matter of personal taste, quite literally in the case of culinary herbs. In addition to those for the kitchen, and those for herbal remedies, a number attract benevolent insects, such as bees and butterflies, and you could just as easily make a herb garden for encouraging wildlife.

Herbs, like other garden plants, divide into those that have woody stems (shrubs and subshrubs like lavender and rosemary), soft-stemmed perennials that come up year after year, such as lemon balm (*Melissa officinalis*) and thyme (*Thymus* spp.), and annuals that are grown every year from seed such as nasturtiums (*Tropaeolum*) and basil (*Ocimum basilicum*).

In a larger garden, herbs can be grown in their own specific border or mixed with other plants in the perennial border. How you grow them, and even buy them, will depend on which group they belong to. Generally speaking, shrubby herbs can be grown from cuttings while annuals are grown from seed.

Using herbs

Herbs for culinary purposes are used fresh or dried. Although dried herbs can be more pungent, when fresh they give dishes a delicious flavour, notably fresh basil with pasta, rosemary with grilled meat and tarragon with chicken.

For medicinal purposes, herbs can be infused or macerated. Herbal teas are made by infusing leaves in boiling water and letting it stand for a few minutes. Macerated herbs are left in oil for 10 days or so, until it becomes infused with the properties of the herb.

Cultivating herbs

Herbs need a good, free-draining soil and a sunny site. They also need some shelter from cold winds. A good solution for tender herbs is to plant them in a container, and then plunge the container in the ground near the backdoor during the summer, overwintering the herbs under glass. Generally, herbs are pest and disease-free and require little maintenance. Herbs from Mediterranean countries will often withstand drought (generally those with small, much-divided leaves) but those with larger, softer leaves (such as mint) will require regular watering in summer. Plant aromatic herbs in a prime position, such as either side of a path – brushing against the leaves releases their scent.

Herbs in containers
Mint can be contained by growing it in a pot which is plunged into the garden border.

Overwintering herbs
Grow tender plants such as parsley in pots and bring them indoors for winter.

Harvesting and storage

Herbs can be picked daily during the growing season, and many can be dried and stored for use throughout the winter months, providing year-round availability.

If the leaves are harvested correctly, the plant will develop a bushier habit. Pinch out the shoot tips and use these first to encourage the plant to form side shoots. Later in the season, you can then harvest the larger leaves from

Storing seeds
Store herbs in fresh air and put in a plastic bag when thoroughly dry to collect seedheads.

Herbs in containers

If you have very little space, there is nothing to prevent you growing some herbs in a window box, for example. The kitchen windowsill is an excellent spot for cultivating a few culinary herbs, and basil (grown from seed), parsley, chives and thyme will all furnish you with as much as you will need for the kitchen from a relatively small container.

More decorative, larger containers can also be used for more substantial herb displays. Remember that some herbs are quite vigorous so take care when you combine different herbs in the same container. Mint, for example, spreads by runners and will rapidly take over an

these shoots as they develop. When harvesting, the general rule is not to remove more than 20 per cent of the leaves at any one time.

Herbs can be dried successfully, and simply, by being hung upside down in a cool place with a good airflow. Damp and cold may cause the herbs to rot before they dry. Once dried, the herbs can be stored in airtight jars. Culinary herbs can also be frozen, but their aroma and flavour is considerably reduced by this method.

Harvesting fresh herbs
Borage flowers can be harvested and used fresh as a flavouring for summer drinks.

entire container, unless you make provision in the shape of a divider. A roof slate, pushed into the container, is a useful divider.

Culinary herb display
A terracotta pot is home to several culinary herbs, including marjoram, thyme, basil (and purple basil) and sage.

Culinary herbs

By adding herbs to food, not only do you enhance flavour, but you also benefit from the important vitamins and minerals these plants contain. As the types of food we eat has changed, influenced by factors such as health and convenience, and the popularity of exotic foods has grown, demand for more unusual herbs has increased. Many varieties, such as thyme, will keep very well in a dried form. However, to get the maximum benefit and the fullest flavour from herbs, they should be used fresh immediately after harvest. Plant culinary herbs close to the kitchen door to allow you to gather them as you cook.

Chives (*Allium schoenoprasum*)

Horseradish (*Armoracia rusticana*)

Dill (*Anethum gravoelens*)

Chervil (*Anthriscus cerefolium*)

CHIVES
Allium schoenoprasum
Alliaceae
H 30cm (1ft)
The stems of this hardy, perennial bulb have a delicate onion-like flavour and are often used raw in salads or with cheeses. It grows best in a light, well-drained soil, and will keep growing well into the winter in a sheltered position. Plant in clumps 25–30cm (10–12in) apart. Can also be grown in a container.

HORSERADISH
Armoracia rusticana
Brassicaceae
H 60cm (2ft)
This herbaceous perennial has pungent, peppery-flavoured, edible roots. The horseradish will grow almost anywhere, but prefers a rich, moist soil. Once established, it is very difficult to remove from the garden. It is served as a condiment, and also complements oily fish, such as mackerel.

DILL
Anethum gravoelens
Apiaceae
H 1.2m (4ft)
The flowerheads and seeds of this tall annual are used to flavour pickles, while its leaves have an anise-like flavour. Dill likes a rich, well-drained soil and plenty of sun. Plant 30–45cm (12–18in) apart.

CHERVIL
Anthriscus cerefolium
Apiaceae
H 45–60cm (10–12in)
This hardy biennial (usually grown as an annual) thrives in most soil types and conditions. The leaves have an aniseed taste and are sprinkled raw on vegetables, soups and salads. Plant 25–30cm (10–12in) apart.

TARRAGON
Artemisia dracunculus
Asteraceae
H 60cm (2ft)
This hardy, bushy perennial has strongly aromatic leaves. Plant 30–45cm (12–18in)

apart, in a light, free-draining soil. A sunny position is vital for this plant to grow well.

BORAGE
Borago officinalis
Boraginaceae
H 50cm (20in)
This hardy perennial has bright blue flowers and hairy leaves, which have a fresh cucumber scent. Borage flowers and leaves are often used in cool drinks. It likes well-drained soil and sun. Plant 30–45cm (12–18in) apart.

CARAWAY
Carum carvi
Apiaceae
H 50cm (20in)
This hardy biennial plant has fine, fern-like leaves, which are an excellent garnish for soups and salads. The strongly flavoured seeds combine well with casseroles and roasted meats and are also used to flavour cakes and breads. Caraway prefers a fertile soil and plants should be about 30–45cm (12–18in) apart.

CORIANDER
Coriandrum sativum
Apiaceae
H 30cm (1ft)
Cultivated for over 3,000 years, coriander is a staple flavouring in curries and Far Eastern cooking. It is also known to aid the digestion. This annual plant flourishes in a light soil containing plenty of organic matter, and prefers full sun. Plant 25–30cm (10–12in) apart.

BAY
Laurus nobilis
Lauraceae
H 3m (10ft)
One of the most widely culti-vated herbs, the spicy, dried leaves of this slow-growing, hardy, evergreen tree are used to flavour both savoury and sweet dishes. It can spread to 5m (15ft) across, and can also be clipped and trained into neat standards and topiary balls. Bay prefers a fertile, well-drained soil, and a hot, sunny, sheltered position.

MINT
Mentha spp.
Lamiaceae
H 45cm (18in)
The most common species of mint is *Mentha spicata*, or spearmint, which is used to flavour drinks, sauces and sal-ads. An invasive herbaceous perennial, it is best grown in a container to keep it under control. Mints grow well in most soils, and prefer a par-tially-shaded site.

BASIL
Ocimum basilicum
Lamiaceae
H 35cm (14in)
Originating from India, this tender, annual herb has bright green, delicately flavoured leaves which are delicious when added fresh to soups, fish, meat dishes and salads. Basil prefers a warm, sheltered site and a light, well-drained soil. Plants should be spaced 30cm (1ft) apart, and watered well dur-ing dry periods.

MARJORAM
Origanum majorana
Lamiaceae
H 45cm (18in)
This hardy perennial shrub-like plant has a sweet yet spicy flavour, which is excel-lent with poultry or in egg dishes. This herb thrives in a well-drained, alkaline soil in full sun. Plant about 30cm (12in) apart to allow room for its spreading habit.

PARSLEY
Petroselinum crispum
Apiaceae
H 60cm (2ft)
Used since Roman times, parsley is a biennial herb which prefers a moist, fertile soil. The densely curled or flat (depending on the vari-ety) leaves are rich in iron and vitamins, and are used as garnishes, as well as to flavour casseroles, sauces and mince. Plants are grown 25–30cm (10–12in) apart.

ROSEMARY
Rosmarinus officinalis
Lamiaceae
H 1m (3ft)
The grey-green, needle-like leaves of this shrubby, half-hardy herb have a distinctive flavour and are often used for stuffings. Rosemary likes a free-draining, alkaline soil and a sheltered, sunny site. Plant about 2m (6ft) apart, as it has a spreading habit.

SAGE
Salvia officinalis
Lamiaceae
H 50cm (20in)
The felted, highly aromatic, grey-green leaves of this hardy perennial act as a dis-infectant to the digestive sys-tem and are often used in stuffings to accompany fatty foods, such as duck. A hardy perennial, sage needs a light, free-draining soil and a sunny position.

THYME
Thymus vulgaris
Lamiaceae
H 15–20cm (6–8in)
The pungent leaves of this half-hardy perennial can be used fresh or dried. It is often used as a seasoning with meats, stocks and stuffings. Thyme should be planted 30cm (12in) apart, and requires a well-drained and sunny position. Clip the plant regularly to prevent it from becoming thin and straggly. Thyme can be grown indoors in winter.

Coriander (*Coriandrum sativum*)

Bay (*Laurus nobilis*)

Spearmint (*Mentha spicata* 'Moroccan')

Basil (*Ocimum basilicum*)

Parsley (*Petroselinum crispum*)

Rosemary (*Rosmarinus officinalis*)

Sage (*Salvia officinalis*)

Medicinal herbs

Lemon verbena
(*Aloysia triphylla*)

Plants have been used for thousands of years to help ease the symptoms of illness, long before chemical drugs became available. Indeed, many of the drugs which are now regarded as common, such as aspirin, had their origins in plants. Even a small garden will hold sufficient plants to make up a basic medicine chest, and by drying and storing them, you will have medicines to hand all year round. The herbs listed are among the most popularly used for common complaints. Warning: consult a herbal medicine practitioner before trying any treatments, as some herbs are toxic and/or have unwanted side effects, particularly in certain illnesses or conditions.

Marshmallow
(*Althaea officinalis*)

LEMON VERBENA
Aloysia triphylla
Verbenaceae
H 1.8m (6ft)
This half-hardy shrub likes full sun and rich soil. It has lance-shaped, lemon-scented foliage and tiny panicles of pale mauve flowers. It can be propagated from semi-ripe cuttings in summer. Its leaves are excellent for infusions for teas as well as for soothing the digestion.

Chamomile (*Chamaemelum nobile*)

Pot marigold (*Calendula officinalis*)

MARSHMALLOW
Althaea officinalis
Malvaceae
H 90cm–1.2m (3–4ft)
This hardy perennial grows well in damp soil in full sun and thrives in seaside conditions. It has grey-green, downy, 5-lobed leaves and pale pink flowers in late summer. Propagate by cuttings in early summer. The root can be taken as an infusion for insomnia or applied as a poultice to swellings. The leaves soothe irritated eyes.

ARNICA
Arnica montana
Asteraceae
H 30–60cm (1–2ft)
Also known as leopard's bane, this daisy-like, hardy perennial likes full sun and rich, acid soil. Small, golden yellow flowers appear from midsummer to early autumn. Sow from seed in autumn. It can be used to make a tincture to relieve bruising and swelling. **Not to be taken internally**.

POT MARIGOLD
Calendula officinalis
Asteraceae
H 30–60cm (1–2ft)
This little annual, with its bright orange, daisy-like flowers from late spring to autumn, likes most soils but prefers full sun. Propagate from seed sown in late spring. Its flowers have antiseptic properties and are used in creams and tinctures, and in cosmetic preparations.

CHAMOMILE
Chamaemelum nobile
Asteraceae
H 30cm (12in)
A hardy perennial, chamomile will grow in partial shade and likes well-drained soil. It has feathery, apple-scented foliage and tiny, daisy-like flowers. It is used to aid digestion, calm nerves and promote relaxation. An infusion of the leaves can be used to relieve pain. The flowers are used in shampoos to lighten hair colour.

PURPLE CONEFLOWER
Echinacea purpurea
Asteraceae
H 30–60cm (1–2ft)
Used by American Indians to cure snake bites, this colourful, purple-flowered herb grows best on fertile soil in sun or partial shade. It can be propagated from seed sown in early summer. Infusions are used for healing skin complaints and it has valuable antibiotic properties.

WITCH HAZEL
Hamamelis virginiana
Hamamelidaceae
H 3m (10ft)
This small, hardy tree produces tiny, yellow, spidery flowers after the leaves have fallen, in mid-winter. It will do well in sun or partial shade in moist soil. Propagate from softwood cuttings in summer. Its astringent properties are well-known, and are particularly good for eye and skin inflammations.

ST. JOHN'S WORT
Hypericum perforatum
Clusiaceae
H 60cm (2ft)

This hardy perennial does well in partial shade or sun, in well-drained soil. It bears bright yellow flowers in summer. Propagate from seed in spring or autumn. Infusions of the leaves can be used for nervousness, insomnia and depression. Fresh leaves can be crushed and rubbed on bites to reduce pain and swelling. The flowers can be macerated in oil, as a rub for rheumatism.

LAVENDER
Lavandula angustifolia
Lamiaceae
H 60cm (2ft)

This half-hardy sub-shrub has wonderfully aromatic flowers in rich purples and mauves and fine, silvery grey foliage. It grows well in poor soil and full sun. Propagate from semi-ripe cuttings in summer or autumn. The essential oil derived from the flowers has a calming, restful effect, and is much used in aromatherapy. It can also be used as an antiseptic to treat insect bites.

LEMON BALM
Melissa officinalis
Lamiaceae
H 60cm (2ft)

This easy-to-grow, hardy perennial has a golden variety, 'Aurea', which has attractive, buttery yellow-splashed leaves. Does well in partial shade and dry soil. Propagate from cuttings in summer. A valuable bee plant, its leaves are used in teas to calm nerves and ease depression. It has a tonic effect on the digestive system.

PEPPERMINT
M. x *piperita*
Lamiaceae
H 60cm (2ft)

This hardy, spreading perennial has tough, green leaves and small, lilac or white flowers in summer. It likes moist soil and full sun or partial shade. Its leaves are highly aromatic and different species have different aromatic properties – applemint (*M. suaveolens*), and eau-de-cologne mint (*M.* x *piperita* var. *citrata*) among them. The leaves are used to make refreshing teas that help soothe the digestion and promote sleep.

WILD BERGAMOT
Monarda fistulosa
Lamiaceae
H 60–90cm (2–3ft)

This hardy perennial has toothed pairs of leaves and small, mauve-pink flowers in late summer. A lemon-scented species (*M. citriodora*) is also well worth growing. They both thrive in full sun or light shade in dryish, well-drained soil. Propagate from cuttings in summer. Use infusions of the leaves for delicately scented teas, which soothe the digestion.

SALAD BURNET
Sanguisorba minor
Rosaceae
H 45cm (18in)

This hardy perennial has been planted for centuries in herb gardens. It has small, attractive leaves, which are good for ground cover, and insignificant flowers. The leaves are eaten in salads and soups, and are used to treat wounds. Steeped in drinks, they guard against infection.

FEVERFEW
Tanacetum parthenium
Asteraceae
H 60cm (2ft)

This daisy-like, hardy perennial flowers from early to late summer and has toothed, aromatic foliage. Propagate from seeds sown in summer. Its dried leaves make a good moth repellent, and can be used as a sedative in an infusion, and for migraines and arthritis (for which it is now a registered medicine). **Not to be taken in pregnancy**.

HEARTSEASE
Viola tricolor
Violaceae
H 10-30cm (4-12in)

This annual has yellow and blue scented flowers from spring to autumn and dark green, toothed leaves. It likes full sun and a fertile soil. Propagate from seed in spring. Thought to aid healing, its peppery tasting flowers are good in salads.

Purple coneflower (*Echinacea purpurea*)

Lemon balm (*Melissa officinalis*)

Peppermint (*M.* x *piperita*)

Salad burnet (*Sanguisorba minor*)

Feverfew (*Tanacetum parthenium*)

Heartsease (*Viola tricolor*)

Index

Acknowledgements

The photographer, publishers and authors would like to thank the following people and organizations who kindly allowed us to photograph their gardens:
Ansells Garden Centre, Horningsea, Cambs; David Austin Roses Ltd, Wolverhampton, West Midlands; Bressingham Gardens, Diss, Norfolk; Broadlands Garden, Hazelbury Bryan, Dorset; Cambridge Alpines, Cottenham, Cambs; Cambridge Garden Plants, Horningsea, Cambs; Capel Manor, Enfield, Middx; Beth Chatto Gardens, Elmstead Market, Essex; Clare College, Cambridge, Cambs; Docwras Manor, Shepreth, Cambs; John Drake, Fen Ditton, Cambs; Mrs Sally Edwards, Horningsea, Cambs; Peter Elliott, Hauxton, Cambs; Mr and Mrs R. Foulser, Cerne Abbas, Dorset; Holkham Garden Centre, Holkham, Norfolk; Kiftsgate Court Gardens, Chipping Campden, Gloucs; Joy Larkcom, Hepworth, Norfolk; Madingley Hall Gardens, Madingley, Cambs; The Manor, Herningford Grey, Cambs; Paradise Centre, Lamarsh, Suffolk; Royal Horticultural Societys Gardens, Wisley, Surrey; Royal National Rose Society, St. Albans, Herts; Scotsdales Garden Centre, Shelford, Cambs; Trevor Scott, Thorpe-le-Soken, Essex; Scarlett s Plants, West Bergholt, Essex; Mr and Mrs M. Stuart-Smith, Cambridge, Cambs; Anthony Surtees, Crondall, Hampshire; University Botanic Gardens, Cambridge, Cambs; Unwins Seeds Ltd, Histon, Cambs; John Wingate and the Golders Green Allotment Association; Wyken Hall, Stanton, Suffolk; Patricia Zaphros, Fen Ditton, Cambs.

The publishers are also grateful to the following for their help and support in the production of this book:
Paul Draycott, Roger Sygrave and the staff of Capel Manor; David Raeburn, John Wingate and the members of the Golders Green Allotment Association; Andrew Lord and the staff of The Garden Picture Library, London SW11.

Suppliers of containers, plants, tools and equipment:
Chiltern Seeds, Ulverston, Cumbria; Granville Garden Centre, London NW2; Squires Garden Centre, Twickenham, Middx.

Picture credits:
(Key: R–Right, L–Left, T–Top, M–Middle, C–Centre, B–Bottom)

Plants for the Garden, p.6–p.65
All pictures by Howard Rice except: *The Complete Guide to Gardening with Containers* (Collins & Brown, 1995): p.7 (BR inset); p.55 (TL, TR). The Garden Picture Library: p.8 (BR); p.9 (BR); p.10 (all); p.12 (BL); p.13 (BL); p.18 (TL); p.28 (TR, BR); p.39 (BR); p.32 (BR); p.33 (BL, BR); p.34 (all), p.50 (BR); p.51 (BL); p.54 (TR, BL); p.55 (BR); p.60 (BR); p.61 (TL). Andrew Lawson: p.13 (BR); p.60 (BR); p.61 (BR). *The New Indoor Gardener* (Collins & Brown, 1998): p.38 (3rd row R). George Taylor: p.13 (TL, T, M, TR); p.28 (BL, CL); p.51 (TL, T, M, TR).

Vegetables, Fruit and Herbs, p.66–p.125
All pictures by Howard Rice except: *The Complete Guide to Gardening with Containers* (Collins & Brown, 1995): p.67 (BR inset); p.120 (BR); p.121 (BR). *The Garden Picture Library*: p.68 (all); p.70 (TR); p.72 (TR); p.77 (TR); p.81 (TR); p.85 (T 2nd L, T 2nd R, TR); p.89 (TC, TR); p.90 (TR); p.91 (TR); p.92 (TC); p.97 (TR); p.99 (TL, TC, TR); p.100 (TL, TR), p.101 (TL); p.102 (TR), p.104 (TR), p.117 (TL); p.118 (TR). *Gardening with Herbs* (Jacqui Hurst for Collins & Brown, 1996): p.122 (TL, third row L, BL); p.123 (2nd row L, 2nd row R, 3rd row L, BL); p.124 (TL, BL); p.125 (TR, 3rd row R). Holt Studios International: p.79 (TL). Photos Horticultural: p.88 (TR); p.89 (TM, TR). George Taylor: p.69 (all); p.71 (all); p.72 (BR); p.73 (all); p.74 (all); p.76 (BL, BM, BR); p; 77 (BL); p.78 (BL, B 2nd L, B 2nd R, BR); p.79 (BR); p.80 (BL, BM, BR); p.81 (BL, BR); p.82 (BL, BR); p.83 (CM, BL, BM, BR); p.84 (BL, BM); p.85 (BL); p.86 (CR); p.86 (BL, BR); p.87 (BL, BM, BR); p.88 (BL, B 2nd L, B 2nd R, BR); p.89 (BL, BM, BR); p.90 (BL, BR); p.91 (BL, BR); p.92 (CR, BL, BM, BR); p.93 (CM, BL, BM); p.94 (BL, BM); p.95 (BR); p.96 (BL, BM, BR); p.97 (BL, BM); p.98 (BL, BM, BR); p.99 (BL); p.100 (BL, BM, BR); p.101 (BL, B 2nd L, B 2nd R, BR); p.102 (all); p.103 (TL, TR, B, CL, BL, BR); p.104 (all); p.105 (all); p.106 (all); p.107 (all); p.108 (BL, BM); p.109 (BL, BM, BR); p.110 (BL, BR); p.111 (CL, BL, BM, BR); p.112 (BL, BR); p.113 (CR, BL, BL inset, BR); p.114 (BL, BR); p.115 (BL, BR); p.116 (CL, BL, BR); p.117 (CL, BR); p.118 (BL, BM); p.119 (TL, BL, BM, BR); p.121 (CL, CM, CR, BL).